# ICARUS

## ALSO BY BRIAN BRIVATI

### AS AUTHOR:

*The Last Optimist in Baghdad*

*The End of Decline: Blair and Brown in Power*

*Lord Goodman: Portrait of a Man of Power*

*Hugh Gaitskell: The First Moderniser*

*The Group 1954–1960: A Time of Hope*

(with Michael Summerskill)

### AS EDITOR:

*The Uncollected Michael Foot: Essays 1945–2000*

*Ernest Bevin* by Alan Bullock

(with Peter Hennessy)

*The Labour Party: A Centenary History*

(with Richard Heffernan)

*Aneurin Bevan, 1897–1960* by Michael Foot

*New Labour in Power: Precedents and Prospects*

(with Tim Bale)

*Guiding Light: The Collected of Speeches of John Smith*

*Anatomy of Decline: The Journalism of Peter Jenkins*

(with Richard Cockett)

*The Contemporary History Handbook*

(with Julia Buxton and Sir Anthony Seldon)

*What Difference Did the War Make?*

(with Harriet Jones)

*From Reconstruction to Integration:*

*Britain and Europe Since 1945*

(with Harriet Jones)

# ICARUS

## THE LIFE AND DEATH OF THE ABRAAJ GROUP

## BRIAN BRIVATI

Biteback Publishing

First published in Great Britain in 2021 by
Biteback Publishing Ltd, London
Copyright © Brian Brivati 2021

Brian Brivati has asserted his right under the Copyright, Designs and Patents
Act 1988 to be identified as the author of this work.

ISBN 978-1-78590-718-0

10 9 8 7 6 5 4 3 2 1

A CIP catalogue record for this book is available from the British Library.

Set in Minion Pro

Printed and bound in Great Britain by
CPI Group (UK) Ltd, Croydon CR0 4YY

MIX
Paper from
responsible sources
FSC
www.fsc.org  FSC® C020471

*For the thousands around the world who did not benefit from impact investment because Abraaj was taken down. I hope this book helps a new generation of investors learn some lessons and make a difference.*

*You need three As to rule Pakistan:*
*The army, America and Allah.*

Former US National Security Advisor
Zbigniew Brzezinski


*I will buy Abraaj for $1. If you accept the offer,*
*all negative media will cease.*

Founder of a prominent US private equity firm
to Abraaj founder Arif Naqvi, March 2018


*Your crime is that you gatecrashed a party*
*that you were not invited to.*

A senior figure in the UAE to Arif Naqvi,
February 2018


*Pakistanis cannot be my partners; Pakistanis*
*are meant to bring in the tea.*

A Gulf Arab when told Arif Naqvi had
bought half his company, 1999


*We can't continue to allow China to rape our country,*
*and that's what they're doing. It's the greatest*
*theft in the history of the world.*

Donald Trump, presidential campaign rally 2016

# Contents

# List of abbreviations

| | |
|---|---|
| ABOF | Abraaj Buy-Out Fund |
| AGHF | Abraaj Global Healthcare Fund |
| AHL | Abraaj Holdings Limited |
| AIIB | Asian Investment Infrastructure Bank |
| AIML | Abraaj Investment Management Limited |
| ANAF | Abraaj North Africa Fund |
| APEF | Abraaj Private Equity Fund |
| AUM | assets under management |
| BMGF | Bill and Melinda Gates Foundation |
| BRI | Belt and Road Initiative |
| CIC | China Investment Corporation |
| CPEC | China–Pakistan Economic Corridor |
| CSR | corporate social responsibility |
| DFI | development finance institution |
| DFSA | Dubai Financial Services Authority |
| DoJ | Department of Justice |
| EBITDA | earnings before interest, taxes, depreciation and amortisation |
| ESG | environment, social and governance |
| GATT | General Agreement on Tariffs and Trade |
| GCC | Gulf Cooperation Council |
| GGM | global growth market |
| GP/GPA | general partner/general partner agreement |

| | |
|---|---|
| IDC | Islamabad Diagnostic Centre |
| IDH | International Diagnostic Holdings (Egypt) |
| IFC | International Finance Corporation |
| IGCF | Infrastructure and Growth Capital Fund |
| IMF | International Monetary Fund |
| IPO | initial public offering |
| JPL | joint provisional liquidators |
| LP/LPA | limited partner/limited partner agreement |
| MoC | multiple of cost |
| OPIC | Overseas Private Investment Corporation |
| IRR | internal rate of return |
| PE | private equity |
| PIFSS | Public Institution for Social Security (Kuwait) |
| PPP | Pakistan People's Party |
| PTI | Pakistan Tehreek-e-Insaf (political party) |
| SDGs | sustainable development goals |
| SDNY | Southern District of New York |
| SEC | Securities and Exchange Commission |
| WASP | white Anglo-Saxon Protestant |
| WTO | World Trade Organization |
| YPO | Young Presidents' Organization |

# Preface

There are lucky and unlucky researchers. I have always been a lucky one. In 1992 when I was writing my PhD I was told by Bill Rodgers (now Lord Rodgers) that Roger Liddle (now Lord Liddle) had some potentially useful boxes in his loft in his house in Hanover Gardens behind Oval Tube Station. When I got these boxes home, I discovered that they contained the entire archive of the Campaign for Democratic Socialism (CDS) – the subject of my PhD. I finished my thesis in record time with the CDS archive in my study.

The *Icarus* project has had two Lord Liddle's loft moments.

My first stroke of luck occurred when, for reasons explained in Chapter 1, I was in Westminster Magistrates' Court in December 2020. I introduced myself to Faaris Naqvi. We then met for a coffee. Faaris and I had a good talk and he remembered me – I suspect as the crazy human rights professor – from when I had approached Arif Naqvi's lawyers before this in November 2020. They rebuffed me, so when I had completed the first draft of this book I sent some material to Arif via Faaris and asked for an interview.

That first draft was completed between January and March 2021 as a result of working lockdown hours and doing little else as all my-face-to-face international training work, my day job since 2009, had been put on hold. Much of the draft was based on the Abraaj archive and acquiring these materials proved to be my second stroke of luck. Following a Zoom interview with a source I was keen to develop, I was contacted by a journalist who had been following the Abraaj saga since the beginning and had been collecting documents with a view to writing a book. The journalist had been provided with a 'dossier' in early March 2018 from an anonymous source and, although they did a few stories initially, their interest in the narrative as it was being 'pushed' was minimal, but they kept collecting material as it became available either from sources or online. Eventually they decided against producing their own book because they felt it was incompatible with their career prospects as a journalist in the Gulf. They offered me the Abraaj archive. It was on a USB stick rather than in an attic. It was a treasure trove. There were some documents, emails and internal memos, a lot of court papers and records, including from the Cayman Islands. Most of the material was already in the public domain and it made for an in-depth crash course in the world of The Abraaj Group.

In response to the pages I sent him via his son Faaris, Arif Naqvi agreed to be interviewed. If talking were a sport, Naqvi could open the bowling for the Pakistani test cricket team. I was the first batsman he had bowled at in a while and he did not know when he would get another game, so he made the most of it. I think that at one point he could have been a spinner, and at times I knew he was spinning. But for the most part he was obviously too overtly damaged, too visibly tired and too mentally pissed-off to bother with spin and that became apparent in his bitingly honest self-analysis. On one occasion he literally struck himself repeatedly on the forehead and said: 'How could I have been so stupid and not seen this coming?' He did not then or later specify what he had not seen coming. In the middle of another discussion, I asked him what his passions were and he reeled off instinctively, 'Islam, family, Pakistan, cricket and then, in no particular order, helping others, making a difference, making an impact, Sufism and Fazal Abbas.' Fazal Abbas, I discovered, is one of his oldest friends. I asked him whether his passions were the same five or ten years ago and he looked at me blankly and said, 'Why should they change? To change passions is to change the meaning of life.' In response, I said that, given what I had read about him, I was surprised that doing deals or making money were not part of that list. He snapped back: 'Don't mix up inputs with outcomes.' A glimpse of the much-feared didacticism.

There are digital echoes of this manifestation of Naqvi online from when he was in his prime. I imagine he must have been infuriating and inspiring in about equal measure. As we talked more, it became obvious that his life now was measured daily in good days and bad days. My wife, Professor Meg Jensen, has literally written the book on trauma and the autobiographical.[1] This was a person with post-traumatic stress disorder (PTSD) telling me the story of his life. The subtitle of Meg's book is 'negotiated truths'. This was a man trying to negotiate between mental illness and truth-telling with visible difficulty, but a palpable courage. This was a man who was suffering. I knew from the court appearances of eminent but opposing psychiatrists that if he were to be extradited Naqvi would be considered a likely candidate for impulsively committing suicide and that he had been diagnosed with trauma and depression. I met him on four occasions, for about eight hours in all, which included a walk outdoors. Four other potential meetings were cancelled at the last moment, another was suddenly cut short because some traumatic memory was triggered or perhaps the whole reality of his situation had descended on him. On one occasion when we were talking he repeatedly lost his train of thought and digressed into telling stories with a manic intensity, walking around and around. In our first meeting he was charming, fluent, funny and had a simply astonishing memory for names and dates. Of course he did, Meg said to me, he is traumatised, he is living in the trauma of being arrested and reliving every circumstance that led to it every waking moment of his life.

By drawing on these ongoing interviews with Naqvi and a wide range of other sources I finished this book in May 2021. I am very grateful to everyone who agreed to speak to me and especially those who pointed me in the direction of further documentary materials. As an archival historian by training, and despite the fact that I have conducted hundreds of source interviews over my career, I am very fond of a document that can be read by others – hence the number of endnotes. You can find all the endnotes with live links to source material on the website that accompanies the publication: www.lifeanddeathofabraaj.com. There is a note on the use of the website at the beginning of the notes and I will use the site to make more materials available over time.

For a supposedly confidential industry, private equity is rather an open book and the volume of material on The Abraaj Group that is available online is astonishing, thanks in part to WikiLeaks, the Paradise Papers and the library of PDFs and PowerPoint presentations that are buried in obscure corners of the internet and on the Wayback Machine. Research in lockdown proved to be remarkably doable.

All interviews were conducted to gather background information unless quotations or specific references are made to them in the text because all of these matters are still part of ongoing litigation in multiple jurisdictions. For this reason, I will not be including a long list of acknowledgments. Friends, enemies, colleagues and business associates of Arif Naqvi and Abraaj have been extremely helpful in providing context and correcting errors. Industry experts, legal specialists and academic colleagues from business studies, human rights, international relations, security studies and international trade have also been patient with my queries. Although I did not interview him, the work of Josh Lerner at Harvard Business School was especially useful on impact investing and private equity. People who were happy for me to reference what they said but did not want to be named are cited, in the tradition of the doyen of contemporary historians, my old friend and former landlord, Peter Hennessy, as 'Private information', i.e. there is a specific source but they do not want to be named. Everything else I have sourced to a publicly available document or a document in the Abraaj archive or is my analysis of the evidence. This book covers a lot of ground and at times delves into a lot of detail.

We will explore the evolution of Abraaj and its unique operating style, impact investing, emerging markets, private equity in general (in the Postscript) and Abraaj specifically throughout. The leadership of Naqvi and the internal civil war that it provoked in Abraaj. The geopolitics and political significance of Karachi Electric, the US–China rivalry, a little Pakistani history and much else. As a professional contemporary historian, I wanted to ensure there was a balanced account based on the available evidence in the public domain. There are a number of reasons why this story matters. The geopolitical reasons are recounted in the text, but there are also people who have been damaged by this story. The people arrested and charged, including Arif Naqvi and other senior staff, lost their reputations, their livelihoods and some may still lose their liberty. Aside from those indicted all the others are now working in other parts of the private equity (PE) industry or in similar roles. Some see their time at Abraaj as a stain on their CVs and have airbrushed it from their LinkedIn profiles. Naqvi's punishment could still be 300 years in jail and the ruin of his family name. The second group of victims are the employees of Abraaj who lost their jobs, pensions and many entitlements to bonuses. The more senior staff may have found new work in the same field, but again there is what they might see as a stain on their CVs. Abraaj was a generous company. Many PAs, secretaries, drivers and support staff, who have nothing to do with any of the decisions made, also lost their jobs in the twenty-odd regional offices dotted around the world. There were between 160 and 200 companies that Abraaj had invested in. Some of these companies lost investments and lost the expertise that Abraaj brought. Many continued with new fund managers and the same levels of engagement and investment, but they may potentially suffer. But the people who matter most, and the reason this story needs to be told, are the people who did not benefit from the impact investment that would have taken place with APEF VI and through the full deployment of the health fund. APEF VI had $3 billion already committed, which was expected to grow to $6 billion, and the health fund had $1 billion. That is a huge amount of potential healthcare, education, clean energy, jobs, goods and services and taxes that do not exist that would have. Moreover, the private equity companies that have come into this space are often more interested in extracting value and less concerned with environmental, social and governance (ESG) concerns than Abraaj seems to have been, so there is a larger detrimental blow to the reputation of impact investing. It is for the people who did not get healthcare, education or a job that we need a balanced account on the record and a reappraisal of the continuing possibility of impact investing in emerging markets. It is an idea whose reputation is too important to leave unprotected.

Despite all the assistance I have received, the views I have formed and the conclusions I have drawn from them along with the mistakes in this book are all entirely my own.

# PART I

# EXPOSITION

# 1

# Shall justice be done?

*It is imperative that prosecutors fulfil their constitutional and ethical
obligations with the same zeal with which they pursue convictions –
not reluctantly, not only after prodding, and not with measured
half-truths. The Court hopes and believes that the attorneys
of United States Attorney's Office will take to heart the lessons of
this case and keep in mind that the prosecutor's first duty is not to
prevail in every case but to ensure that justice shall be done.*

Opinion and order by District Judge Alison J. Nathan on the
conduct of the prosecutors in *United States of America v Ali Sadr
Hashemi Nejad*, September 2020.[1]

In April 2019, prosecutors from the District Attorney's (DA's) office in the
Southern District of New York (SDNY), the same prosecutors censured
by Judge Nathan in the above quote, unsealed an indictment[2] against a
group of Abraaj executives and revised and updated it in June of the same
year. Despite the many critiques of the US justice system and judicial
overreach, there remains an overwhelming force behind allegations from
the US Department of Justice.[3] Headlines across the world picked out

the keywords from the indictment exactly as the prosecutors intended: securities fraud, wire fraud, racketeering conspiracy, money laundering, theft of public funds and theft of employee pension plans. The figures cited were in the hundreds of millions. Some of the laws used were those that had been designed to capture Al Capone.[4] The DA's office laid out the charges and concluded with sixteen counts. If the defendants were to be found guilty, they could be sentenced to several hundred years in prison. If you read this kind of story you tend to assume the people involved are guilty of something. There is no smoke, after all, without fire. When I first read about the Abraaj story, as far as I thought about it all, I assumed the same. The accused must be guilty of something, otherwise why go to all this effort to catch and prosecute them. And if they are not guilty as charged, all of them are rich enough to get good lawyers. But some stories are more complicated than they first appear. The fall of The Abraaj Group is one such story.

For this reason, the reader of this story must come on a journey. It is the same journey that I have been on since September 2020. My own involvement with Abraaj began after hearing about the life story of a man, Arif Naqvi, whose existence was in stasis. Naqvi was the founder of the private equity firm, The Abraaj Group, which was the subject of the Al Capone indictment quoted above. He was arrested at Heathrow airport on 10 April 2019 and subsequently imprisoned, bailed and placed under house arrest. Since his arrest, Naqvi has been living in a kind of modern purgatory. I did not initially look at the facts of his case but rather was struck by the injustice of the demand for his extradition and the uncanny conditions under which he was being held; a personal lockdown as a result of the legal action against him, within a broader national lockdown as a result of the Covid-19 pandemic, based on a treaty, the US–UK extradition treaty, which is not fit for purpose.[5] As I delved into the case more deeply, I became more intrigued. It was probably important to my own journey with this story that I read the skeleton argument presented by Hugo Keith, the QC for Naqvi's defence team in the bail hearings, before reading the indictment.[6] Even so, reading the Department of Justice's indictment against Naqvi and his co-defendants was a significant turning point. There seemed to be no relationship between the actions described in the indictment and the crimes that were alleged to have been committed.

The main crimes that feature in the indictment originated in the campaign against organised crime and were designed to capture those involved in the movement of either stolen money or money that has been obtained by illegal means – for example, the selling of alcohol during Prohibition. We have all seen the movies. To move such funds profitably, you need to have a conspiracy. To indict a criminal involved with such conspiracies, there must be a strong legal logic and compelling argument. At least compelling enough to convince a grand jury, in this case, that a bunch of foreigners were stealing from US pension funds. Indeed, at first glance, the indictment against Naqvi and his colleagues is impressive, and the media coverage has almost universally endorsed it, but even a cursory reading suggested to me that something was not quite right. There was a loose thread hanging off the corner of the document and once I began to pull on that thread this impressive edifice of words began to unravel. The loose thread that first caught my eye was this: despite the charges of conspiring to commit fraud, racketeering, money laundering and theft,[7] there was no actual money missing or unaccounted for at the level of audit from any of the funds under management. In the bail hearing, Arif Naqvi's lawyer stated this clearly and nothing I have read (aside from some misleading media reports, to which we will return), has claimed anything to the contrary, and this was not refuted by the prosecutor during the hearing itself. Creditors made claims for debts, but no one else had stated that anything was actually missing or that monies had disappeared from accounts without being recorded as receivables. This led me to look at the documents filed in the courts of the Cayman Islands when Abraaj was put into a protective restructuring process there, referred to as the appointment of

5

joint provisional liquidators (JPL). When I examined the list of credit-ors in these case filings, I could not find any significant US-based creditors. I say significant because there were claims for a few thousand dollars from various service providers. I kept pulling on the thread. The underlying funds themselves and portfolio companies seemed to be doing just fine – and in fact, continue to do just fine in the main, now under the stewardship of a slew of US and UK PE firms that will benefit from the profits they create. At the moment The Abraaj Group went into liquidation it had assets that were greater than the amounts claimed by the creditors. This was detailed in a witness statement filed in the Cayman courts, which pointed to extensive analysis done by a prominent US-based restructuring firm, Houlihan Lokey, which meant that an orderly restructuring process could have been undertaken to ensure full recovery for each of these creditors. This statement also made clear that all the money that had been given to the fund at the centre of the indictment, the Abraaj Global Healthcare Fund (AGHF), had either been invested as planned or been returned to investors with interest and well above the base rate as of December 2017. An Abraaj executive work-ing on the day-to-day running of that fund stressed that this was done within the time limits set by the agreements in place with the investors and it was done so that it could be drawn down again in the future when investments in health services came up, an undertaking disputing investors in effect reneged on. They proceeded to obtain legal advice from their leading counsel Freshfields that, indeed, their treatment of cash as it stood was in line with the limited partnership agreements with investors. The cash that had already been invested would – at the right time – be returned and the original investors would get their invested money back with a rate of return. As shown in an independent paper prepared by Josh Lerner, the Jacob H. Schiff Professor of Investment Banking at Harvard Business School,[8] Abraaj's track record for return on investment was very good. Indeed, as soon as the money was drawn down, Abraaj started accounting for interest to be paid to investors in that fund at a predetermined hurdle rate – as I learnt, this is a common feature across the global private equity industry. If Abraaj had to delay deploying the funds that had been drawn down from investors, it was already committed to generating a prior preferred return of 8 per cent to the investors, which was detrimental to the company's own economic returns. This return is referred to as 'carried interest' and equated to 20 per cent of investor profits. These were very odd gangsters. Not only did they not steal anything, their 'victims' made a profit.

In a recently released book, journalists from the *Wall Street Journal* argue that the Abraaj affair is a 'key man' story. The advance marketing blurb available at the point that this book went to press describes that they contend that an evil genius at the heart of Abraaj (which means 'towers' or 'towering' in Arabic) was responsible for the collapse of the company because he stole hundreds of millions of dollars and duped the world with his mantra of 'making money and doing good'. The man they refer to is Arif Naqvi. In their view, he is a Muslim Bernie Madoff. A successor to Jho Low of the 1MDB scandal. Their book will repeat the story that was leaked to them over many months, and which they loyally reproduced without knowing the identity of the initial source of the leaks and the emails.[9] It is a compelling tale and perfectly fits the indictment from the Department of Justice (DoJ). On the face of it this entertaining narrative presents a convincing thesis, but it is not the whole story. The whole story is far more complicated and, I would argue, far more interesting and important in two respects that are also the reasons I have avoided the salacious and the gossip-based narrative focusing on the lifestyles of the rich.

The story of Abraaj does not matter because some private equity executives might have self-indulgent lifestyles and adversarial management techniques. *The Key Man* tells these stories because these stories sell newspapers. This story is about injustice and the possibility of harnessing the private sector to address some of the most intractable problems in the world. In terms of injustice, it is about the ability of nation states to act with impunity against individuals and entities that challenge their interests. What happened to Arif Naqvi could happen to any CEO who makes business decisions that challenge geopolitical interests. In terms of impact investment, it matters because the lessons of Abraaj's approach need to be learnt and applied. Individual lives and the lives of communities have been destroyed by the actions of states and their instruments, such as the *Wall Street Journal*. That is the debate this book seeks to address.

Arif Naqvi is clearly a flawed individual who made mistakes – one old friend summed up his character to me as blind optimism – but his company was not some kind of Ponzi scheme that scammed investors. Abraaj was a pioneer of impact investing in emerging markets and the funds it created and the companies it invested in had a multiplier effect in the often poor communities from which they recruited their workers, i.e. the money they invested created more jobs and higher wages, which were spent in these communities, having a classic Keynesian multiplier effect on the local economies. Naqvi has a role to play if we are to accurately understand the collapse of The Abraaj Group, but he is not the sole cause of its demise. He was certainly the target of the destructive legal process and the carefully orchestrated negative media campaign that helped bring the company's intrinsic value down to zero, and it has often been difficult to separate Abraaj from Naqvi, Naqvi from Abraaj, but he is not the whole story. Without doubt, Arif Naqvi suffered from founder's syndrome. As the journalist Atika Rehman put it in a piece in *Dawn* in February 2021 – like Icarus, he flew too close to the sun, taking one risk too many against an enemy that could swat him at will.[10] In 2013, he devised a ten-year plan which he proclaimed publicly to all his colleagues and investors as '10–10–10': within ten years, Abraaj would have grown to ten times its size, becoming one of the top ten private equity firms globally. Naqvi would take Abraaj through an initial public offering (IPO) in London within that period, and thereafter devote himself to an alternative career path. Many speculated that this would be a greater role in the international arena, whilst some said that it would be as head of a separate multinational organisation focused on impact, but the few who knew him well were clear that his future lay in full-time politics in Pakistan.

But then his mortality interfered with his ambitious plans and in 2015 he was diagnosed with colorectal cancer and underwent a seven-hour emergency surgery in Houston. During his convalescence, Naqvi decided that he must accelerate his plan, but maintaining secrecy about his cancer was paramount; if this news got out it would be devastating for Abraaj's growth. Thus, he devised a three-step plan to take the company he founded to an IPO not by 2023 but by 2018.

The first step was that he would follow the successful set of funds launched in the preceding year, 2014, known as the Gen-5 funds with a single global fund, Abraaj Private Equity Fund (APEF) VI. This new fund would centralise the firm, retain the key partners who were core to success, whilst letting those who rested on their laurels go, and take the firm from its long start-up phase, in which everything was ploughed back into the company to fund growth and corporate extravagance, including enormous salaries to attract top talent, to the next stage with an equilibrium of scale and profitability. To get there, the second step in the plan would be to sell the firm's prize asset, Karachi Electric (also known as K-Electric), and the funds from that sale would carry the company through the fundraising period for APEF VI given that Abraaj itself had a significant balance sheet stake of its own in that deal. If needed, the third element of the plan was that there were sufficient additional assets on the balance sheet of Abraaj that could be sold if a bridge was needed to cover any liquidity gaps or to support the IPO by buying back shares in Abraaj Holdings Limited (AHL). Naqvi's strategic bet evolved through 2015 to 2016, but two fatal flaws emerged. First, the juggling act that had to be performed to pull it off was incredibly complex. Second, Naqvi was met with a lack of support from a number of his senior lieutenants, who saw the writing on the wall for their own careers once a central fund and an IPO were achieved. And perhaps this plan was too much for the company to take on. Indeed, some senior figures associated with Abraaj felt that Naqvi lacked the leadership skills to take the company through this kind of a change process. The balls that Naqvi had to juggle to accomplish his sale of Karachi Electric included two superpowers: the United States of America and the People's Republic of China. As he discovered, it was impossible to serve these two masters at the same time. Maybe ego got in the way as he grew rapidly into a public figure. Perhaps the plan was too ambitious, but Naqvi did not know that the race was going to be rigged against him or that his painstakingly created firm and his scheme for its future would be burnt down. The pyrotechnics in this story were not supplied by Abraaj. The company did not set itself alight. Abraaj was torched.

In 2016 the US private equity industry was rewarded for its political donations with a sympathetic regime in Washington. The anti-China lobby, which had been building support under Obama, now also had a new cheerleader in the White House. Abraaj was a victim of a wider campaign to counter the growing influence of China in Pakistan by slowing down both the progress of the Belt and Road Initiative (BRI) and implementation of the China–Pakistan Economic Corridor (CPEC) and, specifically, preventing Karachi Electric from falling into Chinese hands. The knock-on effects of delaying the deal created a cash crunch in Abraaj, the 'Arab' private equity company, run by a Pakistani, shutting it down before it got big enough to achieve stable profitability. If its global fund, APEF VI, had reached its $6 billion close, the company would have reached maturity, with annual management fee income of $120 million from this fund and lower costs because of reduced head count, making it harder for Western firms to break into the emerging markets that Abraaj dominated. It was in everyone else's interests that the towers were left to burn.

Abraaj was taken down in a series of well-timed precision strikes from the autumn of 2017 to the spring of 2018. Each time it appeared as though the company had found a route out of the crisis, another blow landed. Abraaj had been trying to complete the sale of Karachi Electric to Shanghai Electric for $1.77 billion since October 2016, when it signed definitive documentation with Shanghai Electric to conclude the transaction. The deal kept being blocked. A civil war erupted at the top of Abraaj over the Karachi Electric sale to the Chinese and as a result of Naqvi trying to push the deal through despite clear US opposition. Did the news stories feed the civil war in Abraaj? Or were they a product of it, designed to stop the single fund APEF VI being launched or the K-Electric transaction from being completed?

Just as that transaction appeared poised to complete and APEF VI was rolling relentlessly towards a successful first close, an untraceable anonymous email, written in a style that was meant to look like it was from a non-native English speaker, appeared in the inboxes of key stakeholders questioning the commingling of Abraaj funds and other practices. When that failed to stop APEF VI, which did in fact achieve a successful first close, a liquidity pincer was applied. This led to rumours in the US media and a daily assault on the reputation of the firm followed. As a result, it folded. At the centre of it all were the objections led by a small group of investors, mostly US organisations, including the Bill and Melinda Gates Foundation (BMGF) and the Overseas Private Investment Corporation (OPIC), in relation to the use of funds in AGHF. Two independent auditors clarified that indeed all funds had been either invested or returned and no funds were missing although some had been used outside the fund structure. Abraaj in turn argued it was permitted under the fund formation documents to do so. The US-led investors insisted on a third audit by an unknown firm that senior Abraaj managers claim to have never seen but which was quoted in the media.[11] The *Wall Street Journal* and *New York Times* broke this story whilst discussions were in progress with the investors and almost immediately after that, unbeknownst to Abraaj and revealed only when senior executives were being arrested over a year and a half later, the DoJ, in February 2018, opened a file on the company. A data hack or internal leak delivered carefully curated sets of Abraaj emails to the *Wall Street Journal* and possibly other media outlets over the course of the next few months in the form of a dossier. A central question in this case is: who hacked Abraaj or who leaked this material? If it was a hack, who commissioned it? If it was a leak, why did they leak it? The first amendment to the US Constitution and the ability of journalists to protect their sources means we may well never know and the journalists concerned claim that they do not know the identity of everyone who leaked material to them.[12]

A few months later with the fire seemingly out of control, two unsecured creditors vetoed the sale of the firm and restructuring plans that would have repaid them – plans which the secured creditors firmly supported. Instead, these unsecured creditors demanded liquidation, perversely ensuring they would be the last to be paid – a highly irrational thing to do for an unsecured creditor, especially when liquidation in an industry like private equity where reputation is everything brings the intrinsic value of the firm down to almost zero. The appointment of separate liquidators over different parts of Abraaj was perplexing and was bound to lead to a stalemate as they bickered over the size of their respective fees. UK and US firms then took over the Abraaj funds.

So, with Abraaj done for, what of Naqvi? After months of confusion and apparently inept management by two different liquidators, Naqvi remained stubborn and kept hammering away at trying to dispose of Karachi Electric with the backing of its own specific investor group, whilst presenting potential solutions for restructuring Abraaj that were supported by many of the secured investors in the Abraaj estate. At the same time, he kept popping up in the spotlight as a close aide to the new Prime Minister of Pakistan, Imran Khan, and assisting the new government in its economic ambitions. Naqvi was a strong proponent of Pakistan accepting an aid package from the International Monetary Fund (IMF) but only if the terms of that package were conducive to the country's future economic prosperity, and if they were not, then going at it alone. On 10 April 2019, Naqvi was arrested at Heathrow. He was held in prison whilst talks between the IMF and the government of Pakistan were concluded on the IMF's terms. Any momentum that had been gathered by April 2019 in relation to the sale of K-Electric also immediately disappeared. To his enemies, Naqvi was proving to be a tiresome problem: he was not willing to abandon a potential restructuring of Abraaj nor was he willing to abandon the Karachi Electric deal. Now it seemed that he was beginning to interfere in affairs affecting the geostrategic aims of the US in Pakistan again.

Abraaj could not have been taken down without the Karachi Electric deal being blocked and the blocking of this deal was a geostrategic decision, with powerful elements within the private equity industry becoming perhaps unwitting but certainly willing accomplices in the strategy. Private equity players could talk to institutional investors in the US when it became clear that Abraaj was unravelling early in 2018 and make private offers to key individuals inside Abraaj when they knew that Abraaj was going down. US institutional investors could also leak selected information to the Department of Justice and make complaints against Abraaj to put as much distance as possible between themselves, their decisions to invest in Abraaj funds and the media-driven firestorm that was engulfing the firm. They could talk to the media, circulate fake emails and leak others. There is a role for industry participants and competitors in dismantling a player like this, but in the end it takes a state or states to act directly, to encourage their allies to act or deter them from acting and to use the justice system to ensure that no trace is left of their interference. Whether this is the criminalisation of questionable corporate behaviour or an example of judicial overreach; case history is full of examples of such scenarios.[13]

To understand what happened in this case, we need to look at who benefited and who suffered from the collapse of Abraaj. Who benefited and who suffered from stopping the sale of Karachi Electric to the

Chinese? Who picked up the investments in the emerging markets where Abraaj was dominant and who paid the price? China has still not bought Karachi Electric, and it is now rumoured that the utility may be broken up into three constituent parts for which US firms can bid.[14] No US citizens have been arrested or indicted in the case of Abraaj despite their importance in the running and strategy of the firm; indeed, many of the assertions in the indictment are directly linked to the direction provided by some of them. There is powerful circumstantial evidence to suggest that the taking down of Abraaj was an economic hit supported by key US companies and interests within Pakistan, Kuwait and the UAE that are loyal to the United States. It is also apparent that Abraaj was a victim of its own political naivety and in the desperation to save itself in the face of a coordinated campaign to bring it down made serious mistakes.

Abraaj had drunk deeply of the globalisation Kool-Aid. It believed it could somehow operate independently of nation states and for fifteen years it succeeded in doing so, whilst talking grandiosely of a coherent corporate foreign policy.[15] But when the nation states began to strike back, Abraaj had no one to turn to; no lender of last resort, no country that stepped up and claimed writ over the affairs of the group. In terms of private equity, it was also too brown and too black. Of course, there are people of colour in senior positions in US private equity firms, but these are US private equity firms not 'Arab' ones. The people who ran Abraaj were not like other private equity executives and the places they invested were not Silicon Valley start-ups. Abraaj was not, as Margaret Thatcher would have said, 'One of Us'. So not only did Abraaj not have a nation state that could support and make its racial profile irrelevant, but it was also not big enough to save or sustain itself, as it was not an Amazon or Microsoft that could transcend nation states, nor was it white enough to be rescued.

This story became known not because I pulled at a thread that continued to show how it had been deliberately unravelled, but rather because, in the rush to judgement, most analysts did not look at the geopolitics, consider the competing interests, nor explore the complexity that such a multinational enterprise entailed.

This book will set out to provide a balanced account, through a geopolitical and realist interpretation, of the death of The Abraaj Group. We will leave the key man as evil genius thesis for readers of other books and the law courts to judge. In Part I: Exposition, I will explain a little about how I came to write the book and lay out my overall argument. Part II: Rising action describes the remarkable growth and unique nature of The Abraaj Group as a private equity company. In Part III: Climax, I analyse the geopolitics of the Karachi Electric company in the context of the wider superpower conflict over the Belt and Road Initiative and the influence this has on Pakistani politics. In Part IV: Falling action, I describe the stages in the destruction of Abraaj and the role of the different actors in that process. Finally, in Part V: Denouement, I describe the aftermath and legacy of Abraaj and recount a single incident relating to Naqvi's time in prison, which he described to me as we reached the end of our last walk through Hyde Park in a final 'you decide' moment that he left me with as he scurried off home before his curfew began.

I reproduce the incident at the end of the book.

# 2

# 'So, what do you think I am?'

*The Capital which I represent is the State.*

Dario Fo, *Trumpets and Raspberries*

On 10 April 2019, Arif Naqvi, the founder and chief executive of the Dubai-based Abraaj Group, a private equity firm that at its peak had close to $14 billion under management, was arrested when he landed on a British Airways flights from Islamabad. This is how the public story of Arif Naqvi and Abraaj stands at the time of writing. Karachi Electric, a monopoly electricity provider in Pakistan's largest city, has still not been sold to the Chinese, five years after binding contracts were signed. The utility company could well be broken up into three parts and sold off or alternatively it could be renationalised. In which case nobody will take strategic control of this vital geopolitical asset. Meanwhile, hostile creditors who pursued the liquidation of The Abraaj Group against their own interests undermined the chances of a full recovery for the other creditors. The business is in official liquidation. Top Western private equity firms have taken over Abraaj funds, which are all appearing to still be making money for their investors through successful underlying portfolio assets owned within them. The $1 billion AGHF was taken over by the investment firm TPG, Colony Capital acquired Abraaj's Latin America private equity platform, including its $300 million Latin America Fund II, and Franklin Templeton reportedly acquired the $526 million Abraaj Turkey Fund. UK-based Actis acquired five of Abraaj's Africa funds, including the $990 million Africa Fund III – all were acquired for a few million dollars in aggregate value.[1] Some senior executives have already served jail time after being arrested in a US–UK operation that resulted in an indictment being unsealed in the Southern District of New York covering extensive allegations of criminal behaviour. Some senior executives (all of whom were US citizens) were granted immunity from the DoJ investigation, whilst others have turned state's witness to help build a compelling case against the remaining co-defendants in the hope of leniency for themselves. All other money that is alleged to have been misused was returned to limited partners in the AGHF at the end of December 2017, with additional interest paid in early January 2018, even before the initial allegations surfaced in the *Wall Street Journal* in February 2018. Under its new name Evercare, AGHF now operates across Africa and South Asia, including India, Pakistan, Bangladesh, Kenya and Nigeria with investments in twenty-nine hospitals, sixteen clinics, more than seventy diagnostics centres and two brownfield assets; it is one of the largest and most innovative fund strategies deployed in emerging markets history. Globally, new impact investment funds were announced by Western private equity funds to replace the vacuum caused by the collapse of Abraaj and funds under management had reached $502 billion by the end of December 2018.[2] The art market in Dubai, which Abraaj helped create and nurture, collapsed when the firm's significant collection was sold off at a fraction of its value by the liquidators in what was reported as a fire sale,[3] which in turn affected prices for Middle Eastern art across the world.

The DoJ criminal indictment against Abraaj and Arif Naqvi, along with five other senior executives, was made public on 11 April 2019. After three years, Naqvi remains silent. Whenever he is asked for a comment he reiterates a short statement in which he denies all charges and states that he was not involved in any wrongdoing. He will, however, as I discovered, speak to people on very narrow topics that avoid discussing the issues raised in the indictment once he is convinced that they have an open mind, and those conversations are sufficient to raise the questions in at least my mind that appear to be skirted in the mainstream media. His personal public silence and battle against the extradition by the DoJ makes him the only player with an alternative narrative to that of the government of the United States and the US-centric media. He has not told his story because his lawyers advise strongly against it. Every effort by me to engage with his lawyers was met by a stony silence or refusal to comment. The fight against the DoJ centres on extradition to the United States to face a lengthy indictment, with a sentence of close to 300 years under sixteen counts if he is found guilty. Helpfully for the world's media, he has been charged with a series of criminal offences that reads more like a movie script than a legal document, which alleges that he has been conspiring for years to defraud US investors and that this was the goal from the very inception of Abraaj. He has been either in prison or under very restrictive house arrest prohibitions since April 2019.

After I completed the first draft of this book, I sent an overview and some key excerpts to Arif Naqvi and asked to speak to him. To my surprise he agreed to meet to discuss those aspects of the book that did not touch on his case and when we met he remarked that what I had uncovered from the public domain and my interpretation of it was refreshing. Although I was writing a book about Abraaj, it was impossible to separate Abraaj from Naqvi. I had seen hours of online videos of him speaking from stages around the world so I had an idea of what he would be like. He also defined so much of what Abraaj was that I could not help but ask: 'Who is Arif Naqvi?'

If you are Sam Thenya, founder of the Nairobi Women's Hospital, then Naqvi is the guy whose investment of $2.6 million helped increase your number of beds from fifty-seven in 2009 to 256 in 2012.

If you are one of the 10,000 people working for Evercare hospitals, then Naqvi is the guy who created the Abraaj Global Healthcare Fund that supports your job.

If you are the US ambassador to Islamabad, then he is the potential intelligence source and champion of the free market who, against logic and pushback, persisted in trying to sell a key strategic asset to the Chinese against your wishes.

If you are Bill Gates, then Naqvi is the guy your team singled out to invite onto the philanthropic Giving Pledge and who you met repeatedly at Davos. He is the man whose vision of AGHF you bought into, but who you then alleged misused your money before returning it.

If you are the DoJ, Naqvi is the man who should be indicted on sixteen counts and the Pakistani who you are prepared to bend over backwards to get extradited.

If you are the daughter of an elderly parent whose life was saved due to the timely intervention of the ambulance service run by Naqvi's philanthropic Aman Foundation in Pakistan, or the parent of the young man who graduated from its vocational training academy and got a job in Saudi Arabia, you are probably praying that he will overcome his troubles.

If you worked for Abraaj, Naqvi is the guy who lost you your job after demanding a constant 110 per cent from you. The harsh taskmaster who rewarded you when you did well but broke your balls if he thought you were underperforming. Despite this, to many of his former colleagues that I spoke to, Naqvi is a hero: the overwhelming number of messages Naqvi has received whilst under house arrest are from drivers, office assistants, all the way up through the other grades at Abraaj are testament to that. But never once has he received a message from a former partner at the firm; the higher up the food chain you are, the greater your sense of entitlement, I guess. Had Naqvi had the support of the partners in early 2018, would what happened have transpired in the way it did? There is strong evidence that one of Abraaj's senior managers was the source of the leaks that set the whole process of deconstruction going. But who was the instigator and what was their objective?

Arif Naqvi was a perfectionist, egotist, a genius deal maker and he flew his Abraaj towers so close to the sun that they were burnt to a crisp. He was all these things, but his life story is not the story of a crook. It is the story of a man who was certainly flawed and vain and suffered from the delusion that if he could make it around the next corner everything would be OK because it always had been before and because up to that point the usual laws of financial physics had not applied to him. That you could 'do good and make money' was his genuinely visionary mantra, but his good intentions cannot cover up the mistakes he made which may have transgressed the law – and which may ultimately be tried in court. He remains adamant, through his terse and consistent response to any query put to him by the media, that every single transaction at Abraaj was recorded and would ultimately have been reconciled and that no money was missing; that he was, in short, innocent. The wildly exaggerated coverage of his mistakes, which is the dominant narrative in the media at present, should not define his life nor, more importantly, the legacy of the company that he founded. There was much more to him and to Abraaj than the caricature, complete with its racist undertones, which frames this story in the media and in public perception. In fact, he told me and had told others that I have interviewed that he was ready and willing to stand trial in the UK.

When I first interviewed him, he seemed to me neither all hero nor all villain, revealingly brilliant but vulnerable to denial, fragile but occasionally offering glimpses of his inner passion and, despite it all, charming. Whatever he was once, his fragility is now all too apparent. He was sitting on a deep brown sofa positioned in front of a TV screen in his living room in south Kensington – as a work meeting it was allowed by Covid restrictions, but we were kept two metres apart by the size of the sofas. Drone camera images of Dubai would occasionally float across the screen behind him. He consistently refused to answer questions about his case: 'You look for the facts and decide' was all he would say. His frustration at his lawyer-enforced silence was palpable. At times he was fluent, coherent and amusing, especially when it came to the more distant past – growing up in Pakistan, studying at the London School of Economics, creating the Inchcape Middle East deal, the Aman Foundation, the Mustaqbali Foundation and the Abraaj art prize. He was at his most passionate when speaking about impact investing and the difference it can and should make in building back better after Covid-19. His worldview was persuasive and dramatic on a wide canvas, but his persona was reduced – a shadow of the man I had seen in the videos online – he spoke slowly and sighed often, and frequently asked if he was still making sense. He has lost about half his body weight and his face was drawn; his body looked younger, but at times his face looked infinitely older. His youthfulness only reappeared on the few occasions when he laughed or smiled, particularly when talking about his children and grandchildren. Then the PTSD and suicidal depression that had been revealed in court by doctors seemed to physically shrink his body inwards; with his head bowed, he slowly wrapped himself into a foetal position. He recovered to talk about faith, about his own view of what Islam represents in this century, how important his connection to God was in prison. Just before the final haze descended, however, a surge of energy filled out his features, his body became tight under his loose-fitting joggers and T-shirt, he looked right at me and said, 'So, what do you think I am?' I said, 'I don't think you are a crook, but you did make some mistakes, and you should have your day in court to answer your accusers and try to prove your innocence.' I watched the haze of depression descend as he digested my response; it was a grey blanket that he could pull over his head, and he seemed to almost welcome it with relief. He does not have to try any more. It had obviously taken a superhuman effort for him to speak to someone outside his family and legal circle. With the briefest farewell, in his bare feet with his ankle bracelet dragging on the floor, he got up and left. Putting our masks on, his sons saw me out.

Writing about this story began for me because I was originally writing a book about the idea of stasis as defining our political, cultural and social condition. I will return to that book one day, but in researching it I realised that Arif Naqvi, whilst under house arrest and awaiting extradition, was a perfect example of a life in stasis within a society that was itself in a form of stasis imposed by the pandemic.

In the process of looking at the human rights dimensions of Naqvi's case I became increasingly interested in the events surrounding the collapse of Abraaj; something did not feel quite right. When I had a coffee with one of Naqvi's sons whom I met at his final extradition hearing at Westminster Magistrates' Court, I told him that my focus was on stasis and human rights, but that I had become interested in the underlying facts; was there more to Naqvi's case than met the eye? He let down his guard, talked quite openly about his father's case; what struck me most was his absolute lack of guile. This was not how I had expected him to be at all, he was reserved, calm and composed. Of course, in two further meetings with him and one separately with his brother, it was extremely clear that Naqvi's sons were beneficiaries of fantastic lives, upbringings, education and exposure to all the trappings of a high-net-worth individual's lifestyle. But the brothers seemed to be their own men and fundamentally decent human beings. In other words, this was not a case of a patriarch forcing his relatives to do his bidding, nor his colleagues doing the bidding of his relatives. Most of the executives who were arrested or indicted were seasoned professionals who were not part of the founding group of Abraaj – they joined later, had decades of experience in other financial businesses and were big beasts in their own right. Naqvi is clearly a bit of a bully, brash, arrogant and a force to be reckoned with. He had a sizeable ego in his heyday, likes to speak first and last in an interview or a meeting and was an absolute perfectionist – see the rather revealing section in the case study on the Celebration of Entrepreneurship for example. But in his regular business he did not surround himself with mediocrity in an attempt to reflect his own glory, but tried to find the best of the best. Gradually I became less interested in his personality and its flaws as the defining driver of this story – as intriguing as those are – and more by the wider complexity of what happened. During this time various articles had also appeared which made the connection between his arrest, the downfall of Abraaj and geopolitics, but I did not see anyone digging deeper into the case from a geopolitical perspective.[4]

I had attended part of the extradition hearings at Westminster Magistrates' Court and also spoke briefly, whilst walking to the bus stop at the end of the hearing, with a journalist from the *Wall Street Journal* who told me about the book that he was writing, about what he thought of Naqvi and what his thesis was for the story. He described Naqvi as a 'narcissistic c**t', which was not an assessment that I agreed with after reading the skeleton arguments presented by Hugo Keith QC, Naqvi's barrister during the bail hearing, nor the picture that had been painted in the numerous articles and profiles written about him in the decades preceding his fall. It seemed to me then and it seems to be now that the story this journalist was telling me was not the whole story of The Abraaj Group. It was at this point that I became determined to write this book as a more objective account and in an attempt to try to solve the puzzle of what happened to this company for myself. The journalist may have had his own reasons for telling the story of Arif Naqvi, but my impression was that he had decided that Naqvi provided the one-dimensional explanation for the destruction of Abraaj and that he was uninterested in any evidence that might take him in a different direction or complicate his binary narrative of good versus evil. I became increasingly intrigued by this story and luckily found a publisher who felt there was a potential market for two books (I suspect there will be more) that look at the fall of Abraaj and the career of Arif Naqvi. The book by the journalist at the *Wall Street Journal*, as he described it to me, takes his individual perspective and tells the story of his own investigation and, from the material in the public domain at the time of writing, interprets the history of Abraaj through the lens of the individual personality of Naqvi. His ultimate conclusion appeared to be an assertion that Naqvi is a criminal mastermind who schemed for decades to get to the point that he got to in 2017 and was then brought down by his own greed and dishonesty. Suffice to say the journalist does not like Arif Naqvi.

As a biographer I have a certain sympathy with the life narrative approach and one day I might like to write a biography of Arif Naqvi because his is a fascinating human story filled with traits of brilliance, arrogance, empathy, recklessness, generosity, avarice and hubris – all woven into the headlines and the balance sheets and the deals that make up the narrative of his life. The obsession with impact investing, the philanthropy which clearly did enormous good and the commitment to arts and culture are important parts of him no doubt, but he was also a deal maker and businessman par excellence; a purveyor of the idea that greed can do good. And he was an outsider in the ultimate insider's world of private equity, Davos and all the rest. And when it came to crunch time, he was clearly even an outsider in Dubai itself.

The other reason for there being space for another book on Abraaj is the problem that the *Wall Street Journal* was itself an intricate part of the story. The newspaper appears to have been used by forces that were intent on destroying Abraaj to place in the public domain stories based on carefully crafted leaks or expertly carried out hacks. These stories appeared at crucial moments at which the company might have been saved. I am not suggesting that the journalists were doing this intentionally, but standing back and looking carefully at the chronology of events, the timing of leaks, the selective content of those leaks and the editorial policy of the paper it was clearly used as a vital weapon in the armoury of the 'economic hitman' targeting the company. The newspaper was thus a part of the story and not just an observer. Moreover, the geopolitics of the Abraaj story are not reducible to a real-life crime tale with a central villain, and whilst it is completely understandable that every journalist wants to be either Bernstein or Woodward, not every story is a Watergate scandal in which the villains are obvious and the crimes blatant; and not every journalist gets a Pulitzer Prize.

The Abraaj story is something different and it will not be served by a book which tries to fit the narrative of the destruction of Abraaj into the storylines that have appeared over the past decade.

Naqvi compared running Abraaj to flying a jumbo jet at 40,000 feet whilst doing running repairs. I feel the way in which the funds were managed might also be compared to a game of musical chairs. Whilst the music continued, the funds flowed down from investors, were held by Abraaj and then invested under the terms of the limited partner agreements (LPAs), which allowed funds to be commingled if needed. Transactions were carefully recorded in writing and audited, with additional and substantial investments being made outside the fund structure by the holding company with additional co-investment partners. This was not robbing Peter to pay Paul because the money was either in the fund and paying a hurdle rate to its investors or had been drawn down to be invested. But if someone turned the music off at the right moment, then it could be made to look like funds were in places in which they were not intended. Several key players in Abraaj whom I interviewed maintained that all these movements of funds were covered and recorded in investor agreements, which were reviewed by Freshfields and audited by Deloitte and KPMG, and that whenever money moved, it was recorded by the fund as a demand deposit, which in accounting terms is treated as 'cash or cash equivalents', and that each movement between funds had the implicit Abraaj Group guarantee attached to it as far as the third-party limited partners were concerned. When the *New York Times* and the *Wall Street Journal* reported that four investors, the Bill and Melinda Gates Foundation (BMGF), CDC, the International Finance Corporation (IFC) and the French Development Finance

Institution (Proparco), had hired forensic accountants to investigate the commingling, one leading industry blogger commented:

> A reading of the two articles together suggests that there may be some disagreements over the obligation to return called capital – and the time window for doing so – when projects are delayed rather than cancelled. Two hospital projects – one in Karachi and one in Lagos – are said to have been delayed.[5]

Numerous business executives of multinational private equity firms and other companies have confirmed that this was common practice and would usually lead to a regulatory fine if anything were actually wrong. The competing views on what was and what was not allowed by the LPAs will be tested in court, but the timing of the release of the knowledge that questions had been asked was designed to be devastating.

Why would anyone deliberately, and through leaks to the media and perhaps also instructions or requests for actions to key unsecured creditors, turn the music off at the wrong moment and leave things looking as though they were out of place? Especially when Abraaj was doing so much good in the markets in which it was operating by breaking ground in terms of investment, introducing governance and professional services and spreading Western ideas about how to do business in some of the front-line positions against Chinese economic expansion.[6] What was the invisible hand that was influencing ostensibly independent, sovereign or unconnected parties to act in symphony, with one action seamlessly following the other? The city of Karachi plays a vital role in answering this question.

A private equity firm that had grown up in the Middle East but was not linked to any individual nation state purchased a controlling interest in a vital strategic asset in Pakistan – Karachi Electric. It purchased a 56 per cent majority stake of KES Power, which was the consortium entity that itself owned 66.4 per cent (initially 72.58 per cent) of Karachi

Electric. According to the Harvard case study, Abraaj contributed capital through a combination of capital from its own AHL balance sheet (26 per cent) and through its managed fund, Infrastructure and Growth Capital Fund (IGCF, 30 per cent), of which AHL itself owned 23 per cent. It turned that asset into a highly profitable company, indeed one that was the subject of a number of studies by international business schools and was preparing to exit. At the moment of exit a new American government was elected. The primary foreign policy objective of this new government was to challenge and, if possible, stop China's economic and therefore political and military expansion through the Belt and Road Initiative and in all other spheres. This was one part of an overall offensive launched by the US, which included the withdrawal from the Trans-Pacific Partnership trade deal,[7] blacklisting companies such as the telecom giant Huawei from buying American products and drawing up new restrictions on the types of technology – such as biotech and high-performance computing – that could be exported overseas.[8] In those circumstances it would be natural to assume that the US used every lever it had at its disposal to slow down and block the sale of Karachi Electric to the Chinese bidder that had offered the best price and the best long-term investment programme. Indeed, US opposition to projects such as the Nord Stream 2 pipeline, which would bring gas directly from Russia into Germany, has had a fully public element as well as a covert dimension.[9] The public side has seen openly oppositional statements from the Biden administration as soon as it came into power and the upholding of sanctions involved in the pipelines' construction. Covertly, President Biden has been putting personal pressure on German Chancellor Angela Merkel, the main cheerleader for the project, and seeking to target other Russian pipelines such as the Turkestan project.[10] The message of this example seems clear – when there is a bipartisan consensus amongst the US government that your project must fail, they will not hesitate to spend any amount of diplomatic, political or economic capital to stop it. The US will also operate at a deal-by-deal level to counter Chinese influence. Every US embassy in Africa offers a free service to review Chinese contracts and explain to the African side the debt implications of them to discourage the contracts from being signed.[11]

Abraaj had been operating on the assumption that the deal would have been concluded quickly and the $1.77 billion sale price for its controlling stake would have come back to investors, of which $550 million was attributable to AHL itself and the rest as investment return and profit to the other investors. This would have provided significant but, crucially, sufficient liquidity. The pressure on cash flow placed on Abraaj that the failure of this money to arrive created was acute. At this point in its history, The Abraaj Group was trying to move from the dangerous game that start-ups play with big cash burns to grow faster at the expense of long-term profitability via its new global fund, APEF VI, to become stably profitable. But the music stopped, which was compounded by a change of attitude amongst several key US and US-allied stakeholders. The senior management of Abraaj made a series of rushed and at times counter-productive decisions in response to the unfolding crisis, but at the end of 2017 by borrowing, selling off of a number of assets that they were carrying on their balance sheet and the promise from the outgoing Prime Minister of Pakistan, Shahid Abbasi, that the Karachi Electric deal would be concluded by the following May, it looked like the company had solved its cash-flow problem.[12] Instead, what looked like an economic hitman operation was launched against the company from both inside and outside.

The deal remained blocked inside Pakistan, through three successive Prime Ministers – Nawaz Sharif, Shahid Abbasi and the new PM Imran Khan – from 2016 onwards, all of whom had publicly supported the deal being concluded. A series of apparently insurmountable bureaucratic blockages were put in the way of the sale. These blockages could have been removed by the actions of key individuals within the Pakistani government and assurances were given at the highest level that they would be, and that it was in the interests of everybody in Pakistan for the deal to proceed and for the Chinese investment in Karachi Electric to begin. The Pakistani political elite and the Pakistani military, however, represent a complex mix of interests. For starters, there was a complex counter-extremism alignment between the two countries,[13] and the pro-China lobby in Pakistan believed that investment by the Chinese through the BRI was the only viable economic future for the country. China was at loggerheads with India and based on 'my enemies' enemy being my friend', there was considerable strategic support for Chinese investment and even military support through the 'String of Pearls' ports; these are ports around the Arabian Sea that China is acquiring or trying to gain control of, which include Gwadar but also Port Qasim and Karachi itself in Pakistan, described as being so economically and strategically attractive that they are like a string of pearls.[14]

However, other elements in the state and military were and still are closely aligned to the US and the financial, strategic and military support that came from the US. It was not so much that the US was a trusted ally of these elements in the Pakistani elite, but more that they were less distrusted than the Chinese. The interplay between these faceless elements in the political elite and the military establishment at the least muddied the waters around the progression of the deal, and at the most ordered it to be stopped. To this day those obstacles have not been removed and the deal has not been concluded. It appears as if the pro-US and anti-Chinese elements have prevailed or perhaps, as no alternative has as yet emerged, this is a score draw in the great game.

The victim of the score draw in the great game is Arif Naqvi. He is in the position he is in because he challenged the modern American empire. The Abraaj Group grew to be the dominant force and voice of private equity in emerging markets focused on financial returns that generated both money and impact. In the end, making money was not enough for Naqvi. He wanted private equity to be a vehicle for change. He wanted to be a policy maker rather than someone dedicated to making money for his shareholders, investors and employees. So, he set out to write his own rule book that was particular to the markets and impact opportunities he saw ahead of him. In that process, he took his eye off the ball and made a series of mistakes and alienated many people inside and outside Abraaj he should not have; he was clearly not as smart, strategic and important as his self-image or the sycophants around him told him he was. But he was also being hit by a series of calculated precision strikes, Abraaj was eliminated, and its pieces were wolfed up by its US and UK counterparts. Meanwhile, Naqvi is on the highest bail set in the UK's history, awaiting extradition to what would be a show trial in the USA. His lawyers argued in the extradition hearing that his human rights and personal safety cannot be guaranteed. Beyond the conditions he would be subject to if he is extradited, it seems unlikely that 'Pakistani-born' Naqvi – as the US press have repeatedly referred to him alongside the epithet of the 'Muslim Madoff' – is going to receive a fair hearing from an American jury.

The moral of the story is that 'if you do what you are told on the big things then you can get away with the little things'. The Abraaj team ignored the warnings and gave off the appearance of being part of the empire. But history suggests that if you are a WASP (white Anglo-Saxon Protestant) at Goldman Sachs, Barclays Capital, UBS or Deutsche Bank and if you get caught doing what the senior management team of Abraaj is accused of doing then you plead guilty, do a deal, give evidence and hope to get away with a fine or, better still, the firm takes the rap and pays the fine. Goldman Sachs, for example, was fined and ordered to return billions of dollars for its part in the 1MBD scandal.[15] A similar case was recently concluded with Deutsche Bank, the story could well have been written about the case against Naqvi: scratch Deutsche Bank's name out and write Arif Naqvi in its stead and there is not much difference between the two.[16] Financial organisations routinely duck criminal charges by paying fines and life goes on. Only one Wall Street banker was sent to jail because of the 2008 financial crash. The 'system' always appears to close ranks; the outsider remains outside. If an example needs to be made, it is clear where the finger points: the level of example you become depends on the extent to which you heed the warning signs early enough and how embedded you are in the financial empire – that is, whether you are on the fringes of expendability or part of the beating heart.

No US citizens working at the top of Abraaj have been arrested or indicted in this case. In fact, it appears from the DoJ indictment that Mark Bourgeois, a US national who led much of the operational approach to fundraising and valuations for APEF VI was actually the senior US national identified as the 'cooperating witness' who had been granted immunity by the DoJ. Whilst I am not suggesting that Bourgeois did anything wrong, it is striking that he was a central part of the discussions of the valuations which form a central part of the indictments. In contrast, according to sources within Abraaj at the time, Rafique Lakhani and Ashish Dave did not play any role in the development of valuations but are both indicted. In addition, Wahid Hamid, a US national with security clearance and close friendship with Barack Obama, was absent in the indictment and subsequent coverage despite being, as managing partner, at Arif Naqvi's right hand throughout the period under review. Again, I am not suggesting that Hamid did anything wrong, but it is noteworthy that he is the only member of the investment committee, which comprised the four managing partners and was the entity that had the highest-level oversight of all elements of the contested funds, not to have been indicted.

And from those who were charged, some or all are playing the game and doing what is expected of them. Naqvi was also expected to have pled guilty, taken his fine, maybe served a little time and then perhaps he would have been allowed back to work; there are countless examples of US hedge fund executives who have done exactly that. He could have stopped it getting this far if he had heeded the warning signs. What drew me further into this story was the question of why Naqvi had not rolled over and why Abraaj was targeted and not saved.

As a Pakistani-born Muslim, operating out of the Middle East with the glitz of Dubai behind him, Naqvi was always on the fringes and could be rendered expendable if he stepped out of line, no matter how many clearances or accolades he may have received. But there is always a higher clearance and a more connected inner circle. Naqvi had to go for three main reasons: Abraaj began successfully operating beyond the ambit it was being afforded (and the people in the company believed they were too good to fail); they were not seen as 'one of us' in the private equity world (even though they often walked the walk); and, most importantly, the company refused to do Caesar's bidding when it came to the big picture.

After his arrest, Naqvi spent close to two months in Wandsworth prison before his two sons managed to contact various close friends and former associates to secure his £15 million cash bail. House arrest is a form of modern purgatory which exists to save the state money by keeping the prisoner out of jail. Its primary purpose is to mitigate against the risk of flight for someone on bail. It is better than prison, but it has a particular kind of torture to it. Some people living under house arrest can leave their home for set periods daily. Some can move about within areas that do not contain airports and ports. Many can continue working. Almost all must wear electronic tags that do not work well, going off at random times and are in effect a modern form of shackle. House arrest is often part of the process of extradition to countries like the US in which the justice system has been broken by politics. It is the gradual constriction and suffocation of the defendant's ability to fight back. And it does not stop there. In Naqvi's case, until February 2021, twenty-one months after his house arrest commenced, he was only allowed out for a walk for two hours a day.[17] His hard-won concession to be allowed to pray at the mosque on Fridays became the victim of the Covid-19 lockdown. It appears that his house remains monitored. I have spoken to acquaintances, friends and colleagues of his who remain frightened to enter the house for fear of becoming collateral damage if they are seen to associate with Naqvi. His family, all of whom sit as bystanders affected by the ongoing saga, endure their own version of house arrest. The all-encompassing attack on Naqvi has made them all 'un-friendable'.

From the material that is available in the public domain, I would suggest that it is impossible for Arif Naqvi to receive a fair trial if he is extradited to the US. Many of his former colleagues have already done deals with the DoJ to either not be indicted at all in exchange for testimony or, if indicted, to do deals to ensure that they will escape with a lenient punishment. Take, for example, Mustafa Abdel-Wadood who was regarded as Naqvi's number two. A partner and head of private equity of the firm from 2008 right up to 2018, Abdel-Wadood pled guilty to the seven DoJ charges levelled against him and agreed to cooperate. He is out on a $10 million bail and, as is normal in these cases, there is very little chance he will see much, if any, of his potential 125 years in prison.[18] He has played the game. With two children, who were on the cusp of going into high school and university, there was an entire life ahead for him and his family. The fear and threat of the DoJ can be terrifying.

In contrast, Naqvi faces multi-year incarceration in terrible prison conditions even before a trial commences. Due to the volume of documents involved in the discovery process and given the publicity around his case, he will likely be the subject of extortion; there are no secrets in prison. Testimony presented at his extradition hearings described in horrific detail the criminal gangs that operate in prisons that can break the most resolute of people, which, conveniently, would lead to the imposition of solitary confinement for 'his own safety'. Of course, the pressure will eventually become unbearable and Naqvi will inevitably plead guilty to some or all of the charges that he has repeatedly protested his innocence of in order to do a deal with the DoJ and go quietly to jail for a decade or more: this seems the likely outcome unless a judge simply throws the indictment out. This is an anomaly (or unfair advantage depending on your point of view) of the criminal justice system in the US; 96 per cent of federal cases under indictment do not go to court in exchange for a guilty plea. There are multiple issues with the system, but a key one is that it is 'secret and unreviewable'. Judge Jed Rakoff, who presides in the Southern District of New York, summed up the problem in *Why the Innocent Plead Guilty and the Guilty Go Free*:

> Plea bargains are mostly the product of secret negotiations behind closed doors in the prosecutor's office, and are subject to almost no review, either internally or by the courts. Such a secretive system inevitably invites arbitrary results. Indeed, there is great irony in the fact that legislative measures that were designed to rectify the perceived evils of disparity and arbitrariness in sentencing have empowered prosecutors to preside over a plea-bargaining system that is so secretive and without rules that we do not even know whether or not it operates in an arbitrary manner.[19]

But even more than this, Judge Rakoff concluded that 'the prosecutor-dictated plea-bargain system, by creating such inordinate pressures to enter into plea bargains, appears to have led a significant number of defendants to plead guilty to crimes they never actually committed'.

It is probably too late for Naqvi to strike a deal before his extradition appeal is decided by the higher courts in the UK. I am not a judge, a member of a jury or even a journalist, but from the evidence that I have seen, the most that Naqvi and his co-defendants are guilty of are regulatory breaches which should be the subject of regulatory censure. Such crimes should be tried through civil rather than criminal proceedings and Naqvi's life and liberty and that of his co-defendants, should not be being put at risk. I have concluded that there is much more to this story, there is something deeper at work here than just the mistakes of one man or the potentially selfish interests of competing private equity firms. Arif Naqvi is in his house arrest stasis because he did not render unto Caesar that which is Caesar's because, as we shall see, in the US the private sector is the state and the state is the private sector.

The more deeply I investigated this case, the more it seemed to me that the one-sided extradition treaty was not the real story; nor indeed was the way in which the way Arif Naqvi and his colleagues had been treated – though these things are important. This is a politically and economically motivated prosecution of Abraaj executives and arrest, imprisonment and attempted extradition to the United States of Arif Naqvi. There was a wider campaign launched against The Abraaj Group, and the finale of which will be the incarceration of Arif Naqvi with a lengthy prison sentence; a potential death penalty of sorts for a man in his sixties. As I will cover later, Naqvi has become the fall guy for the collapse of Abraaj and has become the subject of selective judicial activism. But collapse is the wrong word. Collapse implies self-implosion. It implies that this was an edifice that with the lightest touch of a hammer would have inevitably fallen to the ground. This company did not collapse. It was taken down.

This is not the story of an individual; this is the story of the geo-politics of global capitalism and the ability of nation states to destroy companies and the lives of people who directly challenge the interests of those nation states.[20] It is also the story of how the media works hand in glove with the interests of the state, unwittingly perhaps at the level of the jobbing journalist, but wittingly higher up the food chain.[21] There are layers of irony here as well. Abraaj was a company that grew out of globalisation and developed an ideology derived from the leading advocates of globalisation. A company that rose as a result of the increasing integration of capital from the Gulf and wider Middle East into the global economy, and a company that invested bravely in places that many other companies would not invest in because it saw them as being 'frontier' or 'emerging' markets. Because something in the global south must always form a frontier to be reached and then transcended by Westerners. Because the Chinese economy is seen as being non-democratic and non-Western, it must be referred to as 'emerging'.

Abraaj was ultimately destroyed because of the rise of economic nationalism in an increasingly isolationist US administration. This was part of the widespread populist rejection of globalisation and integration and can be seen around the world, notably for example, in the UK's vote to leave the EU. But it is also the story of competition within the private equity industry itself between the established and the emerging; between the old way and a new way of deploying private equity – an idea that is itself the subject of a power play between superpowers. What it is not is a simple reimagination of the Bernie Madoff story with Robert de Niro in the title role, or the 1MBD scandal dramatised in the Pulitzer Prize-winning *Billon Dollar Whale*. The DoJ is an extension of US foreign policy and the use of the press is a routine feature of these cases. This strategy was popularised by none other than Rudy Giuliani during his time as US Attorney for the SDNY. Press briefings and media have been utilised as an extremely effective tool by prosecutors, drawn on when needed. To the average person, countries do not get involved in stopping transactions; well, for the US, such an approach is a tool of foreign policy, and corporate history is replete with such examples, especially in nations where the superpower tussle is often balanced on a knife's edge like Pakistan. This book will try to explain why.

The Caesar to whom Naqvi would not bow was the US government. But that was for the future. For now Naqvi, as a Pakistani guest, had to build a company in the Gulf.

PART II

# RISING ACTION – KHALEEJI CAPITALISTS

# 3

# The creation of a Gulf capitalist class

*For those who dare, the rewards are huge;*
*for others, no plaque will be written.*

Arif Naqvi, 11 May 1997[1]

I n 1997, the 37-year-old Arif Naqvi gave a speech at the Private and Family Enterprises Seminar held by the Institute of International Research. His theme was what he called 'corporatising'. Ten days earlier, Tony Blair had been elected as Prime Minister of the UK, confirming that the Thatcher revolution of privatisation and deregulation would not be reversed by New Labour. Naqvi's target audience were the family offices of the wealthy elite of the Gulf and his message was that they themselves needed to modernise to survive in tomorrow's business world. For a young foreigner in his thirties without any history of accomplishment to his name to deliver such a message must have taken considerable chutzpah.

> Corporatising is a part of restructuring that is intrinsic to any living, breathing, dynamic business. Restructuring is vital to

survive and prosper. Corporatising is simply a mechanism of restructuring; it is not done because it is fashionable, and everybody is doing it … We, willingly or unwillingly, are being dragged into this ever-changing, ever-more competitive world. It is only our productivity and efficiency, the quality of our decisions which will allow us to be successful … We can no longer hide behind the boundaries of our countries and plead our special interest cases to governments to save us. We cannot rely on tariffs, or 'nationals-only' business policies of government to survive … We have to adopt our business practices to conform and adapt to the *real world*. For family businesses this is the way to go forward, this is the way to protect the long-term interest of the family. I am not saying that this has always been the case, nor that it always will be. But it is so at this moment. So, seize the moment … Be on constant guard, look around and embrace change as the only permanence in our lives.[2]

Abraaj Capital would not be founded for another five years, but the speech is clear evidence that the company did not arise from the Gulf by accident but was a product of a deep and profound set of changes that Naqvi recognised early on that were fundamentally reshaping the economics of the region. These changes reflected several important forces that combined to propel Abraaj, and its forerunner Cupola, forward. Two decades earlier and these forces would not have been in motion. Two decades later and there might not have been the space for it because so many others were competing for the niche that Abraaj came to fill and, with early-adopter advantage, for a short time, dominate. This was as Naqvi described 'a classic fulfilment of right place, right time' moment. The changes in the geopolitical and socio-economic position and make-up of the Gulf after the First Gulf War formed some of the forces that shaped and worked in favour of Abraaj. These changes entailed a much closer strategic and military alliance and reliance on the United States, which involved the imposition of a neo-liberal economic model to replace the developmental state model, which had been a welfare state driven by energy revenue.[3] In Naqvi's speech he pleaded for businesses to ignore government special interests and the reliance on tariffs or 'nationals-only' business policies to survive. The growing realisation that the oil would run out was a contributing factor in this process of economic modernisation. Professor Adam Hanieh at SOAS London has persuasively described the evolution of Gulf states in the way that Naqvi was outlining. For example, Saudi Arabia emerged in 1932 after being constructed by state-sponsored industrialisation funded by the oil and petrochemical industries. This continued through to the inflation-led oil boom of the 1970s but did not survive the broader global economic realignment of the 1980s and the collapse of the Soviet Union. The roots of the shift to a dual role in the world economy for the Gulf after the 1991 war were laid in the broader shifts of the 1980s. These changes increased in pace and intensity as the region emerged as a centre of finance and services up to and beyond the crash of 2008.[4] Hanieh named these developments of the Gulf as a source of liquidity for the global economy and its role in investment in infrastructure as well as provision of credit in 'Khaleeji Capital' and argued that:

> The key feature of this new phase of internationalization was a further qualitative leap in the importance of finance to the functioning of capitalism and, simultaneously, the construction of a world market based upon fully global manufacturing and distribution chains. Both tendencies had enormous implications for the GCC and helped to underpin the rise of 'Khaleeji Capital' at the onset of the twenty-first century. The economic origins of the new phase of internationalization were found in neo-liberalism's triumphant spread across the world during the previous two decades ... neo-liberalism laid the basis

for a substantial increase in financial flows and the emergence of complicated production chains interlocked through cross-border ownership structures. A major role in this was played by Third World debt, which ... firmly linked poorer countries into the global financial circuits.

There were a number of major steps that created the conditions for Abraaj to flourish and the first was the broad opening of global markets and capital flows. The second major driver of change was the development debt that began to become available for equity markets. This opened up greater scope for leverage in the region, but also created a market in debt and formed another mechanism to drive further capital flows into emerging markets. This was the way that most private equity companies first discovered that the rest of the world existed.

In the late 1980s, when several major debtor countries (notably Chile and Mexico) adopted debt-for-equity plans as part of restructuring debt repayment schedules with commercial banks. These debt-for-equity plans allowed lenders to swap the money they were owed by the debtor country for a stake in a privatized company or asset.

In parallel, the World Bank, the IMF and the IFC developed the idea that having opened their economies and traded their debt, these economies should deepen even further their reliance on markets and market forces by deregulating their financial markets.

This of course opened the door to private equity companies and local stock markets providing a means for localised IPOs as an exit strategy. These changes produced some opportunities for investors if they were prepared to learn to engage in these markets and political systems. Naqvi understood this trend early and Cupola and then Abraaj were designed for this engagement, but this also produced massive problems, especially in debt-ridden economies that offered 100 per cent ownership to outside investors and competed to be the most hospitable to foreign direct investment. However, in other countries this liberalisation produced the beginnings of sustained if unequal economic growth, and rapid industrialisation and consumer purchasing. Global manufacturing interests understood the potential of consumption-led rapid economic growth a long time before private equity. Those markets that by law, custom or hard lessons from the first wave of liberalisation in the 1990s restricted the ability of foreign companies to have 100 per cent ownership and worked on models of partnership, also started to slowly attract private equity. Capital-rich states, like those in the Gulf, which fed the hunger for hydrocarbons in emerging economies, took advantage of the liberalisation to become global investors.

The changes in the structure of the world economy and the flows of capital allowed trillions of dollars of private capital to move more freely into parts of the globe that they had not entered before. Hanieh illustrated the change with some simple numbers: in 1970, foreign investment in emerging states' stock markets was zero. In 1985 it had reached $100 million. By 1994, when Naqvi and his team founded Cupola, it was $39.5 billion.[5] The investment opportunities in these sectors exceeded well over $630 billion, according to an Abraaj Group research report, which formed the basis for the launch of their Infrastructure Growth Capital Fund. The estimate covered a broad range of infrastructure sectors 'that collectively comprise the social and economic fabric of the region'.[6] The report argued that historically the public sector had provided the funding for infrastructure development, but this level of investment could not be met by the public sector on its own. Whilst some of the Middle East, North Africa and South Asia (MENASA) region (such as the GCC) was running budget surpluses up to $400 billon, other states in South Asia had significant budget deficits. The report also found that over 200 privatisations had been announced in the MENASA region across a variety of sectors – and that the privatisation pipeline was expected to reach a value of $1 trillion during the following decade.[7] This was considerably disrupted by the financial crash in 2008, but nevertheless the potential remained strong.

The Gulf states had been transformed. They had come to meet global investments, formed part of them and interacted with them. These social relations were described in Khaleeji Capital as having certain conditions that were unique to the Gulf, within the wider set of emerging markets:

- One is the exceptionally tight intermesh between the ruling families and the state (there is a Department of Private Interests in the Ministry of the Economy in the UAE and the King in Saudi Arabia owns all the oil in the ground).
- The second is the patronage provided by the ruling family to their close associates, such as through land grants, trade concessions, public project contracts and some privatisations.
- The third is the ability – given the ample monopoly profits from oil – of the ruling elite to transform the indigenous working class into a salaried middle class. Hanieh cited figures from the Saudi Central Planning Organization that showed that over 90 per cent of the workforce were Saudi nationals in the early 1960s; this had declined to half by 1980.
- Fourth is the replacement of the local workforce with migrant labour from South Asia and other labour surplus economies in the region, such as Egypt.
- Finally, there are linkages between Khaleeji Capital and global finance capital and the economic and strategic role of the GCC in the world.[8]

In parallel to the development of the role in finance, the social structure of the region changed drastically after the First Gulf War because of the mass expulsion of Yemeni, Palestinian and Egyptian workers. These workers were from nations that had supported the wrong side in the war, but the move away from this workforce had started even before the conflict. Asians were judged to be a much more 'flexible, submissive and obedient workforce because they could not demand rights' – they were not, after all, Arabs.[9] By 2008, 15 million Asians had replaced Arabs in Gulf states, making up between 40 and 90 per cent of the population but having no political and few civil, social or economic rights in what is known as the *kafala* system[10] – the system that has built the stadiums for the 2022 World Cup in Qatar. A key element of the promotion of the new world order was meant to be a linkage between human rights and democracy as the ticket of entry to the world economic club. The reality has been that these standards have been applied unevenly, sometimes even within the same region. GCC states are treated as strategic allies and sources of trade and profitability, whilst blatant racism, virtual slave labour, exploitation and archaic and medieval punishments continue and are ignored. Compare this to Iraq, where a brutal dictatorship must be the subject of regime change and decades of resulting chaos and bloodshed in the name of human rights and democracy ensue.

It is this combination of forces, the Gulf's role in the global financial system, the West's uncritical acceptance of these regimes and the shift of orientation away from other Arab states towards South Asia, which created one part of the environment in which Abraaj could grow. These things did not happen by accident. They were the result of the decade of neo-liberal change that saw deregulation and privatisation led by the UK and the US. It came through the imposition of economic reform and structural adjustment plans and credit and trade agreements between Middle Eastern states and the US, the EU, members of the General Agreement on Tariffs and Trade (GATT) and then its successor the WTO, the IMF and the World Bank.[11] The policies that were to be implemented through these neo-liberal interventions towards globalisation included encouraging free trade, the opening of strategic sectors like finance and telecommunications to foreign direct investment, deregulating or privatising transport and energy provisions and deregulation and often de-unionising of labour relations – which involved abolishing or lowering minimum wages, rolling back job protections and severance pay for migrant workers. The changes produced a 'new regional capitalist class supported by the rise of the Gulf as a global financial and economic hub'.[12]

The Abraaj Group, and to an extent Cupola, were creatures of these deeper forces of globalisation and slowly became more aware of it. The Abraaj Group was to operate at the heart of the intersections of these social relations and was a product of them, and when the forces and ideologies that determined these relations changed, Abraaj was in turn destroyed by them. The irony of the position of companies like Abraaj should not be overlooked. The core team that set up Cupola were Pakistani, but the core group of investors that were gathered for the launch of Abraaj and its first fund were from the Gulf. The core markets that Abraaj began to invest in were emerging markets that were seeing the emergence of a newly affluent middle class in a wide range of new cities. The capital that was being deployed was generated in a Gulf area that had an unwitting by-product of effectively pulling up the ladder of social mobility to the South Asian workforce it had brought in to build its economic position in the new global economy.

On the one hand, the multinational team at Abraaj was providing capital for companies that were building the goods and services that an emerging middle class required, and that this same class benefited from by running the companies populating the growing SME sectors. On the other hand, certainly up until 2012/13, it was deploying capital derived from the Khaleeji Capital system and in which the economic miracle of the desert states was kept afloat on a sea of hydrocarbons and migrant labour. This migrant labour could be deported at will in times of economic crisis, but this also meant the remittances sent back to families in their state of origin were economically significant. Between 2006 and 2018, just under $100 billion was officially transferred from Gulf states to just Pakistan alone.[13] Ask anyone which industry the Gulf states are global leaders in, and the instinctive reply is usually 'oil and gas'. The reality is that they are also world leaders (second only to the US) in the 'remittances' business around outward money flows. This made the Gulf the bedrock of the global *hawala* system of illicit money flows that bypass the banking system. Indeed, despite the glitz and glamour of the UAE and its outward projection, it remains on the Financial Action Task Force's grey list and was the subject of a recent and damning report issued by the Carnegie Foundation.[14]

The formation of what Hanieh calls the 'cross-Gulf capitalist class', who possess capital to deploy internationally and through firms such as Abraaj, is not to say that the individual national identities and differences between the GCC members disappeared.[15] In fact, there was considerable competition between these states to adopt Abraaj as a national champion. These interactions demonstrate how capital, in its formation and its flows, is 'a relation not just a thing'.[16] As a social relation it comprises both relationships in which the 'circuits' of capital matter more than the national identities of the individuals concerned, and a collective nexus in which the combined financial force of the GCC could be increasingly deployed. Cupola and Abraaj exploited these intertwined relationships and grew exponentially; others followed. But in the headlong rush to acquire capital and assets, Abraaj forgot the wisdom of an ancient Arabic proverb: 'I against my brothers; I and my brothers against my cousins; and I and my brothers and cousins against everyone else.'

Cupola was Abraaj before there was Abraaj. From the very first days of Cupola there was talk and gossip around the Pakistani team at the centre of the company as well as the rapid and innovative style of doing business, which was modern by GCC standards. The implication was that without family wealth and/or institutional backing, without large Arab family houses sponsoring and supporting the company, there must be something shady about them. Many people living in the Gulf States take encompassing myths and beliefs when evaluating nationalities with sweeping racist generalities, and I heard the following stereotypes many times: Egyptians and Sudanese are clever and lazy but should be lawyers and accountants, South Asians are inferior and should be labourers, Yemenis are sly, Morocco, Tunisia and Algeria are a source of beautiful women but unscrupulous men, and Indonesians and Filipinos are a source of maids alone. These utterly backward views continue, and it was no surprise to discover that the prevailing stereotype for Pakistanis in the Gulf was that they were 'drug smugglers, money launderers and labourers ... certainly not cutting-edge deal makers!'[17] Imtiaz Hydari, a colleague of Naqvi from Olayan, who became a founding partner of Abraaj, played a part in the Inchcape deal and wrote a self-published account of the deal. In that account he said that

> Cupola had paid investigators, Kroll Associates, $50,000 to do a background check on the key players involved, including board members, to dispel the mounting rumours that the company was a mere front for Pakistani politicians. Some claimed drug money was behind Cupola – it seemed this was part of a calculated campaign to malign the company.[18]

In addition to the regular due diligence done by every investor into its operations, Cupola was also continually vetted at every level throughout its journey and watched, as WikiLeaks revealed, in classified reports that assessed it as a potential partner of the West.[19] From the very beginning, the team who came to form Abraaj were outsiders.

Cupola was set up with a meagre amount of capital (variously reported as $50,000 or $75,000) from Naqvi's formative years in Saudi Arabia working for the Saudi conglomerate, the Olayan Group. I have avoided reciting Naqvi's biographical progression in this book because it has already had much airtime in the media; I have focused on the seminal events that I believe shaped his psyche. Cupola was registered at Jebel Ali Free Zone (a port twenty-five miles outside Dubai), and

Saudi and GCC investors were recruited to back the firm over time. At the beginning of 1995 Naqvi sold half of his stake to Izzat Majeed, chief executive of the UK-based investment firm Alyph Limited, and a former adviser to the then Saudi Oil Minister Hisham Nazer, for over $4 million. This was one significant move into Khaleeji Capital. It was followed by another when Dr Abdullah Basodan, chairman of Nimir Petroleum and former director of the National Commercial Bank in Jeddah, also came in as an investor, extending Cupola's network considerably. Naqvi claimed that 'the deal to inject $6 million into Cupola was done at a restaurant in London with the agreement having been signed on the shirt cuff!'[20] However the deal was done, it was indicative of what was happening more broadly in the Gulf. By 1998 Cupola was based in Al Moosa Tower and comprised a senior team that included Waqar Siddique, Naqvi's brother-in-law; Kokab Mirza, a colleague from Olayan as chief operating officer; Naqvi's cousin Owais Naqvi as head of marketing; Shabbir Jivanji as finance director; and Kazim Awan as business development director. Fayyaz Alimohamed and Nasir Iqbal were also key members of the team. This was a group who had known each other for a long time, trusted each other's abilities and were willing to trust Naqvi's business acumen, whilst working harder and earning less than they could elsewhere: a recipe for success in an entrepreneurial start-up. Cupola introduced franchises into Pakistan – Pizza Express, TGI Fridays, Thomas Cook and Estée Lauder, amongst others.[21] Cupola also provided the operational and financial nucleus of several pioneering concepts in the Middle East. Prominent amongst these were the first venture into outsourcing for banks in Dubai, a novel concept at the time through the creation of a call centre and manufacturing, processing and billing facilities, which has become the core of a regionally focused business process outsourcing; a Visa/MasterCard accredited financial cards manufacturing and personalisation unit which was eventually sold to Oberthur Technologies; and a document management business which was sold to Aramex.[22]

Cupola and the foundational deal it went on to do with the purchase of Inchcape Middle East was emblematic of the formation of the new capitalist class in the GCC. Abraaj, when it was formed, was to ride this wave of change for the decade that followed and more, but, as we shall see, in this moment of initial triumph there were also warning signs that even in the commerce of the Gulf there were limits to which forms of ownership and which social place Pakistanis could occupy.

Within eight years, in 2002, Cupola was registered under a holding company, Gruppe Cupola Luxembourgeoise SA, which directly owned twenty-seven group companies across three business sectors, generating the capital, knowledge and know-how needed for the Cupola team to seize the opportunities across the region. Inchcape Middle East controlled a unique set of assets across the Middle East, which included household brands that were trusted and an integral part of the social fabric of both the Gulf and the wider region.

Inchcape had grown from the middle of the nineteenth century into a wide range of different interests across thirty-two countries. The company's core business was car sales and distribution, but in the Middle East it worked across retail and all kinds of other services. After two very bad years in the mid-1990s, Inchcape commissioned consultants to look at its business and figure out what it should concentrate on and where. The consultants said car distribution in Europe and South East Asia. It was a UK-listed company, and it made the decision to sell off all businesses in Russia, South America and the Middle East. In the Middle East, Inchcape was like the East India Company. It was selling its legacy; it was a big business and it had 49 per cent local ownership. As Naqvi recalled, 'Everyone knew Inchcape because the supermarket you went to was Inchcape; if you bought alcohol it was Inchcape; if you shipped anything it was Inchcape.'[23] For the Cupola team, who would go on to form the nucleus of the Abraaj team, successfully buying the Inchcape brands would at a stroke take them from obscurity to respectability, from being a group of South Asian migrant businessmen to being the owners of the main suppliers of supermarket goods and a range of other products. Most importantly, over a protracted period, they became deal-doers. With the challenge of acquiring Inchcape behind them, no other team in the region could boast similar experience and they had been properly schooled in the trenches. The purchase would announce Cupola's arrival and provide the springboard for further success, but it turned out to be not quite in the way it was planned.

The prospect of Cupola purchasing Inchcape Middle East (IME) were at the outset extremely remote. Naqvi and his colleagues had never been involved in a deal of this size. On paper they lacked the resources and the credibility to launch such a bid. At this point Cupola had invested the bulk of its capital in start-up companies. Naqvi heard about the potential deal in Dubai from Imtiaz Hydari, who was advising one of the potential bidders, the Trans-Arabian Investment Bank. Naqvi was very excited about the prospect of Cupola being able to take over a business which the previous year had a turnover of $562 million. Hydari told him the price for IME was likely to be approximately $150 million.[24] Naqvi now had a clear idea of the size of the challenge ahead and he set to work as quickly as he could on mobilising his team putting together the funds. From the Gulf side there were two figures who were crucial to putting the funding together for such a deal, and Cupola would also need a Western bank to lend money for the leveraged bid. The Gulf figures were Dr Abdullah Basodan and Dr Ahmed Al Malik, both key investors in Cupola; Basodan was chair of Nimir Petroleum and Al Malik was a retired general from the Saudi Arabian armed forces who went on to become the deputy governor at the Saudi Arabian Monetary Agency. Both were extremely well-connected individuals who emerged as crucial supporters of the company at this time. The central issue which was to characterise the entire process of selling Inchcape was the adverse position of the local partners in the firms in the Gulf and in the Levant; and the key question was if someone else won the bid, would the local partners work with them or accept the legality of the deal? Even if the local partners had accepted the legality of the deal, they did not want to work with another external owner and did not believe Inchcape could or should be sold to anyone else except themselves.

Ownership rules in the Gulf were that local partners held 51 per cent of the shares (of which 2 per cent was as nominees of Inchcape), whilst Inchcape, although it managed the companies, held 49 per cent; and 100 per cent of the management rested with Inchcape. The local partners were obviously best placed to purchase the shares owned by IME and most of them felt that they were entitled to do so. But at no point did the management of Inchcape seem to consider the possibility of selling the business to the local partners. Inchcape's judgement, which was proved right, was that the local partners would not pay as high a price as a separate outside bidder would pay for the overall control of each part of their Middle Eastern holdings.

Cupola had not yet identified itself as a private equity firm, but nevertheless it did not intend to run this large group of companies indefinitely. It wanted the local partners to run their own concerns and to manage the group through to a successful IPO on a local stock exchange so it could pay back the capital it had borrowed to make the bid. This kind of leveraged takeover was unheard of in the Middle East at this time. However, once Cupola began to look more closely at the structure of the bid and the nature of the companies involved, the team began to get a sense of the resistance from the local partners to an external bidder and they saw that in fact the value of the group lay in selling key parts of it piecemeal to each of the local partners. The sum was greater than the parts. It was this realisation that allowed the Cupola team to raise the necessary money, pay it back extremely quickly and exit with a profit, but it was not a smooth or pretty process.

Cupola's more immediate concern was that it had missed the deadline to be included on the list of bidders. It took all of Naqvi's persistence and charm to persuade Inchcape that they were a serious proposition and to have them included in the initial bidding round. Naqvi knew that it was the merchant bank Schroders that were handling the sale. He wrangled a meeting with them. According to an individual who was present at the meeting, Naqvi was broadly told:

> You need to show us that you have the money, and we cannot figure out that how you could possibly have the money. Maybe you have friends. But you have to bring a London, city-based bank to certify that you are capable of doing the deal and a firm of city lawyers to do the same and you are already four months behind everyone else, so why don't you put this down as a good learning experience and go away? Thank you.[25]

Next morning, Naqvi started working the phone. A friend said he knew someone at ANZ Grindlays Bank in London. He told them about the deal and, although they had no previous experience in the Middle East, they were interested and agreed to work on a success-fee basis and provided him with the letter he needed. He did a similar deal with a partner at the law firm Norton Rose (now Norton Rose Fulbright) in London. Much to Schroder's surprise, he gave them what they wanted and they gave Cupola access to the data room – a physically secure room containing all the information Inchcape had provided for due diligence by prospective buyers.[26] He flew virtually the whole Cupola team to London, and they camped out in an apartment off Sloane Street with air mattresses and an endless supply of KFC. For eight months they worked at the offices of Slaughter and May, Inchcape's lawyers, from 9 a.m. to midnight. As ANZ did more diligence, they and Cupola were becoming more comfortable with the opportunity. The team also began to realise that the sum of the parts was greater than the whole. They realised that if they took the security down into the underlying asset and sold off companies A, B, C and D, then the bank could be paid back and they would still make a profit. Cupola began to present it as a management buyout, and Inchcape's failure to manage the relationship with the local partners effectively meant that when Cupola was announced as the preferred bidder, many of the larger local partners objected and refused to cooperate with the process. In the end, this allowed the Cupola team to negotiate the price of the overall sale down from $150 million because of the inevitable conflicts with the local partners and the necessity to then consider selling each part of the business rather than float the whole in an IPO. This was lucky because Cupola had significant difficulty in raising the equity that was required as, amongst the more serious family office investors in the region, nobody wanted to get involved until the position of the Inchcape local partners was clarified. However, with the reduction in price to $98 million and with ANZ firmly on side, Cupola managed to complete the bid on April Fool's Day 1999. Once the bid was complete, Cupola then announced that it had separately already negotiated the sale of Spinneys Dubai to the local partner Ali Bawardy for $22 million, all of which went to Inchcape as part-payment for the deal; alongside another $10 million rebate from Inchcape because of certain undisclosed legal constraints on dealing with local partners. With ANZ support, Cupola's own capital was never strained, and it had no need to ask Basodan or Al Malik to put up money. The company acquired Inchcape with only $3 million of its own capital and ANZ was repaid in full within fourteen months, once MMI Dubai, an alcohol retailer, was sold to Emirates Airlines. Cupola then set about selling off the additional individual alcohol-related businesses to local partners. Some of the companies were sold almost immediately, whilst others were sold over the next two and a half to three years. Cupola had done its first deal by leveraging a small amount of capital from its own resources with a much larger amount from a bank as a partner. That meant that when the local partner companies were sold off, the bulk of the proceeds representing profit, after paying back the bank and other fees, came to Cupola directly and represented profits that were in the region of $100 million. Naqvi's reputation had been firmly established.

# 4

# The birth of Abraaj 1.0

After 2001, with many of Inchcape's partner companies now sold, the Cupola team were very well positioned but unsure of what to do next. Naqvi hired McKinsey,[1] a globally recognised consulting firm, to analyse the company and produce a roadmap for the future. McKinsey studied the business and reported that Cupola was operating like a traditional private equity company, if one working in what were still considered non-traditional geographies by the bulk of the industry. Over time this had become a pivotal part of Cupola's strength. By April 2001, Naqvi made the strategic decision to create a new private equity business. McKinsey were closely involved in designing the firm from its inception and consulted frequently thereafter, as we shall see later. McKinsey also played a role in formulating strategy at seminal inflection points as the firm grew. The Inchcape deal was a foundational deal under the name of Cupola and gave it the reputation across the region for having done the first ever leveraged buyout and navigating the local ownership laws successfully. Now Naqvi needed a deal to announce his arrival as a pioneer of private equity, a concept unheard of in the region.

Aramex had been founded as a courier company in Jordan in 1984. With state post offices controlling a monopoly of supply and logistical problems around security, global delivery firms had avoided the Middle

East. Over several decades, Aramex's founders, Fadi Ghandour, and his American partner, Bill Kingston, grew the company to the point at which, in 1996, the Seattle-based Airborne Express, a well-established logistics company acquired a 9 per cent stake, followed by a flotation on NASDAQ. The pair managed to get the company listed, but even with Airborne on board and other international carriers as clients the share price did not perform as they had hoped.

Naqvi had met Ghandour through the Young Presidents' Organization[2] at a Wharton Business School seminar where they were being taught survival skills. Ghandour's competitiveness attracted Naqvi and over the years they did several businesses and public initiatives together.

As Aramex's NASDAQ flotation had not worked as expected, Naqvi proposed to Ghandour to take the company private again; and Naqvi had his first major deal. Using $30 million of Cupola's own capital to leverage the total $60 million needed, Aramex was taken private. Cupola's capital contribution in the Aramex deal was injected into a fund structure to be managed by a new private equity company; it was the first public-to-private transaction for the region and the first private equity deal. The deal was one of the first announced on the New York Stock Exchange after 9/11 and, in the environment of that period, it got a lot of attention, especially as it was one Arab company buying another.[3] In 2005, Abraaj exited the investment through an IPO on the Dubai Financial Market that was intended to raise $270 million but was oversubscribed by a factor of sixty-four.[4] It was an incredible return for investors, the Cupola team, the founders, the management team and the region.

McKinsey had introduced Naqvi to Ali Shihabi, the founder of Rasmala, a small investment company that he felt would provide an Arab 'halo of respectability' to the private equity structure and venture for Cupola. The project was not a success and both Naqvi and Shihabi decided it was better to go it alone and cut ties after a very short period. This was an acrimonious and fractious separation, but Naqvi believed it was justified because almost all of the original Rasmala investors joined his new venture, Abraaj. Shihabi was left bitter and angry. He was not the first business associate to be put off by Naqvi's abrasive, direct and relentless style and he would not be the last. But Naqvi did not look back. 'We went to every conceivable PR agency and rejected hundreds of names,' Naqvi later told the *New York Times*. 'Then one day my colleague, who now works for Deutsche Bank, was making doodles of Emirates Towers – or *Abraaj al Emarat* in Arabic – and said, "Hey, why not just call it Abraaj?" The name brought us good luck.'

Abraaj Investment Management Limited was established in the Cayman Islands in 2002.[5] Private equity firms domicile in this jurisdiction to avoid paying tax, and in the 1990s Dubai allowed this form of registration to free firms from the constraints of local ownership. Given their experience of the local partners during the Inchcape deal, it was natural for Abraaj to use this offshore model.

In its last distributed pitch deck in 2018, Abraaj described the firm's initial growth as 'organic', expanding from Dubai into the wider Middle East, Turkey and South Asia and ultimately Singapore in 2011, with the aim of extending into South East Asia: 'A key driver behind the expansion was growth into markets with similar dynamics and opportunities. Throughout its expansion, Abraaj has remained focused on its core principles: being local everywhere, exemplifying world-class standards, hands-on active value creation, cross platform collaboration and delivering consistency.'[6]

Behind the rhetoric and the sales pitch was the solid foundation that Khaleeji Capital invested in this growth strategy for Abraaj. In 2010 the full board (of which the first seven were founding board members since 2002) included:

- Sheikh Abdulrahman Ali Al-Turki (chairman, Abraaj Holdings Limited; chairman and CEO, A. A. Turki Corporation Trading & Contracting, Saudi Arabia).
- Arif Masood Naqvi (founder and group CEO, The Abraaj Group).

- Hussain J. Al Nowais (vice-chairman, Abraaj Holdings Limited; chairman and managing director, Emirates Holdings, Abu Dhabi).
- Hamid Jafar (Crescent Group, Sharjah).
- Saud Abdulaziz Kanoo (chairman, Oasis Property Developers BSC, Bahrain).
- Sheikh Nawaf Al-Thani (NBK Group, Qatar).
- Saleh Romeih (representing Deutsche Bank, UK).

Independent directors:

- Sean Cleary (chairman, Strategic Concepts (Pty) Ltd, South Africa).
- Sheikh Khaled Bin Zayed Al Nehayan (chairman, Bin Zayed Group, Dubai).
- Sir Paul Judge (director, Standard Bank Group Ltd, UK).
- Fadi Ghandour (founder, president and CEO, Aramex International, Jordan).

Executive directors:

- Mustafa Abdel-Wadood (CEO, Abraaj, Egypt).
- Waqar Siddique (senior partner and chief operating officer, Abraaj, Pakistan).
- Tom Speechley (senior partner, Abraaj, UK).

The geographical spread of these board members indicates that the ownership and strategic direction of Abraaj was distributed across different capital groups throughout the GCC region, with independent oversight from prominent establishment figures in the West – emblematic of a growing firm. In addition, bodies such as the Public Institution for Social Security (Kuwait) and the General Retirement and Pension Authority (Qatar) were also investors and wanted Abraaj to act as an extension of their investment strategies. This soon included other companies from the region that saw the same possibility – such as Air Arabia, a UAE-based quasi-government airline, which had surplus cash on which it wanted to make a return.[7] Abraaj was the answer.

Abraaj established the first Middle East buyout fund in 2002 with the acquisition of Aramex and with commitments of $116 million (Abraaj Buy-Out Fund I, ABOF I), of which the first $30 million were from Cupola, i.e. Naqvi himself was fully invested in the success of the new venture, and this provided reassurance to the newer investors. The fund purchased strategic stakes in some important companies in the Middle East, including Amwal, the leading investment banking firm in Qatar, JorAmco, an aircraft maintenance company privatised by the Jordanian government, and maktoob.com, the leading Arabic internet portal, which after its acquisition by Yahoo spun out a company called Souq, which went on to become the first tech unicorn in the Middle East.

ABOF I was a trailblazing success and it returned its initial investment capital back to investors within eighteen months of its final close in June 2003, with an IRR of over 50 per cent. According to the *Private Equity International*, this early success allowed Abraaj to launch a second fund two years later, ABOF II, which raised $500 million.[8] The years 2002 to 2006 were years spent building Abraaj, developing its international profile in all things linked to Middle Eastern finance, building an effective team and growing the fund management business. Several other funds followed in quick succession, including the Infrastructure Growth Capital Fund[9] in a 2006 joint venture with Deutsche Bank and Ithmaar Bank, which raised $2 billion in a Sharia-compliant fund structure.

In March 2006, Abraaj became the first pure private equity firm to be registered by the Dubai Financial Services Authority to operate out of the Dubai International Financial Centre (DIFC). A subsidiary, Abraaj Capital Limited Dubai, was incorporated in March 2006 and was based in the DIFC, a special 'offshore' economic zone established to build Dubai as a global financial services centre. Dr Omar Bin Sulaiman, director general of the DIFC Authority, welcomed the organisation: 'The track record of this company is second to none. It has been a pioneer in its field, establishing the private equity industry in the UAE and the region, and we are delighted that Abraaj has chosen to come to DIFC as the next stage of its development.'

Naqvi was quoted as saying:

> It is a tremendous achievement to be the first pure private equity firm to be registered by the DFSA. This is doubly significant when you consider that we have never been a regulated business, and it is testament to the high standards of corporate governance that we adhere to that the DFSA has given us this licence.[10]

As a further sign of acceptance, the DIFC invested in Abraaj through its investment arm and a DIFC representative joined the board of directors later in 2006[11] when Abraaj raised its equity base value from $10 million to $1 billion by raising $500 million in fresh equity. Deloitte valued the original equity base at $500 million given the success the firm had enjoyed and the heady nature of investment appetite prior to the global financial crisis of 2008; from $10 million in 2002 to $500 million in less than five years. AIML became a subsidiary of the newly formed holding company, Abraaj Holdings Limited in order to increase capital and diversify the shareholder base of the company. This was again registered in the Cayman Islands. As AIML had a licence to operate as a branch in Dubai, it became the management and expenses vehicle for Abraaj. This allowed for the operating costs and revenues of different sectorial and geographical operations to be brought under one central entity, whereas AHL took over the ownership of all of AIML's investments. The managed funds launched by Abraaj continued to be formed under AIML as the manager of the funds under limited partner and general partner agreements, and the majority of creditors and similar payments were also processed through AIML. AHL provided AIML with the working capital needed to cover operating deficits.

The capital raised by AHL also made an allowance for 10 per cent of the shares to be owned by Naqvi, some of which he gave up in favour of an employee ownership scheme. Board minutes show that on the advice of auditors, given accounting rules that would have led to a financial statement charge to profits if this were held directly, a separate company, AE2L, was established. Owned by Naqvi but held beneficially for the interest of employees and himself, payment for the shares was made by Abraaj, which in turn was to be repaid from dividend proceeds attributable to those shares. By 2017, AE2L built up an equity position of almost 22 per cent, all financed by AHL and recorded as borrowings by AE2L since it also acquired shares from investors who needed liquidity following the financial crash of 2008. Subsequently, the accumulation of reinvested capital and the availability of debt at AHL also allowed the firm to buy back shares from employees as they left, and to invest over and above the normal amounts that private equity firms invest in their own funds. This created considerable balance sheet assets. It also meant that there were pots of capital that could be released from the balance sheet in times of tight liquidity if bridging funds were required or remain on the balance sheet of AHL until just before the IPO when strategic investors could be introduced as part of the price discovery process.

Another innovation was the use of newly raised capital to acquire a controlling stake in the region's largest investment bank, Egyptian Financial Group-Hermes (EFG-Hermes). The idea of 'universal banking' was popular during this time and large commercial banks were busy acquiring asset management entities, insurance companies, brokerages and investment companies in an attempt to create a 'one-stop' solution for investors. Naqvi believed the model could be inverted with private equity firms leading the consolidation charge. Regulators did not share that view and in Lebanon, Pakistan, Jordan and the UAE, Abraaj's efforts to acquire commercial banking operations were rebuffed under the argument that banks needed stable, long-term owners rather than firms with ten-year horizons. Naqvi abandoned the scheme and sold Abraaj's stake in EFG-Hermes fourteen months later and realised almost $700 million in windfall profits for shareholders.[12] It was one of a number of Naqvi's grandiose ideas that fell by the wayside over the years, but nonetheless proved to be a very profitable one.

This approach of raising balance sheet capital was a first in the private equity world and was closely studied by Western counterparts. The subsequent wave of IPOs in private equity firms and hedge funds managed by for example, amongst others, Deutsche Bank, Goldman Sachs, Barclays and Credit Suisse appeared to arise after analysing Abraaj's approach. Part of the purpose of the IPOs was to generate a greater volume of capital on the balance sheet of the firms themselves; this could be invested in funds. Up until this time most fund managers were extremely lightly capitalised (also to avoid liability if the firm collapses) and profits went to the individual partners directly through carried interest arrangements. Local and international media hailed Naqvi as an emerging star investor from a little-known part of the world.

During this period, Abraaj also toyed with the idea of entering the public hedge fund and real estate markets and raised funds for the purpose, even establishing MENASA Capital Management as a spinoff venture with mirrored shareholdings to Abraaj. However, the diversion in management focus was deemed too distracting, and that side of the business never really took hold. It was clear that Abraaj did not have the expertise needed and that the team's skills were best suited to unlocking value from private companies.

By 2007, Abraaj had $5 billion in assets under management rising to $9 billion by the end of 2009; almost 50 per cent of the regional industry. After the successful deployment of IGCF, Abraaj laid claim to expertise in holding majority or minority stakes in greenfield projects, participating in large-scale privatisation, and investing in buy-out and restructuring opportunities across the MENASA region.[13] Before the

2008 crash Abraaj had exited the vast majority of all its big investments across various funds, which limited its exposure to the collapse. As Middle Eastern investment markets froze, Abraaj was able to work with investors to help them through the crisis. Earlier in 2008, Abraaj had launched the successor to IGCF, Abraaj Private Equity Fund IV,[14] and this aimed to raise $4 billion. But the lasting effects of the crash weakened the appetite of investors who had initially committed, and the fund finally closed with only $1.6 billion raised.[15] Many of those initial investors who no longer felt comfortable moving forward were members of the region's elite, and when they reneged on their positions, Abraaj had to take the hit even though contractually it had the right to ask for the money. Abraaj was unable to recover its management fee or cover organisational expenses, especially since it had hired expensive senior professionals to manage the much larger fund that never materialised. Naqvi's determination not to make the same mistake again in 2017, of hiring and replacing and building ahead of fund raising being completed, was a key part of exacerbating the later crises of 2018.

During its first decade, Abraaj became the go-to player in the region's private equity market and a major presence in Dubai itself. Abraaj was embedding further and further into the UAE and was displayed prominently in the DIFC awareness campaigns around the world. At this stage in the life of the company, its bones were still not hardened but certain elements of the strengths and weaknesses of its character had been established. The key target sectors of the firm expanded to include oil and gas, petrochemicals, telecommunications, power, water, healthcare and education, making trophy acquisitions in each of those fields.[16]

After 2006 when Abraaj increased its capital base and formed AHL, its business model combined the best of both worlds. It had the advantage of a well-capitalised holding company corporate structure, as well as the freedom and anonymity afforded by the private equity approach and structure.

Following its substantial capital increase in 2006 and profitable exit from EFG-Hermes a year later, alongside sponsor loans made available to it, AHL had significant resources at its disposal. It continued to make investments with the capital from its own balance sheet. These were either in excess of the contractual requirements, enabling it to sell to later investors as a means of allowing them to acquire 'seasoned primaries' without having to go through the loss-making phases of a new fund, or they were in separate deals with one-off partners. That is the way, for example, in which it directly part-financed the Karachi Electric deal in 2008. The bulk of the profits from these 'balance sheet' transactions was then ploughed back into the company to build new funds, open new offices, recruit teams and experts and enable further growth. This meant that the holding company had the ability to finance growth even when the traditional 2 per cent fund management fees were not sufficient to cover its operating costs and growth capital expenditure; this was unheard of in the traditional private equity industry, but it provided Abraaj with the engine and firepower to expand as it did. Abraaj was at pains to emphasise that the investors in the funds themselves were entirely separate from this process and generally not part of the balance sheet acquisitions and sales.[17] In the aftermath of the 2008 financial crisis, the board also decided to suspend any future payments of dividends in Abraaj Holdings, ploughing all future profits back into growing the business until the firm could list its own IPO.

The initial funds launched by Abraaj reflected both the potential of the region and some of its limits. At inception in 2002, the firm had brought in six regional strategic investors, who formed its original board alongside Deutsche Bank, in exchange for which these individuals and their connections to other business families contributed to capital raised for ABOF I, ABOF II and IGCF (i.e. throughout Abraaj's first decade until the close of APEF IV). Abraaj subsequently referred to these funds as 'legacy funds' to differentiate them from Gen-5 funds that were raised from institutional investors and operated to more stringent documentation. A former senior executive at Abraaj from this time told me that the attitude of these regional investors was very different from the attitudes of larger European and North American institutional investors. They were primarily concerned with receiving a return. They were not used to having funds locked up for ten years at a time. All funds up to APEF IV used block drawdowns, whereby 25 per cent or more of the committed capital would be taken by Abraaj at once rather than on a deal-by-deal basis to ensure that funds were in place when deals were ready to be executed. In this sense, the firm operated like a family office for its client base of wealthy Middle Eastern individuals and a few larger, institutional investors, whilst many of the limited partners within each of the legacy funds were also shareholders of AHL. Limited partners did not always remit monies when requested, but Abraaj chose not to litigate against these delays as this would undermine the relationship that had been cultivated with their investors. Abraaj often had to fill the deficits using its own resources as well as commingle pledged capital from one fund to cover shortfalls in another when required. Commingling was standard practice in the Middle East, with money treated as mutually interchangeable across different funds. These early investors thought they were giving money to Abraaj as an entity, and how it deployed their funds was their business; they trusted the name. Abraaj decided to operate in this way to prioritise long-term partnerships over short-term profitability.

The availability of balance sheet capital also enabled Abraaj to make a broader-based move away from the pure pursuit of profit towards a more ethical, sustainable and impact-driven investment strategy. Year after year, this message was hammered home in the company's marketing materials and annual reports.[18]

Over and above these innovations and business successes, there was something else that marked Abraaj out and made it radically different from traditional private equity firms operating in the West. From its inception, Abraaj's growth model appeared to have political undertones. Naqvi's speeches and writing from 1996 to 2002 seemed more quixotically aspirational rather than grounded in influence or experience, but Cupola was nevertheless a highly successful business. This raises the question, why would Naqvi want to give all that up and move to a private equity model that was untested in the region and with much greater levels of transparency and sharing of profits? The answer seems to lie in what I perceive as his need for constant forward motion. This restlessness was apparent to many people who worked with Naqvi during the Cupola years. Although he achieved success, Cupola was a GCC success story; he wanted more. His experiences at Olayan showed the confluence of business and politics as a nexus of power, and his patriotism for Pakistan led to constant discussions of bringing about lasting change there. For a man in his thirties with no experience or family history in politics, he could have been written off as an idealist, albeit one driven by obvious ambition.

But Naqvi did not go unnoticed. A senior retired general, a friend of Naqvi's at the time, told me that in October 1999, General Pervez Musharraf mounted a coup in Pakistan and invited Naqvi to Islamabad to be interviewed for a ministerial position in a technocratic government.[19] This was a direct response to Naqvi's public profile in the country, which in turn was based almost exclusively on the success of the Inchcape deal. He also told me that although Naqvi declined a position at that stage, he saw where business could take him, and he saw inside the corridors of power for the first time. He also understood power so that when he did join a government, he wanted it to be on his terms. He wrote about Rafik Hariri, a self-made billionaire who rose to be Prime Minister of Lebanon, as a role model and indeed met him several times to learn about his experiences in remodelling his country since Spinneys, which was acquired as part of Inchcape's portfolio, was the largest civil employer in Lebanon at that time. Thereafter, his cultivation of political connections around the world began to look like a strategy. Naqvi had realised the power of money in terms of political profile, and he was determined to play a part on a much bigger stage. The acquisition of Inchcape had given him that stage and access to regional leaders in the political and commercial sphere and he exploited it to grow his ideas and influence; he often differentiated the attitude of Inchcape's previous UK owners as having a colonial approach, whereas he and his team presented a partnership approach.

A close associate of Naqvi from that period, who worked alongside him at Abraaj for many of those early years, explained to me that the GP/LP model at the heart of private equity, explained to Naqvi by McKinsey and his subsequent interactions with practitioners across the world, appealed to him; he saw value in different pools of capital, raised on the back of past performance by an arms'-length difference between investors as limited partners rather than shareholders. In the region at that time shareholders were intrusive and the limitations of a joint stock corporate structure were laid bare through Naqvi's experiences attempting to manage the fallout following the local partner revolts after he acquired Inchcape. He liked the idea of passive economic interests – cloaked in the halo of a legal partnership structure – that would leave him free to innovate.[20]

My read of Naqvi at this time is that he realised that in order to rise, and given the nascent state of emerging markets, access to political power would be essential in a way that conventional Western private equity professionals might not have seen and if they had seen, might not have known how to handle. The Naqvi all-staff emails developed the idea of Abraaj's corporate foreign policy as an extension of his insistence on McKinsey developing a 'Rolls-Royce' blueprint for Abraaj operations and structure rather than a 'Volvo' one.[21] This was also reflected in the way Naqvi set out to surround himself with world-leading talent to ensure that mistakes did not happen. As an outsider, he knew that to maintain his edge he would have to continue to break new ground. Dubai's rapid evolution and business-oriented philosophy was a perfect base for implementing this strategy.

Long-term residents of Dubai told me that Naqvi cultivated his public image from the early days. Every year from 1996 onwards, pre-Inchcape

Cupola would throw an opulent dinner, at which the who's who of local society would be invited and Naqvi would organise entertainers, visiting master chefs and after-dinner speakers. This continued throughout the Abraaj years. Naqvi's speeches would exemplify his charm and charisma, his focus on helping Dubai evolve and his involvement with local philanthropic causes. When Cupola's plastic card factory was nearing completion, he used the fact that the machinery supplier was from South Africa to request that Nelson Mandela inaugurate the facility during a state visit to Dubai. Such actions ensured that state and local government officials began to notice him. Having Mandela open a factory was clearly a coup for a largely unknown business in those pre-Inchcape days. And it was of course a brilliant marketing ploy.[22]

The launch of Abraaj in 2002 was announced at a UAE–Jordan investment summit sponsored by Abraaj. The King of Jordan and the ruler of Dubai joined Naqvi on the stage. He did not know them before the event, but he certainly knew them after. When prominent visitors from the US or Europe visited local leaders and sovereign wealth funds, there would usually be a final time slot in their schedule to be filled, and Naqvi's local knowledge and charisma found willing ears at such meetings. In this way his network was developed further and, as his profile grew, an investment banker told me that Naqvi became known as the 'last-hour guy'.

Being the largest provider of private equity investment in emerging markets placed Abraaj at the front and centre of politics, and the capital surpluses of AHL allowed it to play a proactive role. This happened on a number of different and interconnected levels. Western states knew the sophisticated game Abraaj was playing and encouraged it to do so, even promoting Naqvi to become Prime Minister in Pakistan in a scenario of possible futures.[23] This support was a result of the success of the firm across MENASA and later in the rest of Africa and Latin America. These were geographies that the West wanted to see develop as neo-liberal market economies, and until 2016 it seemed as if Abraaj was doing what the West wanted without need of direction. It was playing the role of a trojan horse for private equity in markets that had rebelled against the debt-driven deregulation of the first wave of globalisation and gone their own way, like Singapore and Malaysia, or had embraced it and were now in recovery, like much of Africa. Naqvi and many in the Abraaj senior management team were in direct contact with heads of state, heads of global bodies and senior ministers frequently – hence the endless panels at Davos and, more importantly, the dinners and meetings. Each partner running one of the funds also had to have excellent relationships with the political leaders of the states in their areas.

As Dubai was Abraaj's home base, the closest relationship Abraaj had to formally maintain was with the government there. This made sense in terms of proximity and, as Abraaj grew, Dubai too was growing as a global financial centre. Beginning with Cupola, the Abraaj team had taken its corporate social responsibility (CSR) role seriously and had projected itself as a good corporate citizen. Cupola began the relation-ship between the team and culture in 1996 when it sponsored an arts workshop at the National College of Arts in Lahore, Pakistan. Later, and with greater resources, it was able to play a more substantial role in the culture of the community of Dubai which was, and to a large extent remains, a cultural desert. Abraaj and Naqvi himself were major sponsors, over the first ten years of its existence, of the Dubai Art Fair, which was an engine of the local art market but also brought a noticeable annual boost to the economy. An analysis in 2019 showed that the art fair brought $33 million to the local economy that year and that 41 per cent of the visitors came from outside Dubai.[24] Abraaj's most significant contribution to regional art was the introduction of the annual Abraaj Art Prize, which was awarded to an artist from the MENASA region and the $1 million annual prize created ripples across the art world. Ten years before the launch of the prize the scene was dominated by the Turner Prize (Britain), the MacArthur (US) and the Archibald (Australia). The Abraaj Prize was awarded to an art concept from the MENASA region and became established alongside the other global art prizes.[25]

> To create an impact on the ground in the MENASA countries,
> a majority of prize-winning artists had to live and work in this
> region for at least the last ten years. Providing an opportunity
> only to the diasporic artists who already have access to the
> network of their host country will not achieve the objective.[26]

It was an extremely effective concept and the art fair and the prize became annual showcases for the role of Abraaj in Dubai and for Dubai to project a more powerful image globally. Sheikh Mohammed bin Rashid Al Maktoum, the ruler of Dubai, made it a point to visit Art Dubai every year and tour it for a couple of hours with Naqvi beside him, which received wide coverage in Arab media. It seemed the symbiotic bond was an effective one.

Similarly, in 2007, Sheikh Mohammed launched an initiative called 'Dubai Cares',[27] which reached 20 million beneficiaries in sixty countries. It was launched amidst much fanfare and Abraaj donated $10 million, the single largest contribution received by the foundation. At the launch Sheikh Mohammed acknowledged this by seating Naqvi next to him. Similarly, Queen Rania of Jordan launched an initiative called Madrasati to improve the physical and educational environment of Jordan's most neglected public schools. Abraaj, at the time investors in Global Education Management System, which was the largest private schooling system in the Middle East, anchored the initiative and Queen Rania named the mascot for the NGO 'Arroof' in recognition of the support from Naqvi.[28]

Beyond the cultural force of Abraaj's multiple sponsorships, there were also more overtly political deals that placed the company as a bridge between governments across the region. Most of these deals were straightforward commercial transactions, but Abraaj, like Cupola before it, always kept at least one toe in the politics of Pakistan as well as in Dubai. Some of Abraaj's investments in Pakistan were general and not especially political, aside from the way in which they contributed to Naqvi's standing in the country. For example, in May 2006, Abraaj announced a joint venture buyout fund of $300 million which was at the time the largest international private equity fund focused on Pakistan. In November 2006, the fund acquired an 80 per cent stake in Mannan Shahid Forgings, Pakistan's leading steel forging house.[29] But as part of the development of the joint venture buyout fund for Pakistan and other interventions, there were also some more geopolitical investments that allowed Abraaj to form a bridge between Dubai and Pakistan, for example in the area of food security.

The implications of the global credit squeeze and crash in 2008 caused significant problems for the Gulf's agricultural product imports, and food prices around the world rose sharply. As a result, GCC members had a significant need for control of cheaper supplies of food. A number of states began investing heavily in the fertile lands of Africa and Asia.[30] Abraaj utilised the Pakistani fund to buy significant holdings of land in Pakistan working with the UAE. Media reports estimated that by the end of 2008 it had invested in 800,000 acres of land.[31] The first Middle East–Pakistan Agriculture and Dairy Investment Forum was held in Dubai in May that year, showcasing Pakistan's agriculture and dairy sectors, and raising more than $3 billion in pledges for new investments. Earlier in March, Abraaj had bought into the Pakistani energy firm Bosicor to tap growing demand for petroleum products in the world's sixth most-populous nation. Other UAE entities also followed Abraaj's lead and made these kinds of strategic investments in food security.[32] As in almost everything else it did throughout the region, Abraaj exploited both its first-mover advantage as well as showing what could be done; where it led, others followed.

A significant element of the growing Abraaj halo effect was, at least in the markets in which they operated, the emerging themes of ESG, impact and a geopolitical awareness, the primacy of which was new to those operating in the corporate sector. The focus on ESG had been developed into Abraaj's '5+5+5' concept: 5 per cent of its net management fees were spent on strategic philanthropic programmes; five days of employee time was spent on volunteer skills; and staff were encouraged to donate

5 per cent of their annual bonus to various community projects supported by Abraaj. From 2005 to 2010 Abraaj spent nearly $60 million working with over sixty NGOs on sustainable programming and community engagement.[33]

Abraaj (with Aureos, which it bought in 2012) invested in nearly 200 companies between 2002 and 2017. Not all of them had a strong impact ethos and not all of them were successful; indeed, Abraaj ran workshops highlighting the failures in its portfolio and what could be learnt from mistakes. But a number of the investments were clearly driven by something more than just economics and impact alone. In 2007, it was widely rumoured that Abraaj had won an auction to privatise the state electricity company in Jordan; but ultimately, the newly formed JD Capital, a joint initiative of the Jordanian and Dubai governments, was awarded it.[34] This could not have happened without Abraaj's assent and political chits were probably banked for the future.

Similarly, Abraaj's investment in the Islamabad Diagnostic Centre (IDC) was the first in Pakistan through AGHF and appears to be its fourth in the global diagnostics space. As a sector of the healthcare industry, and particularly in the context of global growth markets, diagnostics is an often overlooked, underfunded element of care. Having completed AGHF's flagship investment in India through the acquisition of the country's fifth largest hospital group, Naqvi was questioned closely in Islamabad as to why he would deploy capital in India, rather than in Pakistan where healthcare needs were more pressing. IDC was identified as a target and it appears the investment was made in response to outside pressure on Abraaj, according to an ex-AGHF employee. The deal team leader for Abraaj, managing director Hisham Moussa, stated that for Abraaj, the deal was 'an important step for us in building our presence in the diagnostics space across South Asia',[35] and the key elements of the IDC were its 'world class infrastructure and diagnostic technology, and its competent management team'.[36] Quite apart from the gap between referral points and diagnostic service providers mentioned above, healthcare as a whole is an issue of extreme importance in Pakistan. The country is home to over 180 million people and urbanisation of the areas around the country's megacities has only accelerated population pressure. There is an underfunded public health service, which will only come under more strain in the future and, as result, 87 per cent of health-care spending in Pakistan is made out-of-pocket, as people turn to the private sector to fill the gaps.[37] The investment made sense and another objective appeared to be served at the same time.

Naqvi was already known as an innovator in the healthcare space, through his personal philanthropic efforts in Pakistan, having founded the Aman Foundation, again with the help of McKinsey. Naqvi spent over $150 million of his own money creating, amongst other initiatives, a world-class ambulance service in Karachi, a vocational training system, healthcare nutritional support for children from low-income families, maternal and family planning counselling centres for under-privileged women and clinics that provided free medical care in poor areas. Although both Aman and Abraaj executives were at pains to separate the operations of the philanthropic organisation from the commercial one, the political and stakeholder enhancement it brought was obvious even to the unschooled, notwithstanding the fact that, as we have seen, Naqvi suffered from founder syndrome and was hands-on in his support for and the advice he gave to the organisations he established.

None of this was particularly revolutionary in regard to Abraaj's standard operating model, following what had become tried and tested plans for creating impact through successful investment and keeping regional governments onside; especially since Abraaj in particular had a track record of success in healthcare and diagnostics specifically, having deployed over $1.2 billion in twenty-nine different growth markets globally.[38] Even the 2020 Global Justice Now report 'Doing more harm than good: Why CDC must reform for people and planet', which is highly critical of both the concept of investing for impact and of Abraaj specifically, conceded that 'the investment (in Pakistan) was to lead to

30 new diagnostic centres across Punjab ... This appears to have now been completed as IDC states it operates in more than 50 branches in 10 cities.'[39]

I found this interplay between highly profitable investments, impact investing, stakeholder and community engagement and governmental support across the region fascinating. I grilled a former senior Abraaj executive about why Naqvi pursued this overarching approach rather than focusing on personal and company enrichment and fame. He sent me a file containing Naqvi's 'Memos to All Staff', which Naqvi circulated once or twice a year, from 2005, when this individual joined the firm, until 2017, and said:

> This will tell you all you need to know about how he thinks, how he evolved and how he pushed; working for him was a torture and a delight, but you can see in these documents his desperate need to keep everyone who worked at Abraaj involved in his journey.

One can imagine the groans many staff let out when these missives from on high landed in their inboxes – they were not exactly pithy. The documents laid out Naqvi's vision for the firm's direction of travel and the reasoning behind it year after year. Reading them together provides a fascinating insight into the evolution of the Abraaj model, the mistakes and realignments made in organisational structure, the restless energy devoted to mixing things up and keeping the momentum going. Working for Naqvi must have been quite a ride.

Abraaj's utilisation of the capital at its disposal through its various regional or thematic funds was extremely effective: not only was it consistently deployed profitably, but its focus on impact and filling gaps in domestic ecosystems led to all stakeholders, including governments, becoming allies. An investment by Abraaj was often touted as a sign of a nation's capability to pull in respected institutional capital. Even exits by Abraaj could be useful. For example, when Abraaj exited Acibadem

Healthcare in Turkey through a listing in Singapore and Kuala Lumpur, or International Diagnostic Holdings (IDH) in Egypt through a London IPO, the governments in question highlighted the event and proclaimed how their countries welcomed foreign investment but also facilitated their departure at an opportune time. Despite the events which overtook the group in 2018, it remains apparent that Abraaj refined its model, identified the key factors for success in emerging markets and created real impact by planning for the future.

In terms of the specific wider political context that Abraaj cultivated, it is worth revisiting the investment in the EFG-Hermes, which was intended to be a long-term move towards creating a one-stop financial shop but turned into a very successful shorter-term flip instead. EFG was the first locally owned investment bank in Egypt and had been founded in 1984 as an early indication of the changes in capital flows across the region. It was an instrument of the World Bank–IMF–IFC agenda of liberalisation as it managed the government's privatisation process and had become the largest investment bank in the Middle East with a strong regional footprint, including in Dubai, Saudi Arabia and Egypt and was listed on the Egyptian and London stock exchanges. In July 2006, Abraaj bought a 24.62 per cent controlling stake in EFG-Hermes for $505 million, with the objective of expanding the firm's reach in the Gulf region but also inverting the globally touted 'universal banking model'. When the second of those objectives proved to be difficult to implement in practice, Abraaj sold its stake to Dubai Financial Group, the investment arm of the government of Dubai, in December 2007. The transaction valued Abraaj's stake in EFG for $1.4 billion with an IRR of 93 per cent.[40] These balance sheet transactions continued in March 2007 when Abraaj became a co-founder of UAE's Air Arabia when it took part in what was the largest IPO offering in UAE up to that date alongside the government of Sharjah. The identity of both the buyer and seller in the above two examples demonstrate how closely aligned Abraaj was with the government in the UAE.

A more overtly geopolitical investment was the creation of the Riyada Enterprise Development (RED) fund in 2010. RED was sponsored by Abraaj with support of OPIC, the US government's development investor arm, and investment from CISCO, European Investment Bank and IFC. The fund's objectives were to make growth stage, non-majority investments, both directly as well as through individual country sub-funds, in SMEs. The total expected capitalisation was $500 million alongside an OPIC loan guarantee of up to $150 million in principle. The fund fulfilled the promise that Obama had made in a speech in Cairo on 4 June 2009 that the United States would 'launch a new fund to support technological development in Muslim-majority countries'.[41] Abraaj and Naqvi were clearly seen by the US at this stage as figuring prominently in their Middle East initiatives. If this doesn't exemplify Abraaj's status as the go-to private equity firm for outreach to Muslim nations, nothing else can.[42] As part of the development of RED, Abraaj hired Fayez Husseini to lead up to twenty-five Palestinian SME investments over four years and opened an office in Palestine's West Bank. The Ramallah office sourced and managed deals for the Palestine Growth Capital Fund, a Palestinian SME fund that Abraaj established in January 2010 in partnership with the Palestine Investment Fund (PIF) as a subset of RED. Interestingly, from press reports of that period, the government of Israel supported the initiative as an important bridge-building exercise at a time when Arab–Israeli relations were at a low point. It is equally important, if not more so, that after Abraaj pulled the plug on its RED initiative following the acquisition of Aureos in 2012, the Palestine team and office were taken over by the Middle East Quartet, the major diplomatic initiative involving the United States, the United Nations, the European Union and Russia, aimed at mediating the Israeli–Palestinian peace process, led initially by Tony Blair but followed by Kito de Boer, formerly managing partner of McKinsey in the Middle East, who after his Quartet stint joined Abraaj as a managing partner leading its impact investing initiatives.

Abraaj's enduring strength and perhaps its greatest legacy will be the way in which it approached each market differently; as a result, each market claimed that the company was home-grown. Perhaps nothing can exemplify this better than the creation of the Mustaqbali Foundation in Palestine in the wake of the Israeli invasion of Gaza in 2009.[43] Abraaj cancelled its public relations budget and its annual investor conference, reduced its marketing expenditure to zero for the years 2009 and 2010, and from the funds thus saved it augmented additional monies from its balance sheet and launched the foundation with $10 million of its own money. The objective of the foundation was to identify and then look after and nurture children made orphans by the conflict on both sides. The foundation provided for their every need from foster homes, education, health and psychiatric care to toys and vacations; it was an all-encompassing programme. In all, 1,863 children were identified and this 22-year programme is still going strong. Many other partners have joined the programme and after Abraaj's demise in 2018 the oversight of the foundation moved to Bank of Palestine. The Mustaqbali Foundation touched a nerve across the Middle Eastern markets in which Abraaj operated at that time and was widely recognised and embraced as a leading example of business displaying empathy.

Another stream of activism was Naqvi's engagement with a small group of influential business leaders who had started meeting informally through YPO in the aftermath of 9/11, through which he met Christopher Schroeder. Schroeder is a Republican entrepreneur who has taken a close interest in the development of start-ups and other enterprises in the Middle East. He worked on President George Bush's 1988 and 1992 election campaigns and in 2016 he co-led an initiative of the Atlantic Council, under former Secretary of State Madeleine Albright and National Security Advisor Steve Hadley, the Middle East Strategy Task Force's efforts on 'economic recovery and revitalisation'.[44]

But Schroeder's involvement in the Middle East began with his participation in the 'Celebration of Entrepreneurship' event hosted by Abraaj in 2010, which intended to focus global attention on the start-up culture of the region, with Naqvi and Ghandour, as a board member of Abraaj, acting as co-chairs. Coming as it did on the heels of the Obama summit on Muslim entrepreneurs in Washington, US interest in the event was huge and it was attended by numerous officials from the State Department. The event cost Abraaj $6 million. It attracted over 2,400 entrepreneurs and young people, with 2,000 more on a waiting list, and featured 230 speakers, most from outside Dubai. The Celebration of Entrepreneurship took place in November 2010; it focused on opportunities for the youth of the Arab region, it talked about the lack of opportunity and promoted a new initiative from Abraaj called 'Wamda', which would promote an online start-up culture and identify budding entrepreneurs. This was to be managed by Ghandour alongside Abraaj since he was no longer in an executive capacity at Aramex. Following the platform's development, Abraaj and Naqvi together provided 20 per cent of the Wamda fund. Schroeder wrote a book about entrepreneurship in the region in which he credited the festival as being one element in the drivers of the Arab Spring.[45] In addition, the significance of the event was underscored by the fact that Secretary of State Hillary Clinton was briefed on it. Over the next eight years, a source inside Abraaj told me, Schroeder flitted in and out of the Abraaj world, exceedingly well connected, but with motives that remain unclear to my source, who interacted with him frequently, to this day.

On 17 December 2010, Mohamed Bouazizi, a Tunisian street vendor, set himself on fire sparking a wave of demonstrations that began a revolution in Tunisia and set off a series of revolts across the Arab world. In May 2011, the Henry L. Stimson Center published the first systematic report on the Arab Spring, called 'Seismic Shift: Understanding Change in the Middle East'.[46] The report showed that it was not simply the main publications of the foreign policy community that did not see the events coming; neither did the different players in sectors that were supposed to know what was going on in the region – academia, NGOs, think tanks, public opinion polls and risk analysis companies. As this was a protest movement coming from the 'Arab street' one might have expected the myriad of international non-government organisations that lay special claim to knowing the region from a bottom-up perspective to have predicted what was to come. In fact, no NGO anticipated the timing, pace or breadth of turmoil that would engulf the Arab world. Whilst some did foresee the possibility of violent protest in individual countries – for example, in Egypt – none predicted the dynamic of the protest or the way in which it would spread across the region. They described in detail a confluence of mounting regime repression and growing popular agitation over a variety of political and socio-economic issues. But the 'dots were not connected'. The journalists who are experts in the region also failed to see the regional significance of what was happening.

The regional conflagration and the rapid spread of unrest was not anticipated because few were looking at the region as a single political, social or economic space in the way that Abraaj had been doing since 2002. There is an early video in which Naqvi discusses the power of the Arabic language in uniting people from Marrakesh to Muscat, and how the language was breaking down barriers across the region in terms of TV programming, advertising and merchandising and how interconnected the regional emotions and cultures were; this is prescient in light of the Arab Spring, which unfolded later that year.

The fact that the West entirely missed the Arab Spring coming reinforced for many the risks involved in the broader MENASA region. Abraaj was quick to put out the message that it had not predicted what was going to happen but that it understood what was happening and that the underlying economies of the region remained strong – and more importantly, that there was an underserved young population starving to build, to grow, to be served and to consume. In July 2011, Abraaj CEO Mustafa Abdel-Wadood put out the following message:

> With some minor though highly visible exceptions, MENA economies remain fundamentally strong and continue to grow.

The twin engines of high-absorption capacity for investment, in both hard and soft infrastructure, and the significant surpluses from hydro-carbons, against a backdrop of surging demographics and uninterrupted economic reform, give good reason to be optimistic.[47]

To an extent the events caused other private equity firms to pause in their regional ambitions, but Abraaj saw the situation as an opportunity.

Egypt saw an exodus of investors in the wake of the uprising that toppled President Hosni Mubarak, but Abraaj was staying put and planning further investment. 'We are currently studying the acquisition of a firm in the field of petroleum services,' Abdel-Wadood said in an interview published in Egyptian newspaper *Al-Shorouk*, adding that Abraaj had stakes in Egyptian groups Orascom Construction Industries and Al Borg Laboratory.[48] The depth of experience that the team had established and their local knowledge allowed them to bet successfully that business would come through the political crisis. As part of its overall impact investment programme, Abraaj created a healthcare platform, North Africa Hospital Holdings, to buy and roll up hospitals in Egypt and Tunisia. It acquired hospitals in both countries, listed 20 per cent of the Egyptian side of the platform and then listed the Tunisian group.[49]

The company's 2010 annual review opened with the following paragraph:

> The recent political events and the intoxicating triumph of 'people power' has liberated the mindset of the Arab people. Over the long run, these developments will be positive for the region and political transition will reinforce the pace of economic reform. But 'change' also entails short- to medium-term uncertainty. In these exceptional circumstances it is impossible to predict at what borders this movement will stop or indeed, how smooth the transition will be.[50]

Abraaj held its nerve when the political crisis hit and waited for the smoke to clear. In Tunisia, in which the political environment and the level of reforms was judged by Abraaj to be at the right point at which the underlying fundamentals were stronger than the risks, Naqvi told the press that the firm's interest in the country was driven by the government prioritising the private sector's role. He announced plans to invest in pharmaceuticals and agribusiness. 'When you deploy capital, you cannot do so without accepting some measure of risk, and in Tunisia, the level of risk has minimised due to economic reforms,' he said. The depth of experience and the local knowledge of the team allowed them to bet successfully that business would come through politics.

The name Tunisians gave their revolution was the 'Dignity Revolution'. They rejected the foreign naming of it as the 'Jasmine Revolution' as a device to 'cater to the need for exotic imagery',[51] and obscure that at its heart, for Tunisians the aim of the revolution was to 'give an authentic voice to people's dignity … to usher in the age of citizenship in Tunisia'. There can be no better symbol of this reclamation of the dignity of the citizen than the decision in 2020 to issue a 10-dinar note with the face of Dr Tawhida Ben Cheikh upon it. Ben Cheikh was the first female doctor in Tunisia, the vice-president of the Tunisian Red Crescent and the founder of the country's first family planning clinic. Dr Alya El Hedda founded Opalia Pharma in 1988 with the help of Italian entrepreneur Marco Montanari. El Hedda steered it to become one of the top-three generic drug producers in Tunisia and her story, and that of her company, represent an example of the dignity and civic good that Tunisians strove so hard for and Abraaj's role in this field.

Abraaj invested in 2009, with the purpose of being the growth partner El Hedda needed to expand the company's distribution regionally across Francophone Africa. Over the course of the investment, Abraaj helped increase sales of Opalia-produced drugs by 250 per cent. Two years prior to the investment, Opalia had opened a brand-new facility outside Tunis and with Abraaj's support were able to expand their line of over

150 generic drugs to ten countries regionally. Alongside this, Abraaj's capital was able to help El Hedda to empower Tunisian women, with over 60 per cent of Opalia's staff being female.[52] In 2013 Abraaj exited the investment, having seen Opalia expand to more than double its original size, and the Milan-based Recordati acquired 90 per cent of the company, aiming to make it a truly international producer of generic drugs. Abraaj had the confidence and trust in Opalia and El Hedda to stick with them through the turbulence of 2010 and 2011 in Tunisia and were rewarded. Opalia's success not only vindicates Abraaj's judgement that the underlying economic indicators were sound despite the uncertainty; it also shows that in fact uncertainty can open up the possibility of positive change; in this instance the empowerment of women in science dovetailed with the success of a female-led business.

A review of speeches, interviews and reports encompassing Abraaj's first decade shows that it was genuinely attempting to be a global company, always pushing forward. Being created in the aftermath of the globalist moment under the first Clinton administration, and then with the Third Way Blair governments, it developed and grew through the Bush administration's support for the economics of globalisation based on the neo-liberal ideology of the IMF and World Bank and the management of trade through the standards of the World Trade Organization. Globalisation was the mantra of the decades before the financial crash of 2008 and even for some years after. This was also tied to a development rhetoric which looked for the private sector to play an increasing role in development of poorer economies in the belief that it was private sector investment and the creation of successful market economies that would ultimately lead to economic growth and the embedding of the rule of law and democracy.[53]

By 2012, Abraaj had come through the financial crisis and the Arab Spring. Naqvi established a new war room, which usually entailed a group of dedicated full-time professionals from across the group, whilst it worked on its mandate. The word 'war room' was part of the terminology of Abraaj and to be invited to be a member of a particular war room was a badge of honour; it had first been established in 2002 at inception to transition into a private equity mindset, and was then repeated in 2006 and 2009 at seminal moments in the firm's evolution, always guided by and with the participation of McKinsey staff to help drive the analysis, which would define the approach and strategy for this next stage of Abraaj's evolution. In terms of the overall development of the company and the stepping stones to a more global role, the purchase of Aureos Capital was critical in firmly establishing Abraaj as a cornerstone of emerging market investing in the eyes of the investing community globally.

If the deal with Aramex was the signature deal in getting Abraaj's name recognised, building on the foundational deal of the purchase of Inchcape by Cupola, then the 2012 Abraaj purchase of Aureos Capital was the global deal that would cement its leadership position in emerging or growth markets. This global sense of the role of the company became concrete at this point, but it had been building for several years. It is inconceivable that Abraaj would have been allowed to purchase Aureos if the transaction had not been scrutinised and approved by state actors, including the UK and Norwegian governments. At the very least several states would have carried out significant degrees of positive vetting of the company and its key personnel and forensic accounting of its position would have been conducted. The purchase proves that at least up to 2012 Abraaj clearly raised no red flags for Western governments; we know that because at the same time, the Naqvi personal brand was being burnished by US think tanks to prepare for an eventual political role.

Aureos Capital was floated from the UK government's development finance institution, the Commonwealth Development Corporation, and the Norwegian Development Finance Institution, Norfund.[54] Before being purchased by Abraaj, Aureos's investments were focused on SMEs that spanned multiple sectors. Aureos went on to successfully raise new capital, primarily from development finance institutions, governmental entities designed to invest capital in development projects and multilaterals to create seventeen funds, to invest sustainably in SMEs in Latin America, Africa and Asia. From small beginnings in 2001, these seventeen regional funds had by 2012 grown to a range of $1.3 billion of funds under management. In markets where Aureos did not operate, Abraaj's profile was growing – and its returns were growing, too. Aureos looked like an opportunity where perfect complementarity existed. Naqvi rightly perceived this to be a sudden and very warm hug from the Western world.[55]

The entire basis of development agencies funding private equity companies to make investments was controversial within the development sector, which generally distrusted the private sector and its profit motive. This body of criticism came together in a substantial Global Justice Now report, which focused primarily on CDC itself, but which made the general development sector case against the use of private capital almost as a post-mortem after Abraaj had collapsed.

> CDC has demonstrated a near-total resistance to reform by continuing to make more profit than it should and by channelling its investments through tax havens. This 'market knows best' approach to development uses aid money to facilitate the extraction of wealth from the global south to the global north – the exact opposite to what any institution with a development mandate should be doing.[56]

The Aureos–Abraaj partnership was based on the opposite view. The SME sector was central to Abraaj's strategy and dominated the make-up of companies in emerging markets across all sectors. This sector 'diversification' had compounded the development of the SME sector, which makes up the bulk of enterprises in emerging economies. SMEs often provide the highest employment rates and significantly contribute to GDP. By investing in these businesses, Aureos/Abraaj believed that they were working to fill the 'missing middle' in emerging markets.

The 'missing middle' was a term originally coined in 2010 to refer to the absence of affordable housing but spread in usage to describe the development and growth of middle-class, middle-income and middle-sized or growing enterprises and the eco-systems that are needed to support them.[57] Aureos/Abraaj would leverage funds from development finance institutions (DFIs) but also raise funds from more traditional private equity sources. This was the other element in the overall impact picture, aside from the deal-level impact of increasing employment by increasing sales and improving the labour practices of the companies. At a macro level, the profit motive and the transfer of funds from the global north to the global south was defended because of the difference it would make to growth. The volume of investment would be increased if the private equity industry could be encouraged to invest into these markets. Of course, they would get a return on their investment. At a micro level, their expertise would improve the way firms performed, significantly contributing to taxes and wages. This would come either in terms of enhancing the quality of jobs and the conduct of companies so that disposable income would increase and tax takes by states would increase, or in poorer countries by encouraging the growth of formal economies. This relied on private equity companies embracing not only the geographies but also the methods of impact investment. It also relied on the fact that the formalisation of informal economy would help reduce primary poverty, which is a substantially unproven proposition in many instances.[58]

Taking on Aureos would pitch Abraaj into the centre of the cross-currents of these political debates even more deeply than it was already. It is worth pausing here to stress that one of the reasons that Abraaj executives and Naqvi in particular were such a feature of the global merry-go-round of conferences and panels, such as the World Economic Forum's annual meetings in Davos, was to make exactly these kinds of arguments. Both because they believed in the arguments and the evidence for them, but also because the underlying trajectory of the company needed it to keep growing to move from a 'start-up' model to a sustainable model and could start paying substantial dividends and reach the objective of listing the business.

According to an executive responsible for consummating the deal from the Abraaj side, there were two further significant selling points for Abraaj that drove the Aureos move: global coverage and brand. Many of the Aureos investment team were experienced in emerging markets, with the right local knowledge and network needed to underpin the investing Abraaj wanted to do. From ten offices in 2001, the company had grown to a network of twenty-nine offices worldwide by 2012, giving it global coverage. The war room resulted in a consolidation exercise through 2012/13, which was undertaken by Abraaj and closed many of these offices and made a large number of staff redundant. Abraaj wanted the pedigree of the Aureos brand and the office network,[59] specifically in Latin America and South East Asia, that would have taken it a decade to evolve itself; and secondly it wanted to retain the DFI relationships, but not the deals or a large number of the Aureos people. With its background in government development agencies rather than traditional private equity investments, it had the right kind of approach to impact. The relatively small number of portfolio companies it had invested in had benefited from a hands-on intervention which delivered a strong ESG focus. This was also aligned to the Abraaj approach and would allow it to make that case more loudly, across more geographies and to grow more funds.

Abraaj also took the little-known Aureos Sustainability Index (ASI), which was described as a proprietary interactive tool to report development impact over the lifetime of investments and globalised the practice of impact measurement. In the 2012/13 war room, this index was rigorously tested, revised, simplified and relaunched under the same acronym but leading with Abraaj rather than Aureos. The new index measured and rationalised performance against forty indicators across four key pillars covering financial performance, human development, environmental impact and private sector development and corporate governance. These indicators enabled Abraaj partner companies to chart and monitor their own performance through quantitative and qualitative indicators and supported Abraaj's ability to effect change in these companies across both financial and non-financial indicators.[60]

The purchase also brought Sev Vettivetpillai into Abraaj. Vettivetpillai was initially part of CDC and had started its SMEs operation in 1990 to 1992 before leading the spinoff that created Aureos. From 2001, because of its governmental background and development focus, Aureos benefited from government grants and support. It had a strong relationship with the Commonwealth Secretariat, an inter-governmental body, which opened access to funding from the Australian and New Zealand governments to help their Kula Fund for the Pacific to widen its target geography, for example. It also received grants from donors, such as the Norwegian Investment Fund for Developing Countries (Norfund), the Netherlands Development Finance Company, the IFC, the European Investment Bank, the Multilateral Investment Fund of the Inter-American Development Bank, the Gates Foundation, Proparco, the Elma Foundation and the Indian government. The list of investors reads like a who's who of the development finance world. Apart from the World Bank's investment arm, the IFC, all the other institutions were new to Abraaj. Although Sev Vettivetpillai did not indicate it at the time of acquisition, so keen was he on consummating the deal, a close associate of Naqvi told me that Vettivetpillai disliked Actis, which was the 'large-cap' spinoff from CDC and prior to the Aureos acquisition, Actis was being looked at by Abraaj and McKinsey as an acquisition target. The partners at Actis had made fortunes; Vettivetpillai had apparently took exception to what he perceived as the corporate culture given that everyone at Aureos was from the global south and everyone at Actis was English. In his letter of resignation to Naqvi in December 2017, in the midst of investor allegations about misuse of funds,[61] he cited the development of the larger fund APEF VI as one of his reasons for leaving. He had also been replaced as head of impact investing by

Kito de Boer, which was a big downgrade for him, but that was not cited as a reason for his leaving.

Following the purchase of Aureos, the challenge for Abraaj was to cherry-pick the best investment professionals from both firms and ensure that it could raise capital from both the government funds and programmes and additional private capital as well.[62]

Abraaj's public profile showed it had been working in the impact investing space since its inception, but the absorption of Aureos brought in the metrics and the methodologies developed from its interactions with state development agencies. When this combined with the advocacy skills of Abraaj's communications teams and the global status of Naqvi as a leading talking head, the industry took note. But they also took note of the carefully researched analysis of Abraaj's performance that been carried out by Josh Lerner at the Harvard Business School and the Bella Research Group. In a series of published and unpublished papers, Lerner challenged and countered the major objections that traditional private equity companies and the more conservative but larger institutional investors had about both the idea of impact investment and the geographies in which Abraaj had flourished.

In addition to impact investing but closely related to it, geography was the other thing that set Abraaj apart. It had been born in the nexus of the Middle East and South East Asia; in the heartlands of emerging markets. As we will see, Abraaj was also deeply embedded in Pakistan, which was on the front line of the clash between China and the West. To stake its unique claim to these locations, Abraaj repeatedly attempted to refer to them as growth markets rather than emerging markets.[63] Abraaj was right about this instinctively before it was proved right academically, and the terminology was widely adopted by global multinationals commercially. By that time, after the volatility of 2008, the big boys amongst the global private equity firms wanted a piece of the action and looked to access the higher returns that could be achieved by investing in more intrusive ways based around promoting better-run firms. They understood that in the long run the potential growth in Abraaj's markets was very high. Since its demise, numerous players in the industry are now using the term growth markets rather than emerging markets.

By 2013, Abraaj's impact investing philosophy was relatively cemented and the Gen-5 funds served as the rollout of the company's thinking. We have seen from his speeches and writing during the early days of Cupola that Naqvi always believed in the positive impact that the private sector can have on society. He argued that at a macro level, there is a fundamental supply–demand mismatch in many sectors across the emerging growth markets where Abraaj was investing. In Western markets private equity firms faced problems of oversupply and fierce competition. In emerging markets there were shortages of things such as access to energy, healthcare, education, housing and basic consumer goods and there was a huge demand for accessible financial products. The private sector could help supply these things. At the micro level, private equity could help build companies that are not just profitable but sustainable, impactful and role models of corporate governance and best practice.

There is growing evidence that 'good' companies – those with higher ESG standards – are more profitable and valuable.[64] This had been Naqvi's direct experience in terms of deals that first Cupola and then Abraaj invested in, and as a result, he pushed his more 'commercial' colleagues to become pioneers in the adoption and implementation of ESG standards in the Abraaj investment process – from diligence to exit – and across all investment strategies. Naqvi argued continuously in speeches that the idea that there are necessary financial trade-offs in pursuing impact in investment is incorrect, arguing instead that the reality results in a trade-on effect. This effect could also be measured using the Abraaj Sustainability Index tool. But Abraaj argued that this could go further. That you could pursue an intentional impact investing approach with funds that invest for impact, whilst not making financial return concessions. This became the mandate of the impact investing platform created separately from the private equity platform on which the Gen-5 funds sat, and which was rolled out after 2014.

The impact investing strategy was crafted with a significant amount of detail around the impact it was intended to have and how Abraaj would go about executing the strategy. It was presented at seminars, for which I have seen briefing notes and internal emails, to the European DFIs by Naqvi himself, and was repeated in virtually all his speeches from that period onwards. The strategy set out to take an innovative approach to solving problems. Naqvi strongly believed that systemic change was a necessary and achievable critical outcome. He argued incessantly that because Abraaj had a market-leading mantle, it was not a 'nice-to-do' but a 'must-do' as a moral imperative for the firm; a *raison d'être* for justifying growth. He referred to it as a cornerstone of the firm's corporate foreign policy, stating that Abraaj would maximise its impact by adopting five criteria in all of their impact strategies:

- A multi-stakeholder approach, with Abraaj seeking to engage with and invest in relationships with those stakeholders who played a critical role in shaping the future of the relevant ecosystem.
- Addressing systemic shortfalls through a commitment to creating and enhancing sustainable systems, not just finding the 'deal'.
- Catalysing other players by developing opportunities that have the potential to scale and scale rapidly where Abraaj can be a 'force multiplier', since on its own it would never have sufficient capital to have the impact necessary to fund the UN sustainable development goals (SDGs) in its target markets.
- Investing across multiple investment cycles, hence utilising products that must be an active part of solving the 'multi-cycle' investment challenge from inception to permanence.
- Scientifically measuring the resulting impact and committing to having its 'second' bottom line independently defined, measured and monitored.[65]

There remained, of course, many common features that impact investing continued to share with conventional private equity investing, including the need to deliver superior financial returns, achieve scale and channel mainstream external capital into its regional markets. However, the impact investing strategy was shown to have several features that distinguished it from mainstream private equity investing, including more flexible investment mandates, longer term sources of capital and an openness to partner with different stakeholders.

With hindsight, Naqvi's strategy was clearly designed to position Abraaj in the vanguard of impact investing globally. For him, impact investing was much more than just a play on words; he became an evangelist of the cause and eventually an industry spokesperson on the subject, committing publicly to bringing a unique and innovative approach to impact investing, all at a scale that had not been seen before. He openly spoke of the fact that impact investing as a philosophy was too important to leave to NGOs and DFIs; he believes that the private equity industry should be at the vanguard of this impending movement of capital. This appears logical because the industry is, after all, not bound by sector or geography, and its capital is inherently long-term and patient. The ability to build meaningful partnerships in the pursuit of desired outcomes became core to Abraaj's corporate foreign policy as well as its investing philosophy, and Naqvi referred to this as 'partnership capital'.[66] Even when putting the strategy of Aman Foundation together with McKinsey, which he seeded with over $100 million of his own money, Naqvi focused on impact; through building capacity in ambulance emergency healthcare, community health planning and vocational training in a sustainable manner.

Naqvi spoke often on the issue of the impact investing approach leading to a win–win for both business and society, arguing that the inter-generational wealth transfer that was taking place over the next two decades would be the highest in history and that the young inheritors would look for sustainable and impactful ways to invest.

These were to be Abraaj's future clients, and whilst the rationale and impetus for establishing an impact investing business was deeply embedded in Abraaj from its inception, its regional expansion cemented its thinking to encompass the broader, global frameworks that were encouraging this alignment of business and society at that time. Put simply, the sustainable development goals framework presented the business and investment community with a generation-defining opportunity to re-orient itself by delivering financial performance through addressing social challenges. Naqvi embraced that opportunity for the asset management space, well before Blackrock and Allianz and others started articulating similar visions, and his thoughts crystallised the fact that the investment industry could become a force for social good without betraying its return-seeking purpose.

And why was this such an attractive idea? For one simple reason, which is that SDGs identify markets where societal needs outstrip existing investments and available supply of goods and services. That by definition, means that there are either notable market failures or significant market inefficiencies, both of which offer investors the opportunity to achieve considerable returns. Importantly, what the SDG framework makes clear is that social and financial returns are deeply reliant on one another. The framework explodes the false dichotomy of investors having to choose between doing well and doing good because it lays out the path for doing well by doing good.[67]

Abraaj set out to prove this thinking in several ways. It saw a multiplier effect in its markets through the adoption of robust sustainability principles, demonstrated through the jobs it created (both direct and indirect); the healthy workplace environments it insisted upon to support productivity; the investments it made in the supply chains of their 'partner' businesses'; and the hard and soft infrastructure it helped build, which ultimately powers businesses, communities and individuals. And it started issuing annual, sustainability reports that transparently laid out both the hypothesis and implementation across a network of stakeholders. Senior executives served as members of the Global Impact Investing Network, the United Nations Global Compact, Richard Branson's NGO of business leaders 'the B Team', and the Business Commission for Sustainable Development, amongst many others. In recognition of the group's sustainability leadership and consistently applied ESG policies, processes and practices across the investment lifecycle, Abraaj was awarded an A+ rating in 2015, 2016 and 2017 under the UN-backed Principles for Responsible Investment Reporting and Assessment Framework. This was well above the private equity industry score of B for the same category over the same period.[68] The approach was clearly being recognised and this was no longer just about Naqvi; his entire management team, with some notable exceptions, were fully on board and this in turn inspired the wider team.

From inception in 2002 with a dozen employees, by 2007 Abraaj had 135 employees representing twenty-seven nationalities achieving coverage that spanned the Middle East and North Africa. The group had more than 200 investors who had their money in five funds, with an average realised IRR of 50 per cent across more than twenty exits, compared to a US top quartile performance of 25 per cent over a similar period; this is the most transparent of metrics in the industry: its cash-in-cash-out.[69] By the time the 2014/15 review appeared, Abraaj had concluded over 140 investments in more than ten sectors with more than seventy exits. By 2017, more than 200 of these investments were managed through more than twenty offices with 300 employees organised into five regional hubs in Dubai, Istanbul, Nairobi, Singapore and Mexico City overseeing funds of $12.5 billion in 2014/15, rising to just under $14 billion by the end of 2017 – even by the end of its first decade, Abraaj had become a force to reckon with in growth markets.

# 5

# How good was Abraaj?

*We have lost money on five different occasions*
*out of 200 companies.*

Arif Naqvi 2014

Junior staff who were part the 2012/13 war room recall that part of the discussion considered what Abraaj should do next based on an analysis of how good the company really was. The most obvious way to assess the success of Abraaj is to compare its performance as a private equity company with the performance of other private equity companies. Although this is actually the wrong way, or rather the least meaningful way, to read the success of a company in the sector, it is the way the world will form at least an initial judgement. In the case of Abraaj it also matters because the accusation being made against key players in the firm and Naqvi in particular is that the company and his entire life were in effect based on a lie. The key journalistic accusations against Naqvi are summed up in the book *The Key Man*.[1] The blurb from the Penguin site is currently as follows:

In this compelling story of greed, chicanery and tarnished
idealism, two Wall Street Journal reporters investigate a man
who Bill Gates and Western governments entrusted with
hundreds of millions of dollars to make profits and end poverty
but now stands accused of masterminding one of the biggest,
most brazen frauds ever.[2]

The book presents the key man thesis to account for the fall of Abraaj.
It is written by the journalists who broke part of the original story
based on information leaked to them at the *Wall Street Journal*, and it is
designed to present the case from a specific angle that is based on Abraaj
being, as stated in one of the editorial reviews used on Amazon for the
book, a form of 'Ponzi scheme', which is purportedly validated by, or
in turn purportedly validates, the DoJ indictment.[3] To make that thesis
work, the Abraaj story should be a story of smoke and mirrors, it should
be one of a roller-coaster ride, kept on the tracks by dishonesty and lies
until it all came crashing down. If this was the story of Abraaj and the
explanation for the eventual collapse of the firm, then the performance
of Abraaj as a private equity fund would reflect this narrative over an
extended period of time and there would be significant holes in that performance. If this is the story of people under extreme pressure making
mistakes that cost them their livelihoods, freedom and the company
they built over fifteen years, then the performance of the company would
reflect a story of long-term success followed by short-term failure and
sudden collapse.

There are, therefore, at least two levels on which the key man thesis
systemically does not work.

Firstly, it is contradicted by the performance of Abraaj as a private
equity firm in producing results for its investors right up to the present
day, as the funds continue to operate under new management. These
funds would need to show gaps in the financial picture; failing funds and
failed investments that had to be covered up by the misappropriation of

other cash to pay the returns to investors. There were certainly setbacks, funds which did not meet their targets, like Abraaj Real Estate Fund I (AREF I) or Abraaj Buy Out Fund II (ABOF II) and others that suffered because of the financial crash of 2008, but nothing that was either too abnormally perfect or imperfect.

Secondly, it would mean that most of the underlying portfolio companies Abraaj had invested in via its various generation of funds were duds. In fact, the opposite is true and the majority of these funds have performed exceedingly well for their managers, some of whom remain in control to the present day – for example, the Evercare Health Fund, the Latin America Fund II and others. Most importantly it would show a steady run of abnormal success directed and reported from the centre with no major setbacks or failures. It would also need the connivance of at least 300 professionals to work together to provide the con given the decentralised manner in which investments were sourced, diligence was carried out and managed and the different geographical and functional elements that played a part in each investment.

One of the major contributing factors in the final exposure of the American fraudster Bernie Madoff was that over the fifteen years he operated the graph for his fund never deviated from its upward trajectory; even when the financial crash of 2008 came its success was not affected. Objective conditions did not seem to affect Madoff's ability to make money for his investors because there were always more investors to pay the old ones off.

Abraaj's is a markedly different story. It shows a broadly but unevenly successful company, with peaks and troughs, with quite different kinds of returns in different geographies and for different funds. It shows funds that closed undersubscribed, planned IPOs that did not take place and some companies that were invested in but failed. Whilst it shows some amazing successes, there are also some failures. It produced generally good IRRs and at times ones that were best in their class, but also some mediocre exits and performance failures. But the key was it demonstrated that there was a way to do the business of investing private equity differently. In countries in which neither the private equity nor debt markets were mature there was no ability to lever up companies and cut them down because the economies largely depended on the jobs of these companies being retained for both wages and consumer spend to stay in check. Therefore, the kind of growth that Abraaj sometimes achieved in these companies was remarkable compared with its peers in the same market. It achieved the results that it did because of a focus on operational know-how – a new way of being a new partner. Andreessen Horowitz, one of the world's leading venture capital firms, evolved in a similar way in its focus on value creation and getting involved through centralised function support, and there has never been any suggestion that this was ever improper.[4]

The fundamental issue with Abraaj is that there appeared on the face of it to be a blurred distinction between the balance sheet and the fund management business, with the former being capitalised significantly in comparison with its peers, thereby giving it a runway to burn cash and double down on growth at the expense of short-term profits. Therefore, the assumption can be made that there was a blurred distinction between shareholder rights at AHL and investor rights under the LPAs of the funds managed by AIML. But that is for the court to unpack and decide. Ultimately, Abraaj created returns; it was many things but it was certainly not a long con.

The evidence for the period 2002 to 2017 does not in any way indicate a company that was a scam. A detailed media content and salience study shows that of the more than 12,000 articles about Abraaj both from the markets in which it operated and from the Western media, roughly 99 per cent were positive and then suddenly, in 2018, that number reversed completely.[5]

But the level of scrutiny was much more widespread than merely that in the media. Over fifteen years, Abraaj worked with hundreds of service providers, including dozens of prominent law firms, auditors, strategic and operational consultants and all the major banks in the world. The Abraaj Group had over 400 limited partners and over forty shareholders, many of whom did exhaustive due diligence of Abraaj documentation, including valuations. The group's operations were covered by at least four or five regulatory agencies and a dozen or more significant sovereign wealth funds and development finance institutions that were immediate counterparties of the firm and had stringent due diligence and compliance systems and processes. Abraaj pursued a policy of firing between 10 and 12 per cent of its employees every year on performance grounds, many of whom were partners, and it would not be unreasonable to assume that this included individuals who would have knowledge of the company's inner workings. Did this not lead to one whistle-blower complaint? Glassdoor UK is one of the most prominent locations for employees to write anonymous complaints about their employer, but nothing appears there. The firm had hundreds of employees, many of whom occupied very senior positions and would have had grounds to be whistle-blowers when the firm closed had there been cause. It seems very strange that a firm operating with so much publicity and fanfare, with such intrusive regulation and with a visible and highly diversified team did not raise a single alarm bell over fifteen years. It appears that a lot of the material the journalists rely on was provided by two people: one who left Abraaj in public disgrace and one whom the company separated from in 2002. As I said earlier, anything to strengthen a one-dimensional narrative.

Once the negative coverage of Abraaj began it immediately over-shadowed the fifteen years of positive coverage and became the only narrative. Clickbait and scandal sell.

When evaluating how good Abraaj was up to February 2018 it is also necessary to see where it was not good; Abraaj certainly did make some failed investments over time and did not hide that fact. In an interview with a Nigerian newspaper on his first visit to the country in 2014, Naqvi reflected:

> We have lost money on five different occasions out of 200 companies. We lost money either because we forgot our basic principles, or we took risks that were outsized to the level of investment. What we have learnt is how not to do that again. We have learnt that the only way to make investments is in a very disciplined and consistent manner, focusing on both the risk and the opportunity. If you focus on only the opportunity, then you'll end up losing money.[6]

Five failed investments from 2002 to 2014 is probably spin, but even if you double or triple that, it is not an unsuccessful strike rate; having said that, the methodology for choosing what to define as 'failed investments' was transparently disclosed in the footnotes on the Abraaj 'track record' statements that were shared with potential limited partners who were conducting due diligence on the company.

A careful review of this information does not reveal that Abraaj had an outlandishly high and inflated rate of return, with 17.9 per cent net over the period of its investment activities. It was careful in explaining that of the 160 investments shown that were made in the 'private equity investment group' from 2002 to 2016, 138 were in the core sectors of specialisation for Abraaj; namely financial services, industrials, materials and logistics, consumer goods and services and healthcare and education. In addition, it had made twenty-two investments in various other sectors that in fact had a negative IRR of 2 per cent in aggregate; so, as the potential investors would have reviewed and done due diligence on the above, this appears to be laying out the good and the bad; the winners, the losers and the lessons learnt.

Another takeaway from the information is that around 100 of the 160 companies shown as examples had been exited already; and there is little window dressing that can be applied there; it is a simple case of cash in and cash out. Resultant IRR and valuation approaches are of little relevance in looking at those exited investments. Indeed, in over 80 per cent of the companies exited by Abraaj, the exit values were in excess of carrying values, which suggests a reasonably accurate approach based on experience and market realities. Carrying values for investments that are unsold at a reporting date are the subject of numerous debates, accounting standards and are central to the issues that Abraaj executives were charged with under the DoJ indictment. However, my observations are that the approach was subjective not objective, it followed IPEV guidelines and was clearly laid out in the private placement memorandums (PPMs) for prospective investors.[7]

Certainly, some investments may have been carried by opportunistic hope rather than market reality but, as one source with knowledge of the transactions pointed out to me, the carrying value of Karachi Electric was the subject of vigorous debate between Abraaj and its auditors for three years preceding 2016 and the resultant sale value transacted was in excess of carrying value. Harking back to the difference between satisfying investors focused on multiple of cost (MoC) and those focused on the internal rate of return (IRR, discussed in the Postscript), Abraaj followed a very consistent approach of reducing revaluations to only once a year and marking down only investments that were in imminent danger of not reaching their expected exit values. I have seen numerous emails between Abraaj executives showing that this approach had been hammered out and agreed with Hamilton Lane in 2016 and they suggested that if Abraaj executives believed on a commercial basis that the investment would eventually be sold at or around its projected exit value then they should maintain a policy of gradually marking up the investment to the exit value over the period of time leading up to the expected exit date, whilst also cautioning that Abraaj should mark down an investment to zero when it believed that the investment was irreparable and headed towards a write-off.

It appears that within the management team, the biggest proponent of keeping valuations constant, based largely on the necessity to complete fundraising for the first close of APEF VI, was Mark Bourgeois and this was based on his twenty-five years of experience in selling private equity investments to the most sophisticated investors in the world. Bourgeois's views were clearly articulated in emails written by him to senior management from which it is apparent that he drove this approach. It is a simple fact that all those indicted were following this advice. As the only partner at Abraaj who was rewarded annually with a compensation structure based on new funds raised rather than the long-term carried interest that applied to other employees, Bourgeois was clearly incentivised to push the firm into maintaining valuations. Much of the DoJ indictment is based on complaints by a 'US investor', which appears to be Hamilton Lane, around being misled by Abraaj. However, a review of the email correspondence appears to show that the Abraaj valuation principles were framed with input from Hamilton Lane. Whilst Hamilton Lane had recently listed on the NYSE it understandably moved quickly to put distance between itself and The Abraaj Group once the allegations became public, for obvious reasons.

To argue back from the end that the entire story fits the narrative of sustained corruption and theft and that there was a con man at the heart of it all simply does not bear any relationship to reality. At least one measure of that reality should be the performance of Abraaj as a private equity firm. Senior executives did begin to make the fatal mistake of believing their own press releases. Success bred hubris, which is often, if not always, the story of what capitalism does, but what is striking about this company is how it was actually successful.

The most academically reliable way of measuring how a private equity firm performs is called decomposition analysis.[8] In March 2015, Josh Lerner and James Tighe, of the Harvard Business School and the Bella Research Group, performed a decomposition analysis on everything that Abraaj had done as a company. They used a dataset that consisted of over 140 investments supplied by Abraaj, which comprised the full universe of investments that Abraaj had made until that point. In their own words they 'carefully constructed the analyses to provide an impartial assessment of the firm's past performance'. Abraaj and other private equity companies need this kind of analysis to know if they are making a difference, what kind of difference they are making and if they are making that difference in the right sectors. It should inform the decisions that they make about future strategy. Lerner and Tighe highlighted that there are two key advantages of the approach they take. Firstly, that this is a well-understood methodology that 'has been extensively scrutinised' and that given that 'many other funds have been subject to similar analyses, the employed methodology allows us to compare the sources of Abraaj's returns to those of other groups'. The analysis can be replicated, and it can be compared.

There are two sets of studies that have shaped this methodology. In one set of academic papers looking at the impact of private equity, referenced by Lerner and Tighe, 16,500 firms were examined and broadly positive impacts were found, at least with regard to buyouts. Another notable set of papers also questioned the difference that private equity made above and beyond deploying actual additional cash.[9] The methodology does not, therefore, necessarily produce positive results.

These two initial groups of studies examined whether private equity generated value overall; other research looked specifically as to how these generate value. Shourun Guo et al. (2011) and Viral Acharya et al. (2013) used two different methodologies but in both cases attributed returns to the same three sources. Using entirely distinct datasets, both studies came to remarkably similar conclusions.

Guo et al. examined publicly available data on 194 leveraged buyouts completed between 1990 and 2006. From this sample, they identified ninety-four transactions that had post-buyout financial information (typically large US transactions with publicly traded debt). Of the value they attributed to the three identified components of returns, they estimated that approximately 23.79 per cent came from sector growth (measured through increases in industry valuation multiples), 45.43 per cent came from leverage-based tax savings and roughly 30.78 per cent from operating enhancements.

The other study, by Acharya et al., used deal-level data from 395 transactions undertaken by thirty-seven leading private equity firms that had been McKinsey clients across Western Europe between 1991 and 2007. Their sample showed similar results. Sector growth was responsible for approximately 15.12 per cent of the returns, leverage for roughly 49.64 per cent and deal-level abnormal performance for roughly 35.23 per cent.

The paper by Lerner and Tighe stated that Abraaj 'generated the majority of its returns through deal-level abnormal performance (i.e. through the outperformance of portfolio companies relative to peer companies), far more so than is typical of private equity firms in developed markets', finding that:

- Abraaj's exited investments have generated between 53 per cent and 69 per cent of their value on average from firm-level outperformance, compared with 35 per cent in transactions by leading firms in developed countries.
- Abraaj generated a greater proportion of value from sector growth (approximately 42 per cent of exited deals) than has been found in leading firms in developed markets (approximately 15 per cent).
- Much less value was reaped from the use of leverage (less than 5 per cent, as compared with 50 per cent in developed markets).
- For the total set of transactions, including realised and unrealised deals, Abraaj's investments have generated between 35 per cent and 48 per cent of their value on an average from firm-level outperformance.

The paper concluded that the

> results of this decomposition analysis indicate the degree to which The Abraaj Group generates value by selecting high-growth industries in which to invest, by using leverage strategically to enhance returns, or by sourcing and improving companies with high growth potential, respectively ... This

indicates a strong level of portfolio management and focus on value creation through operational expertise rather than financial engineering of the deals themselves ... Intriguingly and speaking to the story of the firm's evolutionary path, we found that Abraaj has created the majority of its returns through abnormal deal-level returns, with sector growth playing an important but secondary role; leverage on the other hand, has had a minimal role in the accretive value creation of the Group's portfolio companies, which is unsurprising given the general scarcity of deal-related debt in emerging markets during much of Abraaj's tenure within its respective regions.

Obviously, positive results are useful for marketing purposes, but there is little point in trying to fudge these returns and the academics concerned would have had no reason to do so because any person reading the paper could attempt to replicate the results using the data provided. To explore in a little more detail the success of the company as a private equity fund it is worth taking a snapshot of the firm at the point at which Naqvi's thinking was moving towards shifting the shape of Abraaj away from regional funds with individual hubs towards a single global fund in a more centralised model, in the process laying the seeds for personal and corporate decomposition that was exploited ruthlessly by those that wanted to let the towers burn.

# 6

# From Abraaj 1.0 to Abraaj 2.0

*Inspirational capitalism at its most enlightened*[1]

The acceleration of the move from Abraaj 1.0 to Abraaj 2.0 was motivated by public and private drivers. The private driver was Naqvi's medical condition, which had forced him to fast-track his ten-year plan and turn it into a five-year plan. This was a closely guarded secret. The public driver was to position the firm to take the lead in emerging markets globally and to make the case that businesses were essential in the achievement of the UN's sustainable development goals to end poverty and protect the planet:[2]

> Companies could unlock at least $12 trillion in market opportunities by 2030 and create up to 380 million jobs by implementing a few key development goals, according to a study by a group including global business and finance leaders ... The Report argued that paying taxes transparently was a key to rebuilding the social contract. It also advocated pricing pollution via carbon trading and reducing food waste, a step that by itself could be worth up to $405 billion.[3]

Overall, this UN report estimated that achieving these goals by 2030 would be achieved only if $2.4 trillion in additional annual investment, especially in infrastructure, could be found. From a financial perspective, the SDGs sold themselves as identifying markets where societal needs outstripped existing investments and the available supply of goods and services. By definition, that would mean that there are either notable market failures or significant market inefficiencies, both of which offer investors the opportunity to achieve considerable financial and social returns, and the SDG framework makes clear that they are deeply reliant upon one another. The money would come from innovative financing from public and private sector sources to raise this amount: 'The global finance system needs to become much better at deploying the trillions of dollars of savings into the sustainable investments that the world needs.' The document reads like the last will and testament of the globaliser's moment. What is striking about the report is that the language is still one of encouragement; of having the argument and persuading the development world itself that the private sector can have a role in building economies in countries that face profound problems of structural inequality. If the history of Abraaj demonstrated anything in the period up to end of 2017, it demonstrated that the private sector could work as a partner of economic development in any context in which it works with local knowledge in close partnership and leaves behind a legacy of improved profitability and improved corporate citizenship.

Following the acquisition of Aureos, Abraaj carefully prepared for the next stage of its growth. It spent a year integrating teams and processes and hired McKinsey (again) to do a strategic review of all aspects of its business. With the Middle East in turmoil after the Arab Spring and a delayed reaction in Dubai to the global financial crisis of 2008, Abraaj was preparing to make its presence felt in the markets previously served by Aureos. It adopted a more centralised model of operation, like much of the private equity industry, with its base in London and an office for client relations in New York.

Although investing activity in the MENASA region continued through the APEF IV fund, sub-Saharan Africa, Latin America, Turkey and Asia became strong areas of growth. These funds came to be known as Gen-5 (North Africa's successor fund was also included). Although McKinsey pushed Abraaj to raise the capital for Gen-5 in the US, it decided that the consolidation meant that the next investment cycle needed to give prominence to the DFIs that were ready, willing and able to invest into Gen-5 funds and to consolidate the relationships with them. The DFI community, like any other development network of donors, is very conservative. It is difficult to get initial funding from these organisations but once you break through for the first grant or project then the conservatism can then work in your favour. Aureos had grown out of the UK government DFI, CDC, so it was inside the community. Abraaj was brought into the fold when it bought Aureos.

Accordingly, and in short order, Abraaj raised Africa Fund III, Latin America Fund II, North Africa Fund II and Abraaj Turkey Fund I and went to work on this transitional phase in the firm's history. For the Gen-5 funds a new structure was developed. Each fund had a separate administrator and custodian who looked after a designated bank account, which was governed by what Abraaj called in its promotional materials a holistic compliance and governance framework designed in conjunction with the Dubai Financial Services Authority. The company spent tens of millions creating this architecture, but it did not retool the compliance architecture for the legacy funds (i.e. those created before 2012 as the only fund still making investments was APEF IV). The legacy investors in APEF IV were joined later in 2015 by Hamilton Lane[4] and the Bank of America, which acquired part of the secondary stakes that were held on the AHL balance sheet as 'excess inventory'. AHL had taken stakes larger than the 5 per cent of the total fund size commitments required because at the time of the financial crash a number of its legacy investors had failed to provide funds. Abraaj took over those positions, winning many firm friends in the process, but it now had 'excess inventory' in APEF IV which it sold, after full due diligence was completed by these two new US investors. In parallel, the Gen-5 funds deployed the capital in the funds, largely from European DFIs, into investments in fifty companies across the world.

APEF VI was eventually launched on the lessons learnt and the experiences of the creation and delivery of APEF IV and the Gen-5 funds so it is worth exploring them in some detail. The firm had raised $1.37 billion in funds in Africa alone, which at the time represented the largest pool of private equity capital raised for the continent. This was split into two funds. Abraaj Africa Fund III (AAF III) closed at $990 million and Abraaj North Africa Fund II (ANAF II) closed at $375 million. The Abraaj annual report stated that this 'demonstrates the continued optimism in the continent and investors belief in the firm's experience, investment approach and consistent record of accomplishment. AAF III focused on well-managed, mid-market businesses which were leaders in their respective market sectors in the core geographies of Nigeria, Ghana, Côte d'Ivoire, South Africa and Kenya'.[5] The fund targeted sectors most likely to benefit from demand driven by the rapid expansion of a young, urban, middle class across Sub-Saharan Africa, including consumer goods and services and consumer finance. ANAF II targeted mid-market businesses that had demonstrated robust growth in the core geographies of Algeria, Egypt, Morocco and Tunisia with the ability to become regional leaders in their field.[6] The fund focused on sectors that were likely to benefit from an expanding middle class and targeted majority and significant minority stakes to influence the strategic decision and growth agenda of its investee companies.[7] Similarly, and with a virtually identical investing hypothesis tailored to local nuances, funds were raised in Turkey and Latin America and, with the Asian fund reaching a final close during this period, the Gen-5 funds raised an aggregate of approximately $2.5 billion.

The Abraaj investment hypothesis and focus on impact was becoming clearer with every passing quarter and was also more effective given the high-budget PR effort mounted by the firm in disseminating its message through Fred Sicre and Mitali Atal. Abraaj was an innovator in the way it used its public affairs teams and PE professionals in an integrated strategic communications approach. They were sleek compared with other PR firms, and Sicre and Atal were an excellent team. Abraaj focused on highlighting the opportunities in 'global growth markets'; indeed, the term was virtually adopted in place of 'emerging markets' at the premier industry event hosted annually by the IFC in Washington where Naqvi gave the keynote speech in 2017.[8] Abraaj brought focus to its 'glocal' approach, highlighting its investment prism through which it filtered potential investment opportunities; hiring senior people from industry that added to the investing skillsets across each region; and articulating clearly its approach revolving around the 'Three Cs and China', discussed in more detail in Chapter 13.[9] This approach identified that in the coming decade the 'Three Cs', namely cities, consumers and commodities, would be the areas of greatest growth and recognised that China was no longer an emerging market but, rather, would soon become the largest economy in the world with the BRI threatening the investing hegemony enjoyed by Western nations in their previous colonies. Some of the approach took investors by surprise – for example, whilst Goldman Sachs was trumpeting the merits of BRIC (Brazil, Russia, India and China), Abraaj was highlighting Mexico, Peru, Colombia and Chile as an alternative aggregated market in South America. This group of countries presented all the opportunities of Brazil without the political and currency risks: the combined GDP of these countries was similar to Brazil's; regional trade bloc alliances were being built in this area; these countries shared Spanish as a common language, which was also the fastest growing language in the US; there was direct access to the Chinese market through the Pacific coastline; and these countries had young urban populations with increasing affluence. It ticked all the boxes as to where and why to invest and, indeed, Abraaj invested in some ground-breaking transactions in those markets as a result. Abraaj also had an inherently political message everywhere it went: 'We are here to invest into your market through people from the market, rather than fly in and take the money from your pension funds and sovereign wealth funds to invest elsewhere.' Policy and decision makers from Nigeria to Indonesia and Algeria to Colombia heard Abraaj's message and embraced it. Abraaj may have used this thinking to drive its marketing momentum, but the underlying ideas were novel and out-of-the-box and are worth repeating to highlight the drivers that made the firm into an attractive investment destination for global investors.

This could be described as the optimal Abraaj iteration and counter-factually it might have been better to retain this devolved and quasi-independent silo structure permanently. But the silo structure puts limits on growth. Within the firm each silo could have gone quietly about its business, creating returns, and not remained so active in geopolitics as a firm even if Naqvi himself was on a trajectory that would take him out of the firm and into politics. It would also have meant that the pressure on the holding company's capital would not have been so acute when the profound liquidity issues emerged in 2017. The internal argument against this route to stable profitability, which won out with the launch of fundraising for the $6 billion APEF VI, was that staying in the silos would have made it more difficult to then break out from being a regionally successful player to a global player that could compete not just in coverage – which it was doing by 2014 to 2015 – but also in scale. For Naqvi in particular, even though he was pursuing a political agenda in Pakistani politics – securing funding for Imran Khan's 2013 election campaign, for example – he wanted the firm to get around the next corner. That meant taking the next step to secure profitability. Naqvi had concerns about the lacklustre performance of some of the individuals who made up Abraaj's regional partners and about the size and bulk that the company had reached. Naqvi's cancer diagnosis in December 2014 also further increased the pace and intensity of change in the company. This debate about the benefits of the regional silos versus a single global firm was rendered moot by the events of 2018.[10]

Abraaj delayed the announcement of many senior redundancies until after the first close of the new Gen-5 funds, which meant that many of the Abraaj team who were old 'DFI chums' were now without employment and some senior officials at the DFIs were furious to have lost their friends in Abraaj. Since the only real power of limited partners exists through limited partner advisory committees (LPACs), which can halt fund deployment until replacements to their satisfaction are hired, this led to some friction at those committee meetings. Fortunately, the rigour of the new investment process served to bring the DFIs onside; however, the tensions in the relationship were never really resolved, they just simmered beneath the surface. When APEF VI was announced, and it was clear that the target investors were institutional and sovereign wealth funds, which inevitably led to the DFI community thinking they had no further role to play, many DFI members were massively aggrieved; after all, the investment performance of Gen-5 funds had also made them look good in their own organisations.

Abraaj's success in distributing strong returns and profits to investors attracted the attention of other regional governments besides Dubai, including Qatar and Saudi Arabia, which in turn tried to court the company to relocate and become part of their strategic investment off-shoots. It appears that Abraaj also had a number of joint ventures and investments alongside governments in the MENASA region. At times, it almost looked like Abraaj was doing favours for these governments and investing in their national assets to demonstrate the strength of those assets to the market.[11] When Abraaj refused to do so, as was the case with a Tunisian telecoms deal in 2018, the warnings signs were sent by the government and displeasure was clearly expressed.

Even though Abraaj was named after the towers of Dubai, which had become symbols of progress across the region, its horizons were not limited to the United Arab Emirates and it grew into a devolved global entity. Perhaps inevitably, relationships with some early investors and executives became strained over time as they began to feel that Abraaj was ignoring them once it started expanding into new markets. There was a deliberate decision to be different, but a key part of Abraaj's success in emerging markets was its closeness to and its local knowledge of the geographies it operated in. It had to retain that powerful comparative advantage whilst fulfilling its growing ambitions to make change happen at a global level. Some investors told me that Abraaj had become arrogant in its approach to the local market but senior executives at the firm still retained strong relationships at the highest of levels throughout this period. It was a balancing act.

Naqvi was heady with the success of having almost completely deployed the Gen-5 funds into more than fifty businesses when he once again started looking ahead. What next? He had much to occupy him in 2013 to 2015: the acquisition and integration of Aureos; raising and investing the Gen-5 funds; keeping Abraaj's public profile visible through near-constant public speaking events; managing the political balance of the firm amongst competing national interests; handling the preparations for the Karachi Electric exit; conceptualising and raising AGHF; hiring and developing impact businesses in clean energy and real estate; creating a London-based credit business that would be a precursor to establishing a significant presence ahead of the IPO; and finally, his own health issues. From the media coverage of Naqvi at this time, it appeared to be too manic a pace to sustain. There is a subtext here worth highlighting; if indeed Naqvi was leading all the above himself, he was also managing a fractious team, which must have felt like he was personally pulling a ship rather than captaining it, and this inevitably led to his desire to accelerate their departure without alarming the limited partner community, whose rule book defined senior management as the 'key men'.

With the strategy on the broader private equity landscape clear, once the Aureos acquisition had been digested, Naqvi began to turn his attention to the UN SDGs, which in his mind were key to enable the private sector to contribute to globalised growth. His aim was to bring his impact investing credentials to bear by creating sector specific funds that resonated with the SDGs, the first of these being AGHF. Abraaj needed prominent partners to buy into that vision for it to be effectively applied at scale. Equally, he understood that the impact investing paradigm needed a separate division from the private equity business in order for both groups to achieve scale independent of each other.

One of the entities that straddles the 'government–private sector–philanthropy' space is the Bill and Melinda Gates Foundation, and it became an Abraaj partner through a circuitous route. In 2012, Bill Gates approached Naqvi and asked him to become a signatory of The Giving Pledge, which describes itself as a commitment by the world's wealthiest individuals and families to dedicate the majority of their wealth to giving back.[12] Naqvi was a perfect candidate for the Giving Pledge PR machine. He was a Pakistani Muslim and instantly diversified the WASPish image of the Giving Pledge. For Naqvi personally, philanthropy had always been important, exemplified in the Aman Foundation, which he had created and through which he spent $150 million of his own money. For Abraaj, it extended the company's image in the communities in which it operated – it was all part of impact investing. Gates and Naqvi became friends and, through Naqvi, Bill and Melinda met the main players in the MENASA region through elaborate dinners and private gatherings organised by Naqvi from amongst his own circle. Most of the Gulf elite were unknown to the BMGF, and Naqvi was not the only person who was approached by the foundation in this manner, just the first. A former executive at The Giving Pledge disclosed that a similar offer was made to Khaled Juffali to open doors in Saudi Arabia, which he did, as did Azim Premji in India, Mohammed Dewji in Kenya and Badr Jafar in Iraq, and this resulted in The Giving Pledge adding almost 10 per cent of its signatories through these anchor individuals.[13] Gates personally and the BMGF collectively were successful in extending their network in the MENASA region at the highest private sector levels.

The connection to Gates was part of the broader evolution within Abraaj. After a dinner for potential Giving Pledge prospects at Naqvi's home in Dubai, the two men had a long debate about the inadequate provision of healthcare across the global growth markets in which Abraaj was operating. This culminated in a verbal agreement to each commit $100 million to a new healthcare fund, the Abraaj Global Healthcare Fund. Sealed with a handshake, the agreement circumvented the layers of bureaucracy that tended to obstruct deals of this kind.[14] In retrospect, the principal-to-principal nature of this deal may have heightened some of the issues later faced by Abraaj. Naqvi was not naive but perhaps thought the personal nature of the agreement was more like those agreed with a family investment office rather than a state entity. Instead, the BMGF saw itself as a cross between the US State Department and the World Health Organization, with a touch of the US Agency for International Development (USAID), operating on a scale beyond that of many nation states.

Naqvi refused to commence marketing AGHF until he was fully confident it could operate within the structures of an investment fund, whilst retaining its evergreen nature and achieve the impact he wanted. The BMGF wanted a fund structure to satisfy its US tax planning requirements, whereas the World Bank's IFC, Phillips and Medtronic preferred the new initiative to be housed under a corporate vehicle. After years of delay, during which Abraaj spent tens of millions of dollars in research, thinking and development, hiring teams and then replacing them, and despite frustration from BMGF officials who wanted things to move more quickly, Naqvi finally thought that his blueprint for AGHF was complete.

Khawar Mann was hired as the CEO of the new entity; a brilliant and passionate advocate of healthcare in emerging markets who shared Naqvi's vision. Mann was looking for a new start after leaving Apax Partners, a UK private equity firm, following the financial crash of 2008.[15] He became the face of AGHF and the concept was finally unveiled to an initially sceptical audience, including doubt from some within the BMGF itself but its momentum won over these initial sceptics.

The final blueprint drawn up by Naqvi and Mann envisaged that AGHF would focus its activities on ten disease profiles in ten cities across Africa, India and Pakistan. The first billion dollars raised by AGHF, alongside leverage from banks, would create a footprint covering those markets. Data technology and partnerships with pharmaceutical companies and equipment providers would look to reduce the cost of doing business in these markets in a way that would make healthcare more affordable, whilst at the same time enabling hundreds of millions of people to enter and benefit from primary healthcare services for the first time. Aside from global historic under-investment in these markets, a rising middle class and urbanisation had resulted in more sedentary lifestyles and dietary changes had led to a double disease burden. Alongside communicable diseases, there was a profound increase in chronic non-communicable diseases – like cancer, diabetes and heart disease – illnesses that can be treated only through effective health systems rather than vaccines.[16] With a shortage of scalable hospitals, clinics and diagnostic labs to invest in, addressing this gap in healthcare required building assets, scaling up existing ones and creating connective ecosystems between them. AGHF was required to meet five core global health impact objectives relating to accessibility, affordability, quality, system strengthening and prevention – which in turn would ensure adherence to the UN's sustainable development goal 3.[17] Each of these five pillars were given two 'backbone' key performance indicators (KPIs) that were to be tracked at a facility level. The targets for each of these ten KPIs were developed in partnership with the management of each of the AGHF hospitals so that there could be consistency in measuring and consolidating platform-wide data. The rationale for acquiring the CARE Hospitals Group and its twelve hospitals in southern India was to provide assistance in formulating the policy blueprint and provide the training and build the experience of personnel for the rollout of the fund in Africa. All of the above was transparently provided to potential investors in marketing materials which I have seen.

The idea was bold and untested, and the complexities of the project required a distinctive process of fund creation and deployment. It was planning to invest in new-build companies and in existing hospitals, all of which would need contrasting degrees of capital injection at different times. Abraaj's structural plan was to create a corporate vehicle named Evercare, which would consolidate and own all the assets, deploy money drawn down from the fund and purchase assets on the fund's behalf. After several years, Evercare would be listed with a suitably increased valuation allowing investors to exit and obtain a sizeable return; whilst the multilaterals and NGOs could remain invested in the public company over a much longer period. This approach had not been tested in private equity before. It was a fund structure overlay to satisfy the tax needs of philanthropic foundations, and policies of DFIs, but the business was being carried out through one overarching subsidiary that could then be listed – therefore also satisfying the needs of short-term investors or those seeking a higher return. According to Abraaj senior management, the intended structure, objectives and methods were all articulated to investors well in advance. Equally fundamentally, Abraaj finessed a unique structure in terms of subrogating its own returns as an investor into the fund to OPIC, thereby allowing the contradictory terms and legal needs of the European DFIs and the IFC on the one hand and OPIC on the other to co-exist in the same fund. This marked the first time that OPIC had ever been able to find a mechanism to invest alongside European DFIs.

AGHF brought together a range of partners to try to fundamentally address and impact poor healthcare outcomes in Africa and Asia. These included healthcare technology companies like Philips and Medtronic, foundations such as the BMGF, double bottom-line seeking investors, including Morgan Stanley, and development financing institutions, such as the World Bank's IFC, CDC and others, to fundamentally address and impact poor healthcare outcomes in Africa and Asia. The fund closed in July 2016 valued at $850 million, and later received $150 million from OPIC as a debt facility. This created a pool of $1 billion of investible capital available to AGHF.[18] Within Abraaj, Sev Vettivetpillai was the managing partner who was tasked with overseeing the impact investing group, which foresaw further funds in clean energy, low-income housing, food security and education for the future, and Mann led AGHF with a strong and dedicated healthcare-focused management team recruited from around the world to manage Evercare. Alongside this, the fund had a dedicated impact committee headed by Sir David Nicholson, the former chief executive of the UK's National Health Service.[19] The idea of financial and social returns working hand in hand with each other was built into the very foundations of AGHF. Naqvi now moved away from the AGHF investment committee and delegated its running to new senior hires.

These steps, the acquisition of Aureos and the conceptualisation of AGHF once again led to the commissioning of another war room and the inevitable presence of McKinsey during 2014/15 to undertake a study to answer the question: 'What will Abraaj 2.0 look like?' This was very similar to Naqvi's question to McKinsey in 2001 when he asked them to look at Cupola and asked 'Who are we?', with a view to creating a roadmap for what Abraaj would become. This was right up McKinsey's alley as they tended to think they worked best when they had a blank canvas to start from.

McKinsey's view was that Abraaj was primed to be the acknowledged global centre for private equity investment in emerging markets. To achieve this the company needed to expand its horizons and broaden and deepen the geographical spread of its investor base. The Middle East family offices had provided hundreds of millions in capital and the DFIs had provided a few billion, but to achieve Abraaj's 10–10–10 plan, a step change was required, even though the target of total market dominance across growth markets was within reach. What needed to change was the type of LP Abraaj worked with. It needed LPs who could deploy hundreds of millions through a single commitment, the pension funds and institutional investors in North America, Europe, China and East Asia. To attract them, the fund size had to be alluring enough and the underlying thesis rigorously tested and backed by hard data and the ultimate proof and validation would come from unearthing investment opportunities of scale across the target markets of Latin America, Africa and Asia. To raise the fund, Abraaj would need to muster a world-class team of fundraising professionals and base them in London, New York and Hong Kong to access the big pools of capital. Internally, the team would have to gear up and create the background material, research and business case for justifying such a move, alongside putting thousands of pages together to ensure full transparency for the online data room, which would be ruthlessly scrutinised once global investors started their due diligence on the fund with a view to investing. The team would also need to ensure that all of the top-tier external professional resources that Abraaj commonly employed to remain best-in-class, from accounting and audit, tax, legal, strategic or organisational perspectives, were deployed. Thus, Abraaj Private Equity Fund VI was born.[20]

The central idea of the fund[21] was to adopt a 'one-platform' vision to dissolve the old model of regional silos with distinct operations and unite the entire enterprise under one organisation. Internally, this represented a move away from a dependency on the Middle East, but also a change in the culture of the company. The McKinsey team worked closely with the senior Abraaj team to articulate the strategy for Abraaj 2.0. The central aim was to draw in investment from Western institutional investors and thereby position Abraaj as the means of guiding Western capital into emerging markets. This would help accelerate the business and promote internal talent, but would also result in a change in the culture of the company.

The move to raise one large global fund was a step away from what had built the success of the company over the previous fifteen years but was based on the ambition to break through to the next level on the premise that scale breeds scale. Toby Mitchenall described the step change in the ambition of Abraaj in *Private Equity International*:

> Large institutional investors are as interested in deploying sizeable slugs of capital as they are in capturing one or two extra basis points of alpha. For a stratum of institutional investors, seeking to commit tickets of more than $100 million per fund but not account for more than 10 per cent of the fund's total, the bigger the fund's target, the better.[22]

That was the logic, rather than create more regional- and country-focused funds; create one unified fund of $6 billion. Abraaj had identified a gap in the market because for investors looking to commit to global emerging markets – and in volume – there were not many options for 'one-stop shopping'. Importantly, although McKinsey always emphasised that the mega fund would appeal to Western institutions, the relationships that had been built with key Chinese companies through the Karachi Electric deal and otherwise over the years also brought in significant potential access to their capital. Alongside the BRI, such companies were only just beginning to flex their muscle on the global investment stage. Everyone who knows Naqvi has described his skill in smelling opportunity, and his relentless drive to prise it open was almost ruthless in execution; he could see demand evolving for his concept from east and west and given his emphasis on corporate foreign policy and not having a nation state backing him, such a structure was immensely appealing for future stability.

Abraaj planned on delivering returns that would be comparable with large buyout funds in developed markets. However, the risk profile of the fund would differ, with less use of leverage and a more diversified portfolio (the fund could invest in up to fifty companies compared with the more typical ten to fifteen per fund until that point).[23] The team could be rationalised down to executives from around the world, who were specialists within their given sectors, all managed centrally, which offered a significant cost reduction. This new approach might have proven to be a step too far but it might also have taken the company to the next level. It appeared to observers that the bet had paid off when Abraaj announced that it was on target with a $3 billion first close in October 2017; however, the fund never proceeded beyond this point following the crisis that almost immediately engulfed the company.

Naqvi was driving down the route to a single global fund, to maximise the skills of a single global investment committee, to utilise the skills of top global industry professionals hired centrally, to change the investing model through the emphasis on technology, to centralise past learnings. He had rejected the idea of a single global fund when McKinsey had proposed it in 2013 and the subsequent success of the Gen-5 funds and the quality of deal flow and cementing of DFI relationships vindicated his approach. However, within that the seeds of future disaster had been planted. In moving to the single fund, Naqvi made enemies of particular senior managers who had an interest in the existence of the company's regional hubs without which they were largely redundant.

The magic ingredient which helped Abraaj to grow so quickly and achieve such excellent results in difficult markets was also the core vulnerability that allowed it to be taken down with such speed and finality. That ingredient was Arif Naqvi. Abraaj was a charisma-led company that developed into a team held together by self-interest, but in the end it was defined by the personality of the founder. Like many other businesses that have grown at exponential pace in recent times, this founder was the catalyst that allowed the funds to become larger and larger. Naqvi's advocacy ensured that Abraaj was seen as the champion of impact investment and that his investment acumen was seen as unchallengeable. These two factors of growth and impact also aroused interest from investors in both the US and China. It was Naqvi's role to manage the conflicting interests of these two superpowers. All these elements together concentrated too much decision-making responsibility in a single person – and that person was also simultaneously laying the foundations for his career after Abraaj. When a founder makes mistakes and suggests courses of action that are wrong it is absolutely essential that there are people around who can question, challenge and contradict them. There are only twenty-four hours in a day and only so much that one person can physically do. There were clearly weaknesses in Naqvi's ability to delegate to other senior members of the team and some of them were not up to the task or could not take the pace at which the company was growing. Most individuals that I spoke to said that both Naqvi and the team itself had weaknesses because, in the final months of Abraaj, there seemed to be no one in the senior management team who could help shoulder the burden or tell Naqvi to stop. It was not that the emperor had no clothes; it was that the emperor did not know what he was up against.

By 2016, Abraaj was a multinational, multiracial, private equity company that was founded on a network of people based locally in the Middle East and later in Africa, Asia and South America. It specialised in making investments in small and medium-sized companies and it had a stellar rise in the first fifteen years of its existence, producing high returns for its investors. Those returns were based on value-added guidance to the companies it acquired by the deployment of teams with local knowledge and networks.

The thematic business focusing exclusively on impact had been successfully launched with the $1 billion AGHF, and new initiatives in energy and low-income housing had been launched. A new credit products business had started operating from London. The business had been internally divided between private equity (led by Mustafa Abdel-Wadood), thematic (led by Sev Vettivetpillai) and credit products (led by Carsten Jorgensen) with an impressive cast of operationally experienced industry executives at the centre (led by Wahid Hamid) to provide support to regional teams and a large thirty-member fundraising team based in

Dubai, London, New York and Hong Kong (led by Mark Bourgeois). Internal company critics stated that the operations team (led by Waqar Siddique) remained somewhat weak and in need of bolstering,[24] but the structure had been honed to support the launch of APEF VI as the final step towards an IPO in London, which would finally allow Naqvi the option to step away from running the business and focus on his ambition to enter politics in Pakistan even if it meant that his only role was as chair of the global investment committee, which in any event was the one role that he cherished the most and that prospective investors in APEF VI most admired him for. During 2016, Abraaj was also focused on developing APEF VI with the aim of commanding the global market of impact investing, with the process coordinated and led internally by Tom Speechley, who assembled a new war room for the purpose and pulled in the brightest minds across the group. Tom had decided to leave the firm following his replacement as head of the global fundraising effort by Mark Bourgeois and this was to be his swansong before going off into the field of medicinal cannabis. Whilst the firm was busy deploying Gen-5 and launching new initiatives, Speechley and his team developed the arguments and hypothesis to launch the new mega fund and took virtually the whole of 2016 to research the business case for justifying such a move, alongside assembling the paperwork and data that would be necessary for future due diligence conducted by prospective investors and ensuring that all of the top-tier external professional resources that Abraaj commonly employed were in order, whether from accounting and audit, tax, legal, strategic or organisational perspectives. Again, McKinsey was consulted throughout this process and validated that the launch of the fund was the logical next step for Abraaj to pursue to capitalise on their position within the private equity space.

In October 2016, when the planning was finally complete, Naqvi convened a meeting in Dubai of all the senior professionals from across all offices globally to announce the new initiative internally – about 120 senior investment professionals, including partners, managing directors and directors, comprising the entire senior team in the private equity silo. Collectively, he encouraged them to embrace this future vision and to debate the potential difficulties of moving from the hub-and-spoke model of regional offices into a centralised machine. And this is where the key-man issues surfaced.

Naqvi and his senior management team knew that the regional model under which the Gen-5 funds had been deployed was weakened by the silo structure, although this was not apparent to either outsiders or the rank and file of the firm. It was weakened by the silo structure in the sense that it could not work at the scale and generate the size of investments that the single global fund could manage because each regional team was too small. The junior and mid-level skillsets that were available locally were strong and supported the political vision of local connections and investing in communities, but all investment decisions were made centrally by an extremely engaged and probing global investment committee, consisting of the three most-senior managing partners in the firm: Abdel-Wadood, Vettivetpillai and Hamid, and chaired by Naqvi. The regional partners saw the value brought by the central execution team, as well as the weaknesses that they exposed when the local investments were subjected to constant scrutiny and common-platform metrics. However, the regional partners were not reflective of the talent below them and acted as a ceiling to their future advancement, whilst aspiring to the high income that funded an 'Abraaj lifestyle', which for Naqvi meant a yacht, a country house and the use of the company jet and for others meant the well-publicised excesses of Wall Street. The senior management of the group viewed the regional managing directors and directors in the firm as the future, not the incumbent partner level, and were delighted by the quality of personnel at those levels. Collectively, these totalled around 120 people who were straining at the bit to make an impact, and for whom a global mega fund made total sense.

Latin America was headed by Miguel Olea, who at sixty-five was looking to retire; Davinder Sikand, who headed Africa, was not widely regarded as being engaged or enthused – a throwback to the Aureos style of working (i.e. the style of government bureaucrats) – and Jacob Kholi, who was another of the partners in Africa, was of a similar mindset; and Ahmed Badreldin, who headed the Middle East and North Africa, was ambitious but became involved in internal conflicts as a result of the constraints imposed by the Abraaj structure. Rumours floated amongst junior staff that Badreldin wanted to break off a fund and coincidentally he was the only partner who managed to do a management buyout of the fund which he managed, ANAF II. It was made clear at the partner level internally that all of the above individuals were being relieved, but they were all 'key men' in their respective Gen-5 funds. Their departure would trigger a halt in investing until someone suitable that had been vetted by the LPAC could be hired – such consultation being the only stage in the fund life where limited partners had a say in decision making, which was something that was cherished by the DFIs as a tool to keep the firm in check, not least because they themselves were accountable to their respective governments and a very critical NGO community.[25] Of course, halting the deployment of Gen-5 funds meant that the APEF VI first close was delayed since it could not officially be closed until the Gen-5 funds had passed a 70 per cent investment threshold; and this was the balancing act that had to be managed throughout 2017.

Through the launch of the global fund therefore, the regional partners knew that their future was uncertain. However much their long-term association with the DFIs could delay the inevitable, the writing was on the wall. But who wants to give up on a gig that is bringing in a seven-figure salary each year? Furthermore, anyone being relieved of a position at the firm at the time of the transition to the global mega fund would have been well aware they were losing out financially. On the assumption that APEF VI would successfully be a $6 billion fund, with a baseline expected return equivalent to the capital invested (the common yardstick in the industry, implying an IRR of just under 8 per cent per annum over the fund life), this would result in an estimated $1.2 billion in carried interest, of which the formula at Abraaj was 25 per cent going to AHL, 37.5 per cent to the central team and the investment committee and 37.5 per cent to the actual teams on the ground that made and monitored the investments. This meant that $450 million in carried interest would have been available to the team – and that was the baseline bare minimum expected return over the lifetime of the fund.[26]

A number of people have stated in interviews that the meeting in Dubai of the senior members of the investment team was a revelation. The difference between the old approach and the new approach was stark and instantly apparent. The non-partner participants were enthusiastic and were identifying transactions that could be consummated through the new fund involving either scale that they could not aspire to before or the consolidation of opportunities that were ripe in the sectors they followed. This gave rise to Abraaj having the opportunity to actually show the prospective created deal-flow to potential investors without anonymising the targets; this in itself was a revolutionary approach and this level of transparency was widely welcomed. After working with investment teams across the world, Abraaj identified approximately thirty companies it hoped to invest in.[27]

The APEF VI fund was launched in early 2017 with a targeted size of $6 billion. It was the fastest fundraise in emerging markets history: within eight months, Abraaj had secured commitments totalling $3 billion, including well over $250 million each from new institutional investors like the Washington State Pension Fund and the Hong Kong Monetary Authority.[28] Being able to attract capital from both Western and Asian investors was a testament to Abraaj's status as a major player in PE by this point, and also its interest in and connections with China. In parallel, Abraaj commissioned JPMorgan to provide a valuation of the firm with a view to appointing the bank as managers of an eventual IPO in 2018 when the APEF VI fund was fully raised. The preliminary report from JPMorgan was delivered in August 2017. It estimated that Abraaj would be worth $2 per share and $3 billion in overall equity as a holding company and its units at the time of IPO – not to be confused with the funds totalling $14 billion under Abraaj management at the time.[29] Gossip inside Abraaj was that firm early interest came from the Saudi Public Investment Fund (PIF) and SoftBank in mid-2017, but the company decided to wait – in hindsight, this was definitely not the right decision given the upcoming battle it would fight; if Abraaj had been absorbed by some monolith at this time, perhaps it would still exist.[30]

This survey of Abraaj's activity is designed to give a flavour of what the firm was doing; this is not an exhaustive company history, but the conclusion should be clear. There was nothing bogus about Abraaj or its precursor Cupola. This was an innovative firm working in challenging places and delivering returns for its investors whilst growing a global footprint with a first-class team that was moving at breakneck speed. It often invested in complex political environments in which it judged that the economic fundamentals were sound. But in the end, there was the metric of 'money-in-money-out', which measured what delivered exit returns were. Not everything worked perfectly but the firm was well marketed through a steady story of growth and success and it delivered a bottom line of achievement. Most telling, Abraaj did not emerge from the 2008 crisis unscathed but, much like the Gulf itself, it weathered that storm better than some old and more established financial institutions and financial centres (such as Lehman Brothers and Wall Street). The management style of the company was extremely demanding but also extremely rewarding, and its record of corporate citizenship was exemplary.

Until the cash-flow crisis of 2017 to 2018, Abraaj was a solid and successful private equity company. It was doing very well but not spectacularly. The last asset management figure reported by the company that could be found in public sources was from 2018 and was $13.6 billion.[31] This is interesting when compared with the top ten private equity companies globally:

1.  The Blackstone Group Inc. – $619 billion total assets under management.
2.  The Carlyle Group Inc. – $260 billion AUM.
3.  KKR & Co. Inc. – $252 billion AUM.
4.  TPG Capital – $91 billion AUM.
5.  CVC Capital Partners – $118 billion AUM, including $82 billion in private equity.
6.  EQT AB – €67 billion AUM ($81 billion).
7.  Vista Equity Partners –$73 billion AUM
8.  Neuberger Berman Group LLC – $405 billion AUM, including $73 billion in private equity.
9.  Advent International – $66 billion AUM
10. Warburg Pincus LLC – $60 billion AUM.[32]

In comparison with these companies, Abraaj was substantial but not an exceptionally sized player; it ranked between forty and sixty in global rankings. Where it was exceptional was in the impact investment that it delivered and the way in which it measured and made that impact transparent. That is what gave it the ability to take to the global stage; it had developed the methodology of managing the risks of investing in geographies that others had not.

Abraaj did not invent impact investing but it certainly turbo-charged it and applied it well, and in the process it made a lot of people a lot of money and helped a lot of companies contribute to the building of a new middle class in emerging markets, which made a practical and real contribution to reducing poverty and building political stability.

PART III

# CLIMAX – FLAG FOLLOWS TRADE

# 7

# A string of pearls

*You're not a star until they can spell your name in Karachi.*

Humphrey Bogart

Western political and financial elites have complex relationships with each other and with outsider companies that are periodically championed from beyond their closed circles of wealth, privilege and power. There is no committee that decides when these elites have used you sufficiently that it is time to dispose of you. It is not surprising that people constantly look for the existence of some kind of single and unified consciousness behind the actions of state and capital. It is not the case that the global elite is divided between the state on the one hand and capital on the other. Within the state there is a political divide between parties that represent alternative ways of doing capitalism and between states that have differing conceptions of pursuing economic interests. The United States pursues profit in ways it describes as overtly capitalist, and it supports its capitalism with blood and gold. It has traditionally used war as both an offensive weapon in support of capital and in defence of its spheres of influence. It has used economic hitmen on a more micro level to promote the interests of US firms. In his classic memoir/study of economic hitmen (EHM), John Perkins wrote that

> activities that would have been viewed as immoral, unacceptable, and illegal in the United States in my EHM days are now standard practice. They may be covered in a patina of oblique rhetoric, but beneath that surface, the same old tools – including a combination of threats, bribes, falsified reports, extortion, sex, and sometimes violence – are applied at the highest levels of business and government. EHMs are ubiquitous ... Corruption at the top has become legitimate because corporate EHMs draft the laws and finance the politicians who pass them.[1]

President Dwight D. Eisenhower identified and was fearful of the force of the military–industrial complex; today there is a private sector–state complex in whose interests the United States acts.

China pursues interests with a different rhetoric and a longer-term planning horizon but underpinning the economic expansion of the country is a clear strategic vision. Chinese commercial entities are more overtly the creatures of the Chinese state and the Communist Party than US entities are of the US state. These states have different modus operandi, ideas and self-images, but they represent, in the end, the same pursuit of nation-state interests and sometimes deploy similar techniques in the defence of those interests.[2] If there is a deep state in active operation in the US and China it is in this differently articulated confluence of economic, political and military power that it functions. And it is at the nexus of these competing interests and clashes that the story of the destruction of The Abraaj Group sits. That nexus occurred in one of the most violent, complex and geopolitically important cities in the world: Karachi.

If we are going to understand what happened to Abraaj then we must understand the city of Karachi and its place in relation to US and

Chinese interests, and more widely its position in Pakistani politics, global politics and the interface between these and global capitalism.

The city is a vital strategic asset so anyone who controls the key assets within it also becomes part of a wider context of competing geopolitical interests and energy policies. In 2008, Abraaj became a central player in the city's economy and therefore its politics and the geopolitics of Pakistan more widely. All explanations, aside from the most simplistic and individualistic ones, which only obscure the interests and actions of nation states, must encompass a set of concentric circles that have at their heart this sprawling mass on the Arabian Sea; Karachi, the twelfth largest beta global city on earth, the place in which all lines of explanation ultimately meet.

Karachi is a place that determines political outcomes in one of the most strategically important countries in the world and, during the war on terror, perhaps the most strategically important country in the world. But Pakistan is important not just because of the war on terror, but also because of its place in China's Belt and Road Initiative.[3] The BRI is playing a significant role in reconstructing the economic basis of many emerging or growth market economies, and that role must be understood as a complex interplay between economic interests and military and strategic interests, most importantly with respect to the control of ports, which determine access to key global choke points. Incidentally, it is also important in terms of countering Islamist extremism because part of the Chinese motivation for the BRI is economic development in its own Western provinces, which have significant Muslim populations and higher levels of poverty compared with the rest of the country. This driver of economic interest requires access to global markets.

China has a global maritime strategy the like of which has not been seen since the British Empire in the eighteenth and nineteenth centuries. It is to build a network of ports around the world through which it can sell its products and deploy its excess capacity in new technology, infrastructure and construction to ensure the economic development of its interests. China either gains entry to ports by building debt and then gaining control of the port as repayment of that debt, as in the case of ports in Kenya and Sri Lanka,[4] or simply through direct investments, as in the case of Gwadar Port – the deepest seaport in Pakistan. Each port is then immediately deepened and rebuilt so that it can accept, if necessary, ships from the Chinese People's Liberation Army Navy as well as its regular traffic of commercial vessels. The process is described as flag following trade:[5] the military following, or having the capacity to follow, commerce. The ports that China is acquiring, or trying to gain control of, around the Arabian Sea, have been described as being so economically and strategically attractive that they are like a 'string of pearls'.[6] Now imagine what Chinese strategists would think if you suggested that they could add Port Qasim and Karachi into that mix? And equally, imagine what US analysts would think if they could see such assets becoming part of the Chinese sphere of influence?

Beyond the impact investment focus of Abraaj, there was one deal that set the company apart from other private equity firms and became the epicentre of the climax of the firm's history and the cause of its ultimate destruction: the purchase of Karachi Electric.

At the time that Abraaj purchased a controlling interest in Karachi Electric, Karachi had an official population of 12.3 million but a total demographic catchment area of between 20 and 22 million with some estimates for its current population now as high as 30 million.[7] It is bigger than eighty countries in the world, having grown from a small fishing village into a centre of the slave trade to become the jewel of the British Empire. Its geographical position also meant that the original fishing village rapidly developed as a port serving both Pakistan and land-locked Afghanistan. The Port of Karachi is the largest in Pakistan and the city itself is the economic powerhouse of the country: whilst Karachi has only 10 per cent of Pakistan's population, it is responsible for 25 per cent of the country's GDP and 65 per cent of the country's tax revenue; a stat that apparently was continuously rattled off by Abraaj senior management.[8]

The main electricity company for Karachi is Karachi Electric. In 2008, Karachi Electric was generating 1,317mW and had 13km of transmission line. It was losing 400mW a month from those lines and making an annual financial loss of 107 billion rupees ($1.5 billion in the 2008 exchange rate). It had a network that spanned 6,500km, supplying electricity to the mixed commercial and residential areas of the centre of Karachi, the richer suburbs and out to the poorer periphery.[9] It also supplied power to the ports of both Karachi and Qasim. Pakistan's domestic energy generation relies primarily on coal power and the majority of these plants are based in the Punjab, which is the most affluent region of the country dominated by the traditional elite. Pakistani coal is inefficient and high in pollutants so much of the supply is imported from external markets using Port Qasim as an entry point. It is therefore almost impossible to overstate the significance of Karachi Electric to the Pakistani government, military and, consequently, the superpowers interested in the region.[10]

Karachi Electric is the only vertically integrated power utility in Pakistan managing all three areas of producing and delivering energy to consumers: generation, transmission and distribution. It was also the only privately owned power generator. It was a classic monopoly provider – heavily subsidised, overstaffed, over-priced, losing billions of rupees in revenues to theft and penalising poorer areas with load shedding (turning supply off in one place to maintain supply in another). The workforce had a 'job for life' mentality. As the monopoly provider of electricity, it had a potential licence to print money because the price of electricity was subsidised by a tariff and because state entities had to buy their electricity from the company. These internal state transfers frequently failed to take place, but the management could take the losses and pay the wages because they were too important to be allowed to fail. The city is controlled more by the resident corps commander of Karachi, who maintains law and order when civilian agencies fail in their responsibility, rather than the mayor. Karachi Electric was directly run by the military from 1999 until 2005 when it was privatised. The direct military control clearly demonstrates the strategic value of Karachi and Karachi Electric to the armed forces who exercise a disproportionate level of influence in Pakistan and have long played a strategic game of balancing the interests of Pakistan's two key allies: the US and China.[11]

In 2005, after six years of management by the army, Karachi Electric was listed on the Karachi, Islamabad and Lahore stock exchanges. The state retained 25.66 per cent, the public bought 1.76 per cent and 72.58 per cent was sold to KES Power, a consortium of Aljomaih Group, a conglomerate based in Saudi Arabia, and National Industries Group (NIG), a Kuwaiti industrial conglomerate, for $293 million.[12] These two entities then hired the Pakistani division of Siemens, the German manufacturing company, to actually run the operation. If anything, Siemens was an equipment provider not a utility operator; and within two years, it had burnt through the capital injected by the new owners. In early 2008, Abraaj was approached by a representative of Aljomaih and NIG, the two private owners of Karachi Electric.

Karachi Electric was a different kind of investment from the other impact initiatives that Abraaj had financed before. This was not an SME but a strategically vital industry in a strategically vital location and Naqvi had the local knowledge and the local connections to understand fully what he was getting into. He was born in Karachi and knew the economic and political context in which Karachi Electric was operating. Naqvi said the following to Harvard academics writing a case study on the deal:

> Almost nothing about the company worked. You could not have designed a more troubled company if you had set your mind to it. But we were aware that if we could invest and make a difference anywhere, that place would be Karachi. In fact, it would be a great ESG opportunity – success with

KESC [Karachi Electric] would accompany longer-term social returns, not just in stability but the economic vitality of the entire country, given the essential nature of electricity. The company was suffering cash losses of $15 million per month and faced issues with the government that had gone unresolved for years. We had been offered the company for one dollar in 2005 and turned it down.

Naqvi called an unusual investment committee meeting. 'It wasn't just the usual executive committee but included all the executive directors,' he said.

Everyone voted for the deal but me. I didn't, because of the 'road-blocks' we had identified, although I said if these were removed by government, I would give my assent. And they were – by the entire federal Cabinet of the government, a commitment sufficiently powerful for us to feel we could rely on it.

For the next nine months, the Abraaj team did their due diligence. Their presence undermined the existing management team, who in September 2008 simply walked out because they realised their time was up and by creating a crisis they hoped the government would intervene and renationalise the company and reinstate them. Instead, Naqvi convinced KES Power to allow him to send in two Abraaj partners, Farrukh Abbas and Tabish Gauhar, who in turn mobilised a thirty-person team from within Abraaj and externally hired other team members to take control and to keep things going even before the actual deal was done. Even though the Abraaj management team was deployed in September 2008, the deal was not signed until full political backing by way of Cabinet approval was forthcoming in May 2009. According to the Harvard case study, Naqvi said: 'By then the team had compiled a record of steady week-by-week progress.' The case study also detailed that Abraaj acquired a controlling stake in KES Power for $50 million with an additional commitment to invest $361 million from Abraaj and partners and raise additional investment of $900 million by 2012 from investors like the IFC and companies like General Electric. As Abraaj's Tabish Gauhar, who had formerly worked at power company AES Corporation, later remarked: 'It had no value as a going concern. The value was all in the improvements we could make. And that was the benefit.' Speaking to *Harvard Business Review*, Naqvi later commented: 'If we could fix it, the benefits would be tremendous. In addition, Pakistan had no energy policy. If we owned [Karachi Electric], we would be able to play a role in creating that.' Between 2008 and 2016, against bitter opposition from unions and by forcing through many controversial decisions, the Abraaj team set about addressing the problems of the company which were judged by *Harvard Business Review* to include:

> Endemic power theft; inadequate supply; rampant black-outs; antiquated tariff structures that did not cover costs; the unwillingness of government agencies to pay bills owed to other agencies (circular debt); and a disorganized staff that was seen as unresponsive at best, corrupt at worst.[13]

A regular and efficient supply of electricity was critical for the Pakistani economy. Sporadic protests would erupt in Karachi when it experienced power outages. This was considered a threat to the stability of the city and the country in general; as such, the civilian government viewed Karachi Electric as an asset of significant importance that could not be allowed to fail because its failure could undermine the experiment in civilian government that had just commenced in Pakistan.

The political ramifications of the acquisition of Karachi Electric by Abraaj were immense and so the team endeavoured to consult all relevant stakeholders before finalising to ensure that it would progress smoothly. This included the armed forces, major banks and all of the prominent political parties on the domestic scene. Additionally, Abraaj lobbied various multilateral financing institutions with interests in Karachi Electric, including the IFC and multiple other international stakeholders. Both General Musharraf, President of Pakistan until August 2008, and his successor Asif Ali Zardari were consulted and gave the deal their approval.

Karachi Electric was a deeply unpopular public utility, which had little trust amongst the people and sections of the Pakistani media were heavily critical of it. This level of scrutiny was natural because of the importance of Karachi Electric to Karachi and Karachi to the country:

> One of the biggest constraints on Pakistan's economic growth was its power supply. In 2006, it ranked 138th in the world in terms of power consumption per capita, largely because the country simply did not produce enough electricity. This paucity reflected the fact that electricity was not priced to provide a return to investors. Widespread under-investment in generation capacity left Pakistan roughly 4,500 megawatts short of fulfilling demand ... (including the unserved population), and its transmission system's losses in 2008 exceeded 38 per cent, compared to an average of 6.5 per cent in the United States. Moreover, many power producers operated below full capacity due to financial constraints, exacerbated by the tendency of customers not to pay their bills. More than half (53 per cent) of the population endured black-outs ... (load-shedding) that lasted at least eight hours a day. Rural areas might face daily interruptions for as long as twenty hours.

The economic impact of this shortage was profound.

> Pakistan's most important export industry, textiles, complained that power interruptions resulted in 100 lost days of production

during 2010, at a loss of $4 billion. Inadequate and unreliable power supplies threatened the very foundation of the economy – the ability to run machines or turn on lights – as well as efficiency-improving innovations, such as computers to speed design and research. Such challenges reduced investor enthusiasm, slowed economic growth, and hindered the country's integration into the broader MENA region. In fact, in Pakistan's context, the state's legitimacy was undermined by its inability to provide basic services such as power and police protection. Citizens took the matter into their own hands by stealing power, which created an increasing sense of alienation from the state.[14]

This was Abraaj's real test. Could it make a real difference in one of its home communities, reverse the sense of widespread distrust and fix an asset that had for years been stuck in the past?

Harvard Business School produced the case study quoted above with Harvard Kennedy School on Karachi Electric, which was subsequently used in institutions around the world as an example of how socially concerned private equity investment can produce excellent outcomes for communities whilst simultaneously securing a commercial return. Karachi Electric therefore attained a global reputation as a benchmark for impact investment and a case study for the future trajectory of the private equity industry and propelled Abraaj's positioning to the top of the private equity industry in emerging markets.

Karachi Electric had not seen new capital investment in infrastructure in over a decade, and its losses due to theft and pilferage were due in part to the systemic corruption plaguing the company. It had not been profitable for twenty years. These issues undoubtedly presented major hurdles to successful investment but Abraaj believed that a management overhaul combined with leverage of the government of Pakistan's capital contributions with debt to raise over $1 billion for capital improvements would help to revitalise the company, bring about improvements for local stakeholders, address chronic energy shortages and ultimately kickstart development in Karachi and the wider economy.

For Abraaj, and specifically Naqvi, the Karachi Electric deal would define the impact credentials of the company and determine its future given the political ramifications of such a transaction, and it was the perfect vehicle for demonstrating the viability of impact investing on a global scale and demonstrating local political impact.

Fast-forward seven years and the company was transformed after Abraaj's involvement. It implemented accountability through structural reforms and change-management programmes. By exempting industrial areas from load shedding, Abraaj improved the economic performance of the city, which increased revenues. It built new generators to increase power generation. In terms of management and governance, Karachi Electric was meant to follow a strict code of governance as a publicly listed company but Abraaj implemented accountability through policy and structural reforms to try to make that compliance a reality. Value and vision statements along with a revised code of conduct were put in place and implemented through a change-management programme. Emphasis was put on transparency and open communication with all stakeholders, including a whistle-blower initiative known as 'Speak Up', whereby anyone could bring any concern (internally and externally) forward with the certainty that it would be independently investigated. Karachi Electric's long-time status as a government entity engendered corruption, entitlement and inefficiency within the workforce, which had made recruiting managers from those ranks difficult. Abraaj implemented an annual performance appraisal process to ensure individual accountability and created a disciplinary cell to address internal corruption. New integrated IT systems and processes allowed for enhanced management information systems and controls.

Abraaj's success in Karachi Electric rested entirely on its ability to implement operational improvements in the context of strong political support. Some of these, such as building new generating plants and improving the efficiency of transmission and distribution systems, were straightforward but still required effective project management and financing – by 2016 there had been four world-class projects executed on budget and on time, resulting in an additional supply of roughly 1,000mW. The key initiative of exempting industrial areas from load shedding had a direct economic impact on the country. Others, such as reducing power theft, incentivising the workforce, securing adequate natural gas supplies and improving management were more difficult. Abraaj successfully piloted a restructured distribution organisation, creating greater accountability, motivated employees and improved processes.

Abraaj made the utility more efficient, but the culture of electricity theft was a more stubborn problem. Theft had become a necessity for people if power was cut off regularly from specific locations, so segmented load shedding to incentivise better customer behaviour and create community pressure was introduced. Karachi Electric also had to address the issue of power theft in 'lawless' areas – which Karachi had a lot of. At the time, Karachi was rife with organised crime, violence and gangs, not to mention the terrorist elements from organisations operating in Afghanistan, such as the Taliban and ISIS; it was natural for them to gravitate to Karachi because the city had millions of people that had migrated as refugees into Pakistan following the Soviet invasion of Afghanistan.[15] One member of the Abraaj team noted:

> We segmented the demand patterns in the city and found that 67 per cent of the city had less than 20 per cent losses theft. So, the remaining third of the city was causing half of those losses. Therefore, we implemented a distribution service provider initiative where we partnered with local service providers who had established businesses in these high-loss areas.

Karachi Electric also calibrated load-shedding (service interruptions) based on a neighbourhood's payment and loss profile. Neighbourhoods with low levels of power theft had minimal interruptions; those with moderate theft may be interrupted for three hours per day; and the bulk of the load shedding occurred in the high-loss areas. Many of the older meters that ran slowly or could easily be tampered with were replaced with modern electrostatic meters. Meter readers, who were underpaid and therefore susceptible to bribery, received higher salaries and a clear zero-tolerance approach to bribery was introduced. Alongside their improved status there was a widespread 'name and shame' campaign in which the names and addresses of known power thieves were posted in the local paper.[16] This was supported by community initiatives to gain stakeholder buy in to these issues and wider corporate social responsibility programme.

Much of what Abraaj did was standard operating procedure for a privatisation and change-management process and the confrontation with unions that occurred was also normal. The utility's workforce was a typical workforce of a nationalised monopoly, suffering from a lack of accountability and redundant workers doing non-core functions (e.g. bill distributors and security staff). Many were overpaid by as much as 50 per cent compared with similar private sector positions. When Abraaj offered a voluntary severance scheme to encourage retirement for roughly 7,000 individuals, the powerful and politically connected unions organised violent strikes that destroyed company property and kept the management team from its offices for three months in 2011. Abraaj's strategy was highly risky given the backdrop of violence that existed in the city and the partisan nature of its politics and affiliations.[17] With Naqvi providing the political clout through constant interactions with the city, provincial and national governments, and against a backdrop of round-the-clock tension, Karachi Electric stuck to its position and eventually the unions backed down.

The resolution of this situation demonstrated that Abraaj's focus on reducing corruption and streamlining service delivery was working. A series of Nielsen surveys confirmed steadily rising opinions of the company.[18] Interestingly, the company had made such strides in power provision and customer regard that the public mostly sided with the company against the unions; clearly, they wanted their power back.

Abraaj also introduced a CSR programme that formed part of the broader ESG policy implemented by the Abraaj team, but it was never about CSR. Karachi Electric's sustainability policy was underpinned by 'a long-term 360-degree value creation model'. During Abraaj's due diligence in early 2008, the firm recognised the need for an engagement strategy that would bring the company into the community that it served and bridge the divide between the utility supplier and its customer base. A number of deliverable programmes were undertaken from 2008 onwards. Tom Speechley and other members of the team stressed that ESG was not a luxury but a necessity for a utility company like Karachi Electric.[19]

In 2012, Abraaj invited the Global Reporting Initiative, which assesses companies on issues such as climate change, human rights, governance and impact on social wellbeing to review and rate them. Karachi Electric became the first Pakistani company to get an A grade and one of the first in the world to get an A at first sitting.[20] By 2013, Karachi Electric was generating 2,700mW, had 31km of transmission lines, had cut monthly loses to 80mW and turned in a profit of $203 million. Abraaj had turned the failing utility company that was critical to the success of Karachi and Pakistan into a profitable enterprise. It was lauded as an example of successful impact investment. It was also attacked by vested interests, bureaucrats and state-run entities because of its success and the projection of that success; whilst large parts of Karachi had largely resolved their load shedding issues, the majority of the rest of the country was experiencing eighteen-hour blackouts; in fact, in the national election campaign of 2013 the main issue was the power shortages plaguing the country.

Karachi Electric powered the city, which powered the economy of Pakistan. Given the critical position of Karachi Electric in the national infrastructure of Pakistan, in which a proxy war is being fought between two global superpowers today, controlling Karachi Electric can be seen as one of the keys to regime change.

In keeping with the private equity model, by 2014 the time had come for Abraaj to find a buyer who would continue to invest in Karachi Electric to improve the lives of the citizens of Karachi. After testing market demand through a placement of some shares on the Pakistan Stock Exchange,[21] both for price discovery and to whet appetite, Abraaj ran a divestment process through Credit Suisse and Citibank. It also used consultants in Pakistan to repeat the stakeholder consultations that had been important in generating the political backing for the initial purchase in 2008. The initial bidding process identified eighteen potential buyers. This long-list was gradually cut down over time on the basis of price offered and commitment to invest.

Those rejected in this initial process were rumoured to include US companies, other private equity firms and major Pakistani business magnates all of whom had strong commercial ties to the US and owned diversified conglomerates who had long-standing relationships with the Pakistani military. In other words, the US lobby and their allies within the Pakistani elite appeared to have been shut out of the deal; the reality, according to Karachi Electric executives at the time, was that the two investment banks independently considered all other bids to be inferior. The two final companies left in the process were those with the highest bids and they were both Chinese. One company withdrew as soon as the two finalists had been announced so as not to compete with the other, probably under pressure from the Chinese government, or if viewed cynically, as part of a pre-agreed internal strategy. This was a classic operation under the Chinese Belt and Road Initiative. The Chinese Communist Party does not take the lead, but a commercial entity will take control of an asset for greater Chinese influence – in this instance in Karachi through controlling the power supply to the Port of Karachi and the largest urban conurbation in the fifth most populous nation on earth.[22] The deal was done in September 2016 and announced almost immediately at the Karachi and Shanghai stock exchanges given that the buyer and the target were both large, listed entities in their respective markets. On paper it seemed to be a 'win–win–win' deal.

But from a commercial perspective this narrowed Abraaj's options and made it clear that the Chinese government wanted Karachi Electric as a strategic asset. In broader geopolitical terms, Abraaj appeared to be picking a side between the US and China. China was committed to building its bridge to make the China–Pakistan Economic Corridor (CPEC) a success and Shanghai Electric's acquisition of Karachi Election would be emblematic of a private sector transaction that was representative of the cooperation between the two states moving forward.

Karachi Electric serves a total market size of 20 million people and has access to generation capacity of 3,600mW. SEP also serves a total market of 20 million people in Shanghai but produces 30,000mW of electricity. The growth potential for the acquirer was clear and this was something that was cited as investment rationale for those closest to the deal. The sale of Abraaj's 66.4 per cent stake in Karachi Electric to SEP for $1.77 billion was agreed and announced publicly in October 2016.[23] The deal was subject to a few bureaucratic conditions. These all appeared to be manageable to the Abraaj team in the autumn of 2016. Five years later, the deal has still not been concluded.

# 8

# The geopolitics of selling Karachi Electric

The deal was blocked using two initial bureaucratic hurdles. Firstly, because the deal was in the energy sector, which was part of critical national infrastructure, it required a national security clearance certificate (NSCC). Secondly, energy is subsidised through a tariff in Pakistan to reduce the price to consumers. That tariff had to be set by the National Electric Power Regulatory Authority (NEPRA). Neither of these should have presented a problem. China and Pakistan were already energy security allies and SEP's parent company was closely involved with Pakistan's nuclear programme.[1] The existence of the CPEC and the strong endorsement of the deal by the government in power, led by Nawaz Sharif as Prime Minister, should have made these issues formalities. The tariff determination exercise was already underway when the deal was signed, the Abraaj team thought that the NSCC had been agreed and the detail of renewing the tariff then in place also seemed a mere formality. To understand what then went wrong we have to understand the position of the military in the power politics of Pakistan, the competing influences on it and the competing lobbies that work tirelessly to swing the pendulum of external influences towards their client states.

Military establishments, like states, do not have permanent friends, only interests, and different parts of military establishments have different kinds of external relationships that are developed over time. The Pakistani military have a long history with the US and with China and with playing them off against each other. In the years immediately after the founding of the state, Pakistan tried hard to ally with the US to secure military aid. India had retained the bulk of the former British imperial military's hardware. Initially, the US tried to keep India within its sphere of influence and ignored the overtures of Pakistan. After nationalisation of the Iranian oil fields in 1952 and the British withdrawal and abandonment of the refinery at Abadan – the precursor, after the Suez Canal debacle, of the more widespread withdrawal of the British from the region east of Suez – the US realised that it needed military assets in the region.

In 1953, the US engineered the formation of a friendly government in Pakistan under three leaders all committed to the US alliance: Governor General Ghulam Muhammad, Home Minister Iskander Mirza and Defence Minister Ayub Khan. The US used food aid and the threat of famine to topple the government of Khwaja Nazimuddin and began arms shipments conditional on them not being deployed against India. From then onwards, elements in the Pakistan military became part of a US lobby in Pakistan but it was not a consistent relationship, and in the decades that followed it depended on the American need to court India, on Pakistan's role during the Soviet invasion of Afghanistan, Pakistan's nuclear programme and on the war on terror after 9/11.[2] In the thirty years from 1958 to 1988, the military ruled Pakistan for all but five years. After a decade of the 'civilian experiment' thereafter, the military assumed control for another decade. It is clear where the power sits in that country.

From the US perspective, India sat in the Soviet sphere of influence because it did not overtly declare allegiance to the US. In the post-Cold War era, President Bush was the first to articulate, 'you are either with us or against us' in the wake of 9/11, but this approach had been a

152

yardstick of US foreign policy since the Second World War. By the late 1950s, failures in Indian five-year plans made the possibility of holding the country for Western alignment a real possibility, which meant there had to be limits placed on the relationship with Pakistan. These tensions came to the fore when Pakistan, seeing that Indian military strength was moving ahead of its own, made a desperate and disastrous attempt to seize Kashmir in 1965.

The move isolated Pakistan from the US and so Pakistan became reliant on arms supplies from China. Military confrontations with India also made China a keen ally of Pakistan. Relations became so close between Pakistan and China that Pakistan called the policy 'tripartism'. It was Pakistan that brokered the detente between the US and China at the end of the 1960s.[3]

Close ties with the US were rekindled after the Soviet invasion of Afghanistan in 1979 made Pakistan a pivotal ally once more. The Reagan administration provided substantial military and soft-power aid to the military regime of General Muhammad Zia-ul-Haq. The Inter-Services Intelligence agency worked with the CIA in supporting the mujahideen to defeat the Soviets, who after the withdrawal of the Soviet Union morphed into the Taliban. The Taliban then became a regional and ethnic security threat to Pakistan itself during the war in Afghanistan, which started in 2002, necessitating a broader alliance between the US and Pakistan during the war on terror. China's role as a major arms supplier for Pakistan had begun in 1962 after it had its own border conflict with India – my enemy's enemy is my friend – and included assistance in building a number of arms factories in Pakistan and supplying complete weapons systems. Beijing sought to build up Pakistan to keep India off-balance. In 1990, the US imposed sanctions on Pakistan because of its nuclear programme but they were unevenly implemented. As Pakistan's leading arms supplier, China now became increasingly an economic partner as well. Military collaboration included personnel training, joint military exercises, intelligence sharing and counter-terrorism efforts. China supplied Pakistan with nuclear technology and assistance, including the blueprint for Pakistan's nuclear bomb. The parallel closer economic ties developed into the 2007 comprehensive free trade agreement, which opened Pakistan's markets to Chinese imports. Bilateral trade between the two states reached $17.2 billion in 2017/18 as Chinese exports to Pakistan grew from $3.5 billion in 2006/07 to $15.7 billion in 2017/18.[4]

After 9/11, military and economic aid from the US to Pakistan began again and has steadily increased. Between 2002 and 2011, the US provided $18 billion in assistance for the war on terror, with $8 billion coming directly into Pakistan's treasury to be used, amongst other things, to pay salaries, including for those military personnel in civilian roles. In 2011, Pakistan was the fourth-highest recipient of total assistance from the US after Afghanistan, Israel and Iraq. President Obama signed the Enhanced Partnership with Pakistan Act of 2009, better known as the Kerry–Lugar Bill, which tripled non-military aid to the country and allocated $7.5 billion to Pakistan from 2010 to 2014, investing in areas such as healthcare, education, social services and humanitarian assistance.[5]

In parallel, from 2012 onwards, deals in the China–Pakistan Economic Corridor[6] – a central plank of the overall Chinese BRI programme – were signed and widely publicised; the rhetoric was that China and Pakistan were becoming increasingly close. China had pledged $46 billion to Pakistan through economic and infrastructure projects in the CPEC plan alone, rising to $60 billion; the entire US aid budget to Pakistan, including coalition support, from 1948 to 2010 had been $96 billion.[7] The BRI has two central dimensions: the Silk Road Economic Belt and the 21st-Century Maritime Silk Road. The plan encompasses sixty countries across Eurasia and the Pacific. The belt runs through the continents of Asia, Europe and Africa, connecting China, central Asia, Russia and Europe in the north and linking China with the Persian Gulf and the Mediterranean Sea through Pakistan. The maritime route starts from

China's south coast and terminates in western Europe passing through the Indian Ocean and the South China Sea on one side and the South Pacific on the other. Together it contains a network of 4.4 billion people with $2.1 trillion GDP representing 63 per cent of the world's population and 29 per cent of its GDP.[8] At no point does it touch the territory of the United States but at every point it is directed to compete with the economic, strategic and political interests of the United States.

The sea road around the Indian Ocean and up the coast of Africa requires ports along its route that can be used for trade but also as resupply points for the Chinese Navy, the so-called string of pearls. A key pearl is the port of Gwadar, which is about ten hours' drive from Karachi in an isolated and poor region called Balochistan. Balochistan is an ethically distinct and remote area that has a strong separatist movement allegedly funded by India to keep Pakistan in an unsettled state; as such, the only force that can keep the separatist tribal chieftains at bay is the Pakistan Army with the civilian provincial government having a nominal sway at best. It borders Iran and sits adjacent to the Strait of Hormuz, the 21-mile-wide waterway through which, in 2018, daily oil flow averaged 21 million barrels per day or the equivalent of about 21 per cent of global liquid petroleum consumption.[9]

The Pakistan Army chief, during a visit to Gwadar in July 2015, said: 'Gwadar Port and CPEC will be built as the most strategic deep seaport in the region, at all costs.' Pakistan purchased Gwadar from the Sultan of Oman for $3 million in 1958. In the 1970s, the Nixon administration was offered the chance of building a port at Gwadar. This was turned down because of economic viability and potential controversy.

The port that has been constructed at Gwadar has hardly any cargoes going through it as the roads connecting it overland to China have not been completed. With separatist violence on the rise, these roads might not be completed in the short term. From the perspective of Chinese trade this is obviously suboptimal, from the perspective of the flag it is fine. The facility that could be required for resupply of navy ships has taken its place on the maritime road. There are several requirements for the next phase of the trade project to develop. One of those is to provide better access to water and to electricity for the district in which the port sits. Karachi Electric is the nearest and largest energy provider which already supplies areas within Balochistan, such as the economic hub where numerous refineries and other industries are located. Therefore, SEP can wait patiently for the deal to be concluded because of the long-term strategic importance of both Karachi and Balochistan.

The focus on Gwadar has obscured the fact that even before that facility was open, a Chinese nuclear submarine had sailed through the Indian Ocean and docked in Karachi in May 2015, causing considerable disquiet in India and in the United States.[10] The Indian media covered the story extensively.

> These seminal developments call for an objective assessment in terms of China's intent underlying its submarine deployments in the Indian Ocean and its implications for India … these deployments may be seen in context of the growing volatility of the security environment in the South China Sea, including the increasing brinkmanship between China and the United States. In case of a maritime conflict in the area, China's energy shipments transiting the Indian Ocean are strategically vulnerable.[11]

There are broadly two views of why China launched the BRI: containment or isolationism. Either the BRI was a response to Obama's pivot-to-Asia strategy that was announced in 2011 and called 'Rebalance to Asia':

> The pivot includes two main security and economic arms – to redeploy 60 per cent US air and sea power to Asia by 2020, surrounding China, and to negotiate the Trans-Pacific Partnership Agreement with allies, excluding China. The

de facto containment effects of these policies prevent China
from expanding its influence to the East and South.[12]

Or the BRI was a response to US isolationism which began under Obama
and became the central pillar of US foreign policy under Trump. The
deployment of nuclear submarines suggests that China was perceived
to be moving into a political and strategic vacuum left by the US. The US
government under Obama was concerned about China's rise and the
election of Trump heightened animosity to new levels. Every iteration
of Trump's administration was filled with China hawks, whilst a closer
US alignment with India has elevated concerns in security circles that
China is seeking to control the Indian Ocean. As a result, the United
States, Australia, Japan and India created Quadrilateral Security Dia-
logue alliance, which was designed to counter the maritime threat
posed by China in Asia. The election of President Joe Biden has, if anything, reinforced the long-held view that China remains the largest
economic and security threat to the US.[13] As such, it is clear to see how the
intelligence services would have briefed Obama, Trump and now Biden
about the threat posed by China in Pakistan to US interests, including if
Karachi Electric had fallen into Chinese hands.

Abraaj's ties to the US government were strong during Obama's tenure;
especially when Abraaj hired senior people who had connections not just
in the US private equity industry but also in government. As late as May
2016, Naqvi was being received at the State Department by the head of
the Bureau of Economic and Business Affairs. He was sitting on various
boards where his advice about how to harness emerging markets was
valued.[14] The company was praised and supported and Abraaj's leadership
spoke on the platforms of the global elite. USAID partnered with it
on joint projects and investments and OPIC provided credit facilities
whenever asked. The question all of this now raises is what the US wanted
and expected in return. When would the bill be issued? Or did Naqvi
have a covert understanding with the US that made him a bankable ally?

Between 2008, when Abraaj invested in Karachi Electric, and 2016, when Trump was elected, the world had changed. In the beginning the US had welcomed and worked to enable Abraaj's investment in Karachi Electric. WikiLeaks identified that the US embassy in Islamabad identified the development of Karachi Electric as a core pillar of Pakistani stability in a cable on 25 August 2009. The cable highlighted:

> Abraaj Capital is the largest private equity firm in the Middle East and South Asia. Headed by a Pakistani national, Arif Masood Naqvi, the majority of the board is from the UAE and Saudi Arabia. Abraaj invested in KESC under its ten-year, $2 billion Infrastructure and Growth Capital Fund, managed by Executive Director Tabish Gahaur. The majority of Abraaj's 210 investors are based in the Middle East, including a number of Gulf State sovereign wealth and royalty funds, according to Ismail.[15]

'Ismail' was Naveed Ismail, the CEO of KESC installed by Abraaj, who told the Americans that he needed $4 to $5 billion in capital investment over the next five years to fully upgrade its operation. To get this money the embassy was asking the State Department to mobilise the consulate in Dubai to informally assess how additional private and public capital could be mobilised. The US administration feted the Abraaj team in Washington in September that year and continued to support and build Naqvi up as an example of Muslim businessmen with whom they could work at a specially convened summit in Washington.

There had been considerable support within the US for, and approval of, the acquisition of Karachi Electric by Abraaj. A Western-orientated private equity company taking control of the strategically vital asset seemed to be aligned with the United States' own policy and agenda in Pakistan. During this period, the US was predominantly focused on solving issues in Afghanistan, with Pakistan viewed as an increasingly unreliable ally in the war on terror. Despite doubts, the US had made a concerted bid for influence on the country with the Kerry–Lugar Bill in 2009 that expanded the provision of military and civilian aid to the country. The K-Electric deal was viewed as a private sector venture that supported US efforts to reform Pakistan's energy industry since $1 billion of the Kerry–Lugar funding was earmarked for energy sector reform as a central plank:

> The United States and Pakistan have a strong history of energy cooperation, dating to US support for construction of the Mangla and Tarbela hydropower dams in the 1960s and 1970s. More recently, in line with the Enhanced Partnership with Pakistan Act of 2009 (also known as Kerry–Lugar–Berman), the United States committed more than US$1 billion to support energy sector cooperation with the Government of Pakistan. These cooperative efforts made almost 2,300 additional mega-watts (MW) available to Pakistan's national grid from 2009 to 2015, benefiting some 26 million Pakistanis and increasing the revenue of the country's distribution companies by over $400 million annually. This complements Pakistan's broader, homegrown efforts to expand generation, improve distribution and transmission, diversify its energy mix, and achieve full cost recovery in the energy sector.[16]

In the years after the Karachi Electric purchase, key US diplomats reinforced to the Abraaj team the centrality of energy sector reform to US interests in the country. It was widely known that Rick Olson, US ambassador to the UAE and later Pakistan, and Richard Holbrooke, special envoy for Pakistan and Afghanistan, had told senior Abraaj executives that the US would tacitly support Karachi Electric as Abraaj's endeavours were good for the country and for US efforts to promote stability in Pakistan.[17] After 2008, the engagement with Abraaj and Naqvi in particular stepped up.

President Obama fulfilled a pledge he made in 2009 in his speech to the Muslim world in Cairo by inviting key business leaders to a Presidential Summit on Entrepreneurship in 2010. Panellists at the summit included Naqvi alongside Eric Schmitt, CEO of Google, and Muhammad Yunus of Grameen Bank. In his 4 June 2009 Cairo speech, Obama had said he wanted to 'create a new corps of business volunteers to partner with counterparts in Muslim-majority countries'.[18]

The courtship continued in 2011 when the foreign policy establishment anointed Naqvi as the possible future leader of Pakistan in a scenario which even highlighted the importance of upgrading the power generation industry. It was organised by the Council for Foreign Relations, the Center for Global Affairs, New York University and the EastWest Institute and was funded by the Carnegie Foundation. It was organised and attended by members of the institutional foreign policy establishment. The idea was to consider three potential scenarios for the future of Pakistan over the coming decade: radicalisation, fragmentation and reform over a ten-year period ending in 2021.[19] The vision of the reformist imagined future was interesting and illustrative of the way in which the US elite saw Naqvi operating at this time. The scenario predicted that Pakistan's political system would be transformed by the founding of a National Justice Party, which would be economically liberal, moderately Islamic and base its approach on policies and solutions and would be led by Naqvi, who would become Pakistan's leader and lead Pakistan into prosperity. To project this future for a businessman with no known political aspirations at the time was a bold move and was interpreted as such.

In 2013, USAID launched the Pakistan Private Investment Initiative, aiming to raise $150 million in private equity investment for small and medium-sized firms in Pakistan.[20] The administrator of the programme Rajiv Shah had endorsed Abraaj's work in Pakistan as a prime example of spreading US corporate values to emerging markets. Speaking at the launch event of a US government-sponsored investment conference on Pakistan, Shah said that USAID was committed to Pakistan's development:

Pooled funds will initially be $100 million which we expect will grow many folds into hundreds of millions of dollars in investment for small and medium businesses. By partnering with Abraaj and JS Private Equity Management, USAID capitalizes on these companies' expertise to make smart investment decisions that will grow the Pakistani economy, create jobs, and generate profits for investors who seize the economic opportunities that Pakistan presents.

The period of 2012 to 2015 saw further overtures from the US, including rumours of direct approaches to Arif Naqvi to nudge his political aspirations forward. Naqvi was in increasing demand as a member of global bodies – for example, the UN General Secretary appointed him to the board of Global Compact, the UN network for CEOs, Bill Gates had brought him into the Giving Pledge and he had been working closely with McKinsey since 2002.

In the meantime, Abraaj continued to boost its senior ranks with key hires from the US to exploit this courtship further. The senior appointments within Abraaj included Pradeep Ramamurthy, who joined Abraaj in 2012 and described himself on his LinkedIn page as a 'private equity professional with a background in national security. Like organisations that are at inflection points. Thrive at the intersection of strategy, brand building, and scaling partnerships.'[21] He began his career in the FBI counter-terrorism department before joining first the Bush and then the Obama administrations as senior director for global engagement on the National Security Council. Abraaj also hired Wahid Hamid as managing partner in February 2012. Hamid had been President Obama's roommate and close friend at Occidental College and they travelled together through Hamid's native Pakistan for three weeks. Hamid had top US security clearances and had worked at various multinational billion-dollar companies holding senior executive positions. Naqvi asked Hamid, as the most senior Pakistani in Abraaj after Naqvi himself, to sit on the board of Karachi Electric but according to a source close to the Karachi Electric oversight process, Hamid consistently refused to take a place on a public company board in Pakistan during the sale process, citing US government reluctance to green-light him.

In December 2016, Alan Jones and Mary Fanning published a paper with the Center for Security Policy, entitled 'What could possibly go wrong? Secret deal allows company tied to Saddam's Nuclear bombmaker, Iran and UAE to manage key Florida port facilities'. The paper for the right-wing think tank was a product of deep Republican muckraking on the Clintons and Obama. The paper, however, linked Hamid to the Jafar family via their shareholding in and membership of the board of Abraaj.[22] It also outlined in detail the direct links between Hamid and the US government:

> The Jafar family also has direct business connections with two of President Barack Obama's lifelong friends and college roommates – former foreign students Vinai Thummalapally of Hyderabad, India and Wahid Hamid of Karachi, Pakistan. Thummalapally and Hamid both bundled campaign contributions for Barack Obama and attended Barack and Michelle's wedding. In 2015 Wahid Hamid spent time with President Obama at the White House, aboard Marine One, and at Camp David. Wahid Hamid was also a member of the Pentagon's Defense Business Board under President Obama. Wahid Hamid, along with Mohammed Hasan Chandoo (aka Chandio), another one of Obama's Pakistani college roommates, allegedly met Obama at the Karachi airport in 1981 at the beginning of Obama's mysterious tour of Pakistan. Hamid Jafar and his son, Gulftainer executive Badr Jafar, who is the nephew of nuclear physicist Dr Jafar, both have served on the board of directors at UAE-based private equity firm The Abraaj Group. Wahid Hamid is a Partner at The Abraaj

Group. Badr Jafar also has ties to SelectUSA Director Vinai Thummalapally.

Abraaj also hired Vinay Chawla, who had been deputy coordinator for economic and development assistance at the US embassy in Islamabad and was described as:

> A seasoned US diplomat with close to twenty years of experience across the Middle East and South Asia. His work focuses on the intersection of foreign and economic policy in global growth markets. With the State Department, he has a proven track record of developing economic growth initiatives in war-torn areas and difficult markets. He successfully negotiated strategic partnerships with both public and private sector stakeholders to advance American interests.[23]

Mark Bourgeois also joined Abraaj as a managing partner in charge of all fundraising in 2016, after he had spent much of the previous three years working closely with Abraaj despite being the CEO of a prominent US placement firm called Atlantic-Pacific Capital. A source in the investor coverage team told me that at the time Bourgeois received substantial 'consulting fees' for introducing Hamilton Lane and ensuring their investment into Gen-5 funds in 2015.[24] He was a staunch Trump supporter and closely observed the ongoing sale process of Karachi Electric to Shanghai Electric, including joining Naqvi on trips to China.[25] The fifth American involved with Abraaj was Matthew McGuire, who was hired in from the World Bank at the request of Jim Kim, the president of the bank. From 2015 to 2017 McGuire was the US executive director of the World Bank Group, sitting on the board of the IFC. He also served in the Obama administration at the Department of Commerce and the Treasury Department. In the endgame of Abraaj as people were jumping ship in February and March 2018, McGuire's willingness to stay close to

Naqvi resulted in him being appointed chief operating officer of AIML prior to its separation from AHL. McGuire orchestrated the ultimate sale of AGHF to TPG. He then joined TPG as part of their growth and rise impact funds team, which focuses on emerging markets investing.

There were many others, but together this senior group of five were probably the closest to Naqvi in terms of strategy; I have been repeatedly told by multiple sources that one or more of these individuals were constantly by Naqvi's side from January 2017 through to the collapse of Abraaj. They formed a pro-US lobby inside Abraaj, and they opposed the sale of Karachi Electric to the Chinese. What is clear from their backgrounds is that they clearly had access to the upper echelons of US intelligence – as did Kito de Boer – and this suggests that either Naqvi was totally naive in his choices of whom he hired or that he was somehow required to bring on people that could ensure that Abraaj's mission remained aligned to US state and intelligence interests. Whatever the reason, when the time came, these individuals clearly knew where their individual and collective interests lay. Even more interesting is that none of these names appear in the US indictment that listed virtually every other senior executive at Abraaj.

There is a final chapter in the US courtship of Naqvi – a courtship which ended abruptly with the Karachi Electric deal. I was told by a senior source in the Abraaj management team that Naqvi was introduced to John Kerry by his close friend (and perhaps mentor) Kito de Boer, whilst Kerry was still the US Secretary of State. Kerry had a significant role in defining the Obama administration's stance on China, the Iran entente, Afghanistan and Pakistan (AfPac as they were known) and the region more widely, and this was also where his focus lay during the administration's last two years. De Boer had overseen the McKinsey work on Abraaj from inception until the post-Aureos acquisition in 2012/13 after which he ran the quartet based in Jerusalem as a direct appointee of John Kerry at the State Department. As the Obama administration was coming to an end, both de Boer and Kerry started planning their post-transition roles. De Boer had agreed to join Abraaj as head of impact investments in place of Vettivetpillai in 2017, but prior to that, according to emails I have seen, he and Naqvi spent almost a full year actively developing what they called the 'Kerry Plan', assisted by Tom Speechley, Vinay Chawla and Derek Brooks; a blueprint to rebuild infrastructure across a Middle East region ravaged by two decades of almost constant conflict.[26] The plan was grandiose and expansive, envisaging $10 billion to be raised from the Arab region's sovereign wealth funds. Naqvi met Kerry on a number of occasions to discuss the Kerry Plan, alongside discussions on the evolution of Abraaj in general and the sale of Karachi Electric to the Chinese – such discussions included a meeting on the side lines of Davos three days before the new Trump administration took office. Kerry was excited and enthused by the idea and even attended the Abraaj investor conference in March 2017 as the keynote speaker, which got widespread coverage. However, the GCC states were firmly behind Trump's new policies and unlikely to support Kerry in his envisaged new role. By early 2017, Abraaj and Naqvi were clearly being perceived as *persona non grata* at the US State Department. Had Kerry been briefed following his Dubai trip? If so, he would surely have wanted to stay clear of the fallout that was to come.[27] Indeed, very soon after the trip, he withdrew from the initiative with the Abraaj team, and the plan itself made little progress until something like it was pushed by Jared Kushner.

Whilst Naqvi was building strong relationships with the Obama White House and being cultivated as an asset for US values, the Chinese were closely watching Abraaj's progress as well. Abraaj executives were frequent visitors to Beijing, and an early indication of their approval of the Abraaj business model came when the China Investment Corporation (CIC), the Chinese sovereign wealth fund, agreed to partner with Abraaj in 2009 in buying a strategic stake in DP World, the largest port operator in the world, which is listed in Dubai and London and owned by the government of Dubai. The deal was structured to effectively provide liquidity to the Dubai government in the aftermath of the 2008 financial crisis, which had hit Dubai particularly hard.[28] Although the Dubai government backed out of the deal at the last minute, Naqvi continued to build the China relationship directly with the chairman of CIC, Gao Xiqing.

According to a source who was present, Abraaj hosted a private dinner for senior Chinese executives visiting the UAE in 2015 at the request of Shaukat Aziz, the former Prime Minister of Pakistan. They included the chairman of the China International Capital Corporation (CICC), the chairman of the China International Trust Investment Corporation and senior officials. The chemistry was strong and the Chinese decided to take a closer look at Abraaj. Discussions started in relation to the Chinese taking a significant stake in Abraaj and in the funds managed by it to enable China to navigate emerging markets investing by proxy as well as directly through the BRI. These discussions on many fronts continued through 2015 and 2016, during which period Abraaj was not raising any new funds, except potentially in energy prior to the launch of APEF VI in early 2017.[29]

The Asian Infrastructure Investment Bank (AIIB) was formed with support from 100 countries in 2016 with the principal aim of acting as a counterpoint to the World Bank. The chair was Jin Liqun, who had previously been chairman of CICC and had developed a good relationship with Naqvi following an initial meeting over the above-mentioned dinner in 2015 and the pair had met a number of times subsequently at World Economic Forum events to discuss how Chinese entities could start investing in Abraaj products. Jin was sure that the Abraaj expertise in emerging markets and its footprint was similar to that of the BRI and he insinuated that the Chinese had monitored the company's growth closely with a view to becoming partners.[30]

When Abraaj decided to divest itself of Karachi Electric in early 2015 and appointed financial advisers, Jin suggested to Naqvi at Davos that he enter into a direct discussion with a state-nominated Chinese company to agree sale parameters. This first strong indication of interest eventually culminated in the signing of a binding transaction with SEP, which was a subsidiary of China's State Power Investment Corporation (SPIC), the major state holding company in the power sector. At the same time, parallel discussions were taking place between SPIC and Abraaj to make it the anchor in Abraaj's future impact investing initiatives, including in energy and housing; the Chinese were particularly keen to invest with Abraaj in South America and Africa. An investment banker present at a glittering banquet in Beijing to announce the Karachi Electric deal told me that the chairman of SPIC, Wang Binghua, announced the transaction as the first in a series of joint ventures between Chinese state enterprises and Abraaj. He also said that CIC were a co-investor in the Karachi Electric transaction and were considering taking a strategic stake in Abraaj itself.[31] If it is true that the Chinese were going to take a strategic stake in Abraaj, this must have been in the works for months before the dinner and it would have compounded the unease felt by those who were against the sale of Karachi Electric to the Chinese. When I asked Naqvi about this, he changed the subject and refused to engage. What he did say was that it was during the same trip that discussions between Abraaj and China's State Administration of Foreign Exchange commenced in relation to avenues for investment, which culminated in the Hong Kong Monetary Authority committing $300 million and becoming the largest investor in the first closing of APEF VI, with the State Administration of Foreign Exchange itself indicating that it would participate in the final close with an estimated $500 million. However, events at Abraaj in 2018 overtook this outcome and prevented any further closings of APEF VI.

The increasing closeness between Abraaj and Chinese interests was being observed in the US. Abraaj was building a bridge between both sides of the superpower geopolitical divide. Listening to Naqvi's speeches on YouTube, it seems that he had been warning about Chinese superiority since 2011, which over time became an endorsement of the BRI as being the 'equivalent of fifteen Marshall Plans'. Given Naqvi's proximity to members of the Obama administration, his endorsement of the BRI was perceived to be manageable had Clinton won. All this was put on ice when the SEP deal to acquire Karachi Electric was announced and shortly thereafter Donald Trump was elected as the forty-fifth US President. It was becoming clear that all bets were off. The hubris with which Naqvi attempted to juggle and to an extent play super-powers off one another was breathtakingly audacious and its inevitable consequences would be devastating for himself and his firm.

# 9

# More than meets the eye

*If Abraaj had been allowed to sell its shares in K-Electric to Shanghai, Arif would be a free man today. You tell me: a man who had deep contacts with the most powerful people in the country was unable to resolve administrative hurdles in the sale of his shares – a transaction which had no financial implications for Pakistan and that was hugely beneficial to the country. There is more here than meets the eye. How and why?[1]*

This was the response of former Prime Minister Shahid Khaqan Abbasi when Naqvi's efforts to fight his extradition failed in the first instance at Westminster Magistrates' Court in January 2021, quoted in Pakistan's leading newspaper.

An increasing number of analysts are now speculating that the answer to Prime Minister Abbasi's how and why question lies in America's deep displeasure over China's growing influence in Pakistan. It is an intriguing question: in a country where everything is made possible for powerful men who knock on the right doors, why was this an impossible task? Did the Americans thwart the Karachi Electric deal? Even if the deal had gone through, would Abraaj have been allowed to survive and let Chinese capital flood emerging markets through a private equity side door?

The original announcement of the sale to a Chinese state enterprise was met with consternation in the US embassy in Islamabad and in Washington. Clear messages were delivered directly to the top of the company and echoed by senior US nationals who had been brought on board to cement and enhance US relationships for Abraaj: do not sell to the Chinese. It appears that at this point the interests of the US state and the interests of The Abraaj Group diverged drastically. The key question is what actions were set in train as a result of this. Abraaj had agreed a deal to sell Karachi Electric. That is what private equity companies do when their investment period ends. The US would have preferred that Naqvi stay in place and be the channel for Gulf investment into the Pakistani energy sector to fuel further economic development that would pave the way for a reformist takeover and clean-up of the country; what prevented Abraaj from doing the US's bidding were the limited partnership structures in private equity through which funds must be returned to investors within a ten-year time frame. Abraaj decided that the geographic, technological and financial logic of the Karachi Electric–Shanghai Electric deal achieved both their own commercial and geopolitical objectives. These corporate geopolitical objectives included opening the door to Chinese capital investing through Abraaj more widely. For Naqvi personally, involvement in Pakistan, since the days of investments made by Cupola (which was the precursor to Abraaj), played the double role of making business sense and enhancing the potential of his eventual political career. There was a parallel move in US foreign policy against China and a growing suspicion of Chinese ambitions, motives and objectives, but Chinese money in US public relations firms kept a lid on this until the Trump years when the confrontation became open.

The US foreign policy establishment decided that The Abraaj Group could not be controlled and an attack on Abraaj found willing accomplices in the established blue-chip US private equity firms that were competing with Abraaj in various emerging markets. This might not have amounted to much if it had taken place at a time when the old establishment and the old relationship between the White House and private equity existed. But there was a new establishment that was about to take over Washington, which perceived Abraaj as being too cosy with their rivals in the upcoming 2016 presidential elections. Trump supporters in the right-wing blogosphere separately launched an attack on Abraaj by releasing documents through Breitbart News and WikiLeaks that showed large donations to the Clinton Global Initiative and alleged that these were in some way connected to the award of contracts to Abraaj and one of its shareholders.[2] This was in parallel with Naqvi speaking at several events in Washington that had been arranged in his honour and at which he vocally cautioned attendees against a Trump administration because of its effect on US relations with the emerging world. Throughout 2017, Naqvi was also fundraising for the new global fund APEF VI. As part of that effort, he was using the relationship with SEP's parent company to attract Chinese investors into what would have been the largest private equity fund in emerging markets in the world. The largest committed investors in APEF VI were the Hong Kong Monetary Authority ($300 million) and the Chinese State Administration of Foreign Exchange (SAFE), which had indicated it would also commit $500 million. This is interesting because this profile is contrary to what the public perception of a US-majority fund looked like.

If the Obama administration had been suspicious of Chinese intentions then the Trump administration, which won the US election weeks after the Karachi Electric deal was announced, was paranoid about both Pakistan and China. The Trump administration was not interested in globalisation. It generally favoured India as a partner over Pakistan, and Trump was frequently rude about Pakistan, including one famous Twitter attack in January 2018.[3] In this Twitter blast, Trump called Pakistan a 'safe haven' for terrorists:

The United States has foolishly given Pakistan more than
33 billion dollars in aid over the last 15 years, and they have given
us nothing but lies & deceit, thinking of our leaders as fools.
They give safe haven to the terrorists we hunt in Afghanistan,
with little help. No more!

This rhetoric was indicative of Trump's 'America First' ideology that meant that any deal which did not appear to be in the primary interests of American capitalism was suspect. The situation shifted therefore from the US government expressing a more passive-aggressive objection on geopolitical grounds to the sale of Karachi Electric to the Chinese, to an active ideological opposition to any expansion in Chinese interests in any strategically important location around the world where an American interest could be substituted in its place. This policy shift in Washington in 2017 coincided with several other significant global changes. Abraaj went from having multiple warm, personal and professional relationships with members of the Obama administration at all levels, to having no network whatsoever in the incoming administration.

Links between the US lobby within Abraaj and their former employers, including elements of the US intelligence agencies, would of course have remained intact had Trump not been elected. But the new team in the US administration adopted a hard line towards any state or non-state actor that was not completely loyal to the US and in the stomping of feet and 'America First' approach that virtually collapsed European alliances they ramped up their opposition to China as well as anyone connected to the Chinese, particularly through commercial dealings. OPIC, a clear extension of the US government, had agreed in principle a ten-year funding stream to Karachi Electric in October 2015 but this was cancelled as soon as the deal with the Chinese was announced.[4] OPIC cited its own charter that would not allow it to fund any entities that were owned by foreign states.[5] One OPIC official, who took a leadership position after Trump took office, told a senior Karachi Electric official that 'you are either with us or against us now' and stated that the funds could not be used for any projects in relation to CPEC. What was of course embarrassing to OPIC was that a few weeks prior to the sale of Karachi Electric being announced, it had finalised and announced a new $150 million credit facility to AGHF as well. This process was commenced and completed by OPIC under Elizabeth Littlefield, an Obama appointee who was reported to be close to Naqvi.[6] This overt embarrassment must have caused consternation in OPIC, which the Trump administration was making a more overtly political institution (it was replaced in December 2019 by the DFC). Perhaps in part because of this embarrassment, OPIC joining the BMGF revolt against Abraaj management practices for AGHF.

On a macro level, Trump's tweet in January 2018 that Pakistan was a rogue state was further validated through the IMF talks that Pakistan held later in 2018 when Mike Pompeo flew to Pakistan to meet the government and advised that the US would not support any IMF terms that allowed funds to be used for CPEC-related projects.[7]

From Pakistan's perspective, CPEC would provide a significant investment into the infrastructure of the country – creating roads, railways, sanitation and power to all motors of a modern economy. There were many critics of the initiative within Pakistan, who could point to the example of Gwadar Port. Gwadar was not built by inward investment creating local jobs in a poor province. Instead, Chinese companies were being funded locally by Chinese banks and importing equipment and labour into Pakistan, thereby exacerbating the current balance of payments crisis and leading to value being extracted from the country. In parallel, the provision of soft long-term loans with good commercial rates created debt dependency. This dependency had been used in other countries to gain control of ports and other facilities, such as in Kenya and Sri Lanka. It is a modern-day form of debt imperialism.[8] And China's socio-political global narrative was not getting any better as mainstream media covered brutal conditions for workers across its joint investments in various countries around the world.

The US lobby in Pakistan sought to encourage back-tracking on some of the initiatives outlined under the CPEC framework because of the need to secure financial support for the Pakistan economy from Western institutions. This included a bid for support from the IMF. It was reported that Arif Naqvi was part of the team involved in evaluating the IMF terms as a member of an advisory group to the new Prime Minister Imran Khan from August 2018 onwards. Abraaj's fires had already started burning earlier that year, which prevented him from being part of the election campaign according to sources within Imran Khan's political party; however, the two men remained close and the advisory group encouraged the new government to seek more favourable terms than those on offer as well as articulating alternative plans in case the IMF discussions failed. At the same time, Trump had launched his trade war with China.[9] Many CPEC projects had been delayed or stalled by the actions of the Pakistani state bureaucracy and because of security concerns in Balochistan in which separatist violence had flared up.[10] Decades after Cold War proxy battles, Pakistan has again, by design and function, become a battleground for supremacy between the United States and China, and into this superpower battle came the new government of Imran Khan. Khan promised to be different to leaders of the past. His political party (Pakistan Tehreek-e-Insaf, PTI) was not plagued with the same historical issues as the two leading dynastic parties – the Pakistan People's Party (PPP) and the Pakistan Muslim League-Nawaz (PML-N). It promised radical change – it published an election manifesto which promised equality and opportunity. The PTI was made up of intellectuals and not the same battle-hardened, politically smooth veterans of the PPP and PML-N – one of its core principles is to eradicate the endemic corruption within the system – clearly putting forward the message that nobody, no matter how senior, is unaccountable. Therefore, as part of its sweeping changes, the government began to investigate a number of initiatives and deals that had been consummated in the past – leading to arrests of prominent political figures, including the effective heads of the PPP (Asif Ali Zardari) and PML-N (Nawaz Sharif). Khan has been heavily criticised in sections of the Pakistan media as the country has not moved forward during his tenure, and hostile elements of the media claim that his 'witch hunt' is a personal vendetta against these other parties. This has been evident through the various arrests that have taken place of high-profile former politicians, businessmen, media magnates and their friends.

Many of the CPEC projects have gone through this same investigative process and come out 'clean' according to Asad Umar, Finance Minister of Pakistan, who announced this in a speech[11] countering the shrill attacks on CPEC launched by Alice Wells, the US State Department representative overseeing the US–Pakistan relationship. Umar's very immediate and defensive response was a clear indication that Pakistan was still, at least as far as the civilian government was concerned, clinging to hopes of tripartism and ensuring that its other ally, China, did not take affront, illustrating not only that the CPEC projects did not have governance and corruption issues but were judged to be good for the country as whole.[12] Many of the deals in CPEC 1.0, however, continue to be stalled, delayed or otherwise blocked by those elements within the system opposed to the BRI. Undeterred, Khan signed an additional $11 billion[13] of deals to kickstart what was heralded in the pro-government element of the Pakistani media as CPEC 2.0.[14] This raises the question: whatever happened to CPEC 1.0? In some instances, the notion of a completed project from the Chinese perspective may not be the same as the notion of a completed project from the Pakistani or other external perspectives. This can also explain the strategic patience of which the Chinese are certainly capable. For example, the Chinese have patiently sat waiting for the K-Electric transaction irrespective of five years' worth of delays around bureaucratic hurdles. China sees the big picture.

The significance of Karachi Electric was fully understood by the US not least because Naqvi had briefed them repeatedly and extensively on it and subsequently reported his conversations to partners within Abraaj.

Naqvi would brief US State Department officials, who consistently had an interest and had supported the initial investment by Abraaj. The WikiLeaks notes pertaining to the Karachi Electric transaction and its significance highlight this.[15]

The deal was obstructed despite the clear commercial, development and political benefits that it would bring to the country and civilian government. Three successive administrations and three successive Prime Ministers of Pakistan between 2016 and 2019 publicly proclaimed that they wanted the transaction to be completed because of its importance to Pakistan. But when the deal with Shanghai Electric was done, the US stopped seeing Abraaj as either pro-US or even neutral. Public actions by the US government were necessarily limited in scope; the US government does not overtly fight with foreign companies, but rather, in the background, the alternatives are considered. The Pakistan Private Investment Initiative was quietly dropped and the OPIC loan to Karachi Electric was cancelled as the company was being sold to a Chinese company. The incident was written up in Karachi Electric's annual report in 2017:

> OPIC … had signed a USD 250 Million financing agreement with the Company in February 2016, primarily to fund a major transmission project. After signing of the Sale and Purchase Agreement … between KES Power and Shanghai Electric Power Company, a Chinese state-owned corporation, financing agreement with OPIC had to be terminated as OPIC's charter does not allow to lend to an organisation controlled by a state-owned entity. The major portion of the gap, arising due to exit of OPIC, was filled through a Rs.23.5 Billion syndicated facility from a consortium of 6 local commercial banks in November 2018.[16]

Privately, the forces aligned against the deal were much more significant, of which the most important was the pro-US lobby existing in the military and government civil service establishment. The army's interest to assist the US in curbing Chinese influence married with its own objectives to stop the Karachi Electric transaction from being completed so as to place limits on Chinese influence growing yet further in Pakistan. Sections of the Pakistani army are heavily influenced and funded by the US. Bureaucrats are often paid by the US state indirectly and their children's education is frequently financed by scholarships from US universities.[17] Although the military has officially endorsed CPEC, the army is acutely aware of the need to balance China's influence with the influence of the US. The key is maintaining the flow of external influence that supports the balance of power that has kept the military at the apex of decision-making circles since 1948, the so-called tripartism kept in place by the Pakistani establishment. The fact that CPEC finally started to gain momentum after the Khan government appointed a former army general to head it is indicative of the army's desire to maintain control. Even an immediate outburst in the media against such overt interference and allegations of corruption against the former general were glossed over and suppressed.

The interests of the Pakistani military are not only geopolitical. The Pakistan Army officer corps, as with officer corps in many other militaries, have economic interests to protect in the national economy. In Pakistan, the military's influence on the state, and long periods of direct rule of that state, has meant that its security role has been blended with an economic role. According to a recent academic analysis, 'the military has expanded its role in the economy by active involvement in industry, commerce, and business, developing a stake in government policies and industrial and commercial strategies'.[18] The military's economic role also extends to social and welfare roles through Pakistan's large charity system.[19] Combined, these give the Pakistani military 'a large stake in the economy, as well as some financial independence from the government, at least with regard to welfare, pensions, and trusts'. In *Military Inc.*, Ayesha Siddiqa called these sources of military revenue 'Milbus', referring to extra-budgetary 'military capital that is used for the personal benefit of the military fraternity'.[20] This large amount of capital and economic power makes Pakistan's military 'one of the dominant economic players in the private and public sectors of the economy'. Indeed, I was told by a political figure within Pakistan's ruling party, PTI, that a running joke amongst frustrated democrats in the living rooms in urban Pakistan is the lament that in Pakistan 'the state exists for the benefit of the military, as opposed to everywhere else, where the military exists for the benefit of the state'.

It would be near impossible, in the absence of another WikiLeaks-type moment, to establish firmly that the US leaned on the Pakistan civil bureaucracy–military complex (referred to within Pakistanis almost universally as the 'establishment') to block the Karachi Electric deal; backroom conversations between elements of the intelligence fraternity do not happen over email. I surmise that the request to block the deal would have been delivered by the relevant intelligence chief-of-mission at the US embassy in Islamabad to his official military intelligence counterpart; or perhaps to a senior 'asset' depending on how far you want to go in developing the narrative. Thereafter, a key civilian bureaucrat would have been told to stall negotiations and introduce impediments to prevent the deal from proceeding; in effect, covertly signalling and encouraging either Abraaj or the Chinese to withdraw from the deal if government consent was not forthcoming. There would never be more than two or three people of seniority or rank involved in this process and none would acknowledge that such a strategy was being implemented. But the power of the army establishment in Pakistan is such that its ability to exercise control over the key levers of government is absolute and nothing happens without its assent, irrespective of who is running the government. That is just the way it is. Let us see how this was blocked.

The deal to sell Karachi Electric to SEP was announced in October 2016 and was expected to close within a few months pending what the

Abraaj team expected to be 'fairly vanilla' commercial and regulatory condition precedents – events that had to take place before the deal was done. The deal would have produced a great return, making $618 million in exchange for a $300 million investment made by IGCF as part of the $1.77 billion sale price, and it would have provided $550 million cash for AHL itself between its direct holdings in Karachi Electric, its interests as a limited partner in IGCF and amounts owed to it by KES Power. Not only would the transaction have created a fantastic case study for APEF VI, for which Abraaj was totally focused on raising funds for during that period, but it would also alleviate all the financial pressure that Abraaj had come to face as a direct result of the delay in the return of this capital. Finally, the deal itself would be good for Pakistan if SEP fulfilled its pledge to invest a further $9 billion in upgrading and enhancing capacity and infrastructure. Abraaj would have emerged with an additional impact investment fund backed by fresh Chinese capital ready to replicate and develop on a global scale – utilising its economic and political resources to make true infrastructural and societal change that touched the end consumer across emerging markets. In preparation for that, a senior team within Abraaj had already commenced negotiations with the government in Mozambique to build a new 'gas city' modelled on Dubai and entered discussions with the UAE government on food security initiatives in that country.

Once the deal had been signed in October 2016, the two major issues that remained to be resolved were the new seven-year tariff regime under which the company would operate (this had a direct bearing on its future profitability as its level would either confirm or re-determine the price that SEP was willing to pay) and the NSCC.[21] Elements within the Pakistani bureaucracy–military complex used the tools at its disposal – specifically regulatory obstacles – to ensure a limit was placed on Chinese expansion in Pakistan; perhaps in their own narrow self-interest, perhaps at the behest of the US.[22]

There was little that could be used in terms of criticising Abraaj's management of Karachi Electric; by 2016, the utility was generating EBITDA over $200 million per annum and had delivered $1 billion in infrastructure investment. Loss of electricity through transmission had been reduced from 38 per cent (unofficially 50 per cent) to an audited 18 per cent. A once mistrusted, inefficient public utility company was now a thriving commercial enterprise, providing a dependable service for millions of consumers, facilitating lasting development across Karachi and Pakistan more broadly. SEP had not only endorsed Karachi Electric's success but was knocking on its door to allow the largest ever amount of foreign direct investment in the city to be deployed. The first instrument of delay was the chairman of NEPRA, Tariq Sadozai, a retired army brigadier whose inaction contributed to the scuppering of the transaction and, in his role as chairman, he had constitutional protection against being fired by the government for not doing its bidding and approving the tariff. The relationship between NEPRA and the central government has not been an easy one but it is legally and constitutionally independent and would remain so even if recent changes were implemented. The point is that the government has limited powers to instruct NEPRA what to do, which gives it considerable powers to presume its own line on certain issues.[23] Executives involved in the negotiations believe that Sadozai did not have the domestic strength to resist the government onslaught unless he was specifically promised protection in the murky, byzantine way the Pakistani state operates.

The 2016 tariff determination was delayed by Sadozai by a year and, when issued, was significantly below Abraaj and SEP expectations. The requested tariff was Rs.15.8 and the approved tariff was determined by Sadozai at Rs.12. This could have precipitated the collapse of the SEP deal. Karachi Electric appealed against the determination, but this was heard by the same body that had set the original tariff. The result was a slight improvement to Rs.13. The Prime Minister at the time, Shahid Abbasi, was committed to the deal happening and he took the unprecedented step of having the federal government appeal the decision on the tariff on behalf of Karachi Electric in an effort to move the deal forward.[24] NEPRA kept silent on the government's request until after the incumbent government left office and a caretaker government was appointed to preside over the 2018 elections. This government had no mandate to influence the outcome one way or the other. Once the caretaker government was in place, Sadozai announced the tariff as remaining unchanged. NEPRA's decision had clearly blocked the deal.

Whilst this was happening, the army leadership assured the government of Abbasi that it supported the deal and Naqvi himself was given similar assurances separately. It was unthinkable that a former senior army officer would have gone against the wishes of the army leadership. By setting such a low tariff for Karachi Electric, in spite of the successful trajectory the company had been on for the previous eight years, it appears that elements within the military elite were set on disrupting the deal. Indeed, given the way in which Pakistani power politics work and the way in which the military continue to function in the civilian realm, it is highly unlikely that Sadozai would have taken this stance without clearance.[25] For the establishment, undermining the sale of Karachi Electric, whilst clearly not in the national interest as the civilian governments perceived it, would go a long way to appeasing the US without permanently disrupting the wider CPEC initiative, which, in any event, was hitting roadblocks and slowing down because of direct US governmental lobbying and obstruction; if that was the understanding that they had reached in the background.[26]

In tandem with the tariff issue, SEP also needed to obtain an NSCC. However, this was not granted by the privatisation secretary because the 'relevant' departments had not provided the clearances (the specific departments that were being disruptive were not identified).[27] Naqvi met repeatedly with Prime Minister Abbasi and, given that this roadblock was a national security issue, with the director general of the ISI.[28] Over a period of two to three months, KES thought they had brought the deal back on track despite a wider crisis unfolding back in Dubai and London courtesy of the *Wall Street Journal* and the *New York Times*, which started in February 2018. He was helped by the strategic patience of the Chinese but hindered every time the deal took a step forward in Pakistan by something negative happening elsewhere. The coordinated attacks on Abraaj in the US press were a major setback and the coverage was directly repeated almost verbatim in key elements within the Pakistani media known to be 'establishment-backed'. This led to yet another slowdown in the approval process but despite the outgoing Prime Minister taking the issue directly into the federal Cabinet for approval to overrule the privatisation secretary, going public with his support for Karachi Electric and condemning bureaucrats for destroying the government's ability to implement decisions, still, nothing moved.[29] Two individuals, the chair of NEPRA and the secretary of the privatisation commission – ostensibly unconnected – had together thwarted the largest single inward investment in Pakistan's history. They cannot have done this by accident.

As far as the Pakistani media were concerned, Naqvi had chosen sides within the Pakistan party system. The fact that outgoing Prime Minister Abbasi supported the deal despite Naqvi's friendship with his political opponent speaks volumes for his commitment. Having said that, I spoke to a number of people across the political divide in Pakistan and found that Naqvi had friends in all the major political parties; but perhaps that's just how Pakistan works. Naqvi and his friends in Dubai had supported Imran Khan's 2013 election campaign[30] and he was also privately working on ideas for what would be Khan's first government, including, as it was reported, helping on developing the 'Agenda for Economic Revival 2018–2023',[31] a summary delivered by PTI supporters from academia and the private sector on how to stimulate growth in Pakistan. This was regarded by many as a kind of economic manifesto for the PTI. The agenda covered a range of proposals, including fiscal policy, the development of the housing sector, a reform of the public sector and how to reform the system of government in Pakistan. It also contained a chapter on how to maximise the value of CPEC from a Pakistani perspective. Many of these proposals were antithetical to established interests in Pakistan, principally within influential elements of the Pakistani bureaucracy–military complex.[32] There was a clear perception that Naqvi was aligned with the PTI and much speculation about this exact role existed, especially after Imran Khan's ex-wife released a book during the election campaign designed and timed to disrupt Khan's electoral chances in which she discussed Khan and Naqvi's closeness. This was further confirmed when he openly started visiting Islamabad weekly as part of Khan's trusted inner circle of advisers after he became Prime Minister, including being party to the extensive debates on the negotiations with the IMF.[33] This role was publicly reported and called into question in the media at the time because Naqvi had no official party affiliation or government role. Every report on Naqvi advising Khan duly repeated the *Wall Street Journal* allegations. One journalist in Pakistan told me that a *Wall Street Journal* reporter kept calling local journalists, urging them to report his stories.

It was also reported in the Pakistani media that Naqvi had played a role in helping develop policy for the new government and that in particular he had taken responsibility for delivering a policy which envisioned all public sector enterprises to come into a corporate fund structure that would be the basis of a future sovereign wealth fund and that he was a major advocate of the PTI's drive to stimulate economic reform and asked Masood Ahmed, a recently retired senior IMF official, to assist the Pakistani team tasked with the negotiations with the IMF.

This approach by Pakistan to the IMF was initially supported by Mike Pompeo, but he was adamant that IMF funding could not be used to support CPEC projects or subsidise debt repayments.[34] He told a CBS News interview: 'Make no mistake. We will be watching what the IMF does. There's no rationale for IMF tax dollars and associated with that American dollars that are part of the IMF funding, for those to go to bail out Chinese bondholders or China itself.' This followed an equally testy exchange at the first meeting between Khan and Pompeo. The subtext was clear: it would be fine if the IMF assistance were provided under US-imposed conditions that ensured no benefit to China. Khan was in a quandary. Any deal with the IMF could not be used just to push a problem down the road and saddle Pakistan with additional debt whilst undermining the country's autonomy. But he needed the cash. Pakistani's previous IMF deal, agreed in 2013, granted a $6.6 billion bailout to the country, conditional on strict restructuring and rationalisation efforts. The new iteration contained similar conditions, which would devalue the currency precipitously.[35] The Prime Minister was advised by his inner team to seek supporting finance from Saudi Arabia, the UAE and China to buy more time, which he did, providing space for Pakistan to negotiate more favourable terms with the IMF. Reuters reported in December 2018 that the UAE was to deposit $3 billion in Pakistan's central bank in the next few days, this followed an October loan from Saudi Arabia of $6 billion, which included a '$3 billion deposit for its foreign currency reserves and another $3 billion in deferred oil payments'. This was an extension of blockade politics in an attempt to reduce Pakistani dependence on LNG from Qatar.[36]

Naqvi with a few other trusted aides of PM Imran Khan met with senior World Bank officials to further discuss alternatives to the punishing IMF deal. They suggested to the officials that if the IMF deal was accepted, Pakistan needed to adopt a hard stance in relation to autonomy on the exchange rate in a fiscal deficit that supported the economic priorities of the PTI government. By this point he had a target painted on his forehead as a potential obstacle to the IMF negotiations.

The Prime Minister was receiving contradictory advice from his advisers who were clearly not all on the same page as the local media outlets reported on each day with glee. Whilst Khan deliberated on which concessions to give to the IMF to get the package approved, Naqvi returned to London against the wishes of Khan, who wanted him to stay in Islamabad. According to Naqvi's call logs, Khan was the last person he spoke to before he took off from Islamabad to London on his flight via Doha. He was arrested and detained on 10 April 2019 at Heathrow airport. Soon thereafter, Pakistan agreed to the IMF deal on what the media described as unfavourable terms; the Finance Minister was sacked and a trusted confidant of the establishment, Hafeez Sheikh, was imported into the government as a replacement – a steady hand.[37] Naqvi remained incarcerated for a period of close to eight weeks until 28 May 2019, seeking to collect funds to post bail in what was at the time the highest bail amount ever demanded in UK courts – £15 million in cash, along with £650,000 submitted by sureties publicly and a 24/7 curfew monitored by a tag. It now definitely seemed that he was *persona non grata* as the Crown Prosecution Service signalled, incorrectly as it turns out, to the magistrate about how he had apparently fled the country on a private jet earlier in the week. When Naqvi's barrister presented his boarding card for the Pakistan International Airlines flight he took to Islamabad, the barrister for the CPS simply said it could be a fake. The CPS also said Naqvi had phoned Khan after he was arrested, whereas his counsel clarified the call had been made the evening before he boarded his flight. His subsequent house arrest (which is still in place) makes it impossible for him to contribute to the political process in Pakistan. Having been courted by the US, Naqvi is now positioned in their eyes as an opponent to the Atlantic capitalist instrument of neo-liberalism, the IMF and by extension the American-led development industry based on that Atlantic model. He was projected as a firm supporter of CPEC, Chinese investment strategy in Pakistan and an advocate of a policy of moving away from dependence on the West so that Pakistan could become more autonomous with support from other Muslim nations. In my opinion, it was this toxic combination that motivated the US to obstruct the Karachi Electric deal in 2017 and then destroy Abraaj itself in 2018 when Naqvi not only refused to shift ground but continued battling to save Abraaj, consummate the Karachi Electric deal and, to make matters worse, repeatedly popped up in Pakistan as Imran Khan's adviser. Naqvi was an irritant and the speed with which an indictment was brought, and the severity of its content, suggests that he was cropping up in too many different places and therefore needed to be dealt with, once and for all. The fly had to be swatted.

PART IV

# FALLING ACTION – LET THE TOWERS BURN

# 10

# Strangled by a string of pearls

A braaj could have been strangled by either party in the string of pearls geopolitical conflict because it allowed itself to become vulnerable to both internal and external attack in the winter of 2017 and the spring of 2018. If you were going to take down Abraaj this was the perfect moment. You could only have known it was the perfect moment if you were a senior figure near the top of the Abraaj or were hacking internal email traffic on a regular basis. You would only have had the right tools to do the job if you were a nation state. Abraaj's vulnerability had been created by Naqvi's relentless drive for change, especially in his aim to complete a ten-year plan for an IPO in five years. This pace of change exposed the differences in the nature of Abraaj's investor base. The move to a different kind of investor base to achieve the global fund which would be the basis for the IPO had two consequences. Firstly, US and other Western institutional investors expected adherence to different operating standards from Middle East family offices; and the legacy funds were run differently. Secondly, the creation of more unified new global funds, like the planned APEF VI, threatened the positions of the existing senior management and contributed to an internal civil war. Alongside this, the failure to consummate the Karachi Electric deal was at the root of an ongoing cash-flow crisis that really got crunchy in 2017 and seemed to have been resolved by the end of that year before it came to a head in the spring of 2018.

Much of what follows has been synthesised through interviewing ex-Abraaj executives, trawling media articles that were appearing virtually daily throughout the first half of 2018, examining emails contained in the Abraaj archive and speaking to bankers that worked in creditor institutions of AHL at the time. The management of cash flow across the group and its funds, particularly AGHF, initially caused a small number of specific investors to ask questions and the inability to sell treasury shares and take other measures to ease the liquidity position accentuated a growing loss of confidence in early 2018. This was accentuated by Hamilton Lane jumping into the equation by asking questions about APEF IV. It was the revelation by the media that these questions were even being asked that precipitated the crisis. Therefore, the leaking of material to the media and its publication was the initial instrument of destruction. The company might have withstood all of this if two key unsecured creditors, the Jafar family and the PIFSS in Kuwait, had not pursued the repayment of their debt in such a way that precipitated the liquidation of the company and ensured its complete inability to repay its debts. Experienced investors would be expected to think very hard before seeking the return of their funds in this way. Additionally, these actions were compounded by well-timed anonymous emails and equally well-timed leaks to the DoJ and the media that then continued to undercut the restructuring and rescue plans that were attempted – each of which was signed off by global experts as not only being attainable, but probable, in the event that rational behaviour on the part of all stakeholders prevailed. But it was the reports stating that questions were being asked by investors and additional audits of funds were being demanded that were the catalysts because asking such questions was enough to begin the deconstruction of the foundations of investor confidence on which the business was based. The speed, logical progress and orchestrated manner of the attacks suggest that potentially a senior internal source may or may have not been involved, but a well-resourced external agency certainly was the driver given the technological sophistication necessary to access secure systems and to send virtually untraceable emails, alongside the expense involved and the logistics. From the vantage point of stepping back from the trees into forming a view of the entire forest and with the benefit of hindsight, the fall of Abraaj looks more like a controlled explosion bringing down a neglected building onto its foundations rather than one that imploded and collapsed because its foundations were rotten.

The way in which you read the events that occurred because of the cash-flow and liquidity issues that beset Abraaj is governed by perception. It is like the parable of the six blind men and the elephant. Each takes hold of a different part of the elephant and decides what the elephant is like from the part of the elephant they can touch: it is like a wall or a snake or a spear or a cow or a carpet or a rope. Your point of view depends on what you can touch from the place in which you stand (i.e. the part of the elephant that you can feel). It will be the job of judges and juries to decide how the Abraaj story plays out. Each participant in this tale thinks they know the truth from the part that they can see. From what I have seen, and that is by no means all the evidence a judge will see, the dispute comes down to an interpretation of what was and what was not allowed by the limited partner agreements and the manner in which valuations are conducted in this industry. The fact that all the money was logged into the accounting system and no money was actually unaccounted for suggests that these charges will drop away, and because the bribery allegations were not linked to any charges, they were included more to paint the picture and fill in the scenery because the Southern District of New York did not actually have a case. The indictment is window dressing to achieve extradition utilising the hyperbole of the prohibition era laws used to construct the counts. It seems clear from the actions of the Abraaj team, in, for example, handing over the evidence to the Dubai Financial Services

191

Authority, voluntarily opening their books to separate audits in turn by KPMG then Deloitte and subsequently, under protest to Ankura, checking their processes with law firms like Freshfields and Allen & Overy, that they believed their actions were legal and legitimate – they were running a complex global business. Moreover, their law firms and global accountancy firms told them that what they were doing was permissible; maybe sanctionable through civil processes if they got it wrong or a judge agreed with the other side in their interpretation of the LPAs, but certainly not criminal in intent. Only six out of 400 investors questioned the way Abraaj operated at the outset and they were led by US investors and one creditor, OPIC. If what was happening was an elaborate criminal conspiracy over two decades, then why was this so? There are a number of dimensions involved in understanding why no investors outside the US (except CDC and Proparco) and no investors who had worked with Abraaj for longer than the period since 2015 complained about the operation of the funds; and if indeed the creditors at AHL were concerned around repayment, not a single one of those were from the US or US based. The implication of the indictment is that a significant number of US creditors were involved and that this established DOJ jurisdiction in the case, and yet the DoJ indictment seems to suggest that the affront was that non-US creditors remained unpaid and it was its duty to figure out why. Of course, once the rumour mill started churning and the firm began unravelling and executives began running away from the conflagration as fast as they could, many different entities jumped in ostensibly to ensure that their interests were protected, but often simply to have a ringside seat at what was arguably the most explosive financial industry story in a long time.

It is clear that APEF IV was the transitional fund between Abraaj 1.0 and Abraaj 2.0. Abraaj 2.0 was initiated with AGHF and Gen-5 funds. No complaints have arisen about Gen-5 funds but only for AGHF. Abraaj's interpretation of the LPA itself had been upheld by Freshfields so the company was entitled to rely on that opinion and the culmination of

Abraaj 2.0 would have come with the closing of the single global fund APEF VI. It also appears that all but six of the investors in APEF IV were legacy investors. They came from the original and early adopting group of investors. If you asked them what was the entity in which they were investing and in which they placed their trust, they would have said Abraaj Capital or maybe just Abraaj. They would have known that this entity was now called The Abraaj Group, which constituted distinctive elements and multiple funds, but that was not their partner. For them, if their funds were not yet invested in portfolio companies they were held by the entity itself, Abraaj. If their funds had not been put to work they could have had them back but after they had been drawn down they were earning a preferred return that ensured they would get their money back before Abraaj did – they trusted Abraaj and there was no reason for them to think in a contrary manner – this, for example, was exactly what happened in the case of Prince Khalid bin Sultan of Saudi Arabia, amongst others, who preferred sending full commitments rather than being bothered by periodic drawdowns. As the thing they were investing in was Abraaj Capital the investors did not care and, further, they gave permission in the LPAs for their money to be held within Abraaj overall as an entity and used at the discretion of the Abraaj team. They allowed this because this also worked the other way around. If they could not meet the required commitments when a drawdown was requested and they delayed the honouring of it, Abraaj would step in with its own funds to make up the shortfall as it had done to a significant extent in APEF IV. The investors had faith that Abraaj would produce the returns that they desired. They tended to be agnostic about the details of how that came about. In fact, how it came about was governed by a defined legal relationship that both sides treated with some flexibility to mutual benefit. The LPAs required that the investors provided funds when requested for investments. The Abraaj Group, as the general partner, could have legally enforced that condition. But it never did. There was an understanding between the two parties; this was the way business was conducted in the Middle East. As the general partner, Abraaj also had a considerable balance sheet of its own which it could deploy to fill those gaps. This was unusual for a private equity firm, but it gave Abraaj an enviable strategic flexibility when crises, such as the crash in 2008 or the Arab Spring in 2011, spooked investors. Given this underlying understanding, there was also considerable leeway in the LPAs and in custom and practice for the way in which funds were used once drawn down but before they were directly invested into a portfolio company and in the timing of distributions from the sale of assets when Abraaj exited. This flexibility was not written down but was based on at least two decades worth of precedent dealing with Khaleeji Capitalists. For some of the core players in the Abraaj funds it was a powerful and overriding precedent that actually also defined the culture of the company. But cultures in companies like cultures in every human entity change and evolve over time or those entities die out. This is the heart of the matter and the nexus of why APEF IV and AGHF made Abraaj vulnerable to external attack as those who were looking at the conduct of the company did not have the full picture and an understanding of the Abraaj's operating precedent. This can be illustrated in two ways in particular. Firstly, in the way in which Abraaj behaved during the unfolding crisis with respect to the legal options it had to enforce its position on its investors. Secondly, in understanding the difference in the relationship the company had with Abraaj 2.0 investors.

The US investors in Abraaj 2.0 did not operate on the basis of flexible reciprocity in this crisis, whereas at two defining moments Abraaj continued to do so. In response to the questioning of its conduct of the AGHF by four investors, Abraaj could have refused their request for another audit, when the fund had already passed one, and challenged in court the investors' legal right to the information they were demanding. Instead, they returned the funds to the investors with interest. Secondly, as pressure mounted on Abraaj, rather than attempt to power through, which might indeed have been possible, and close APEF VI at that point with just the $3 billion raised in the first close and enforce the legal commitments of those who had made undertakings to invest, Abraaj freed all investors from their commitments to the fund. This was entirely consistent with the way in which Abraaj 1.0 had always done business based on flexibility and reciprocity; it had done so with APEF IV in the financial crisis of 2008; it had done so when acquiring almost $1 billion of IGCF initial assets through its own resources before limited partner funds arrived; it had done so when it acquired the CARE Hospitals Group prior to the closing of AGHF with its own credit lines. In contrast, Abraaj 2.0 was not dealing with entities that would reciprocate but only litigate. Concessions in this context were catastrophic to the viability of the company.

It was catastrophic because the relationship between Abraaj 1.0 and newer Abraaj 2.0 investors was different. At least six of the investors in these two funds (IGCF and APEF IV) were not legacy investors. They had not grown up alongside, with and through Abraaj, they were the investors that were being brought in and to an extent were shaping Abraaj 2.0 as expressed in the APEF VI global fund. Abraaj needed investors of their size to achieve its step up to the next level of sustainability and investors needed the inherent juicy upside of acquiring secondary stakes at deep discounts. Meanwhile, DFI-type investors like CDC, although they did not provide as much in terms of volume, provided reassurance to other new entrants from the US. If you asked this new group of investors what entity they were investing in, their answers, which fashioned the nomenclature used in the Securities and Exchange Commission (SEC) civil indictment and the DoJ criminal indictment, would have been that it was the APEF IV, AGHF or APEF VI, not The Abraaj Group.

In personnel terms, whereas the – mostly pre-2012 – legacy investors of Abraaj 1.0 had relationships with and telephone access to Naqvi as the key man, who was the person on whom the success of the funds rested and whose involvement the investors insisted upon, for the later investors – post-2012 – i.e. Abraaj 2.0, it was not envisaged that the 'key man clauses' would refer to individuals; they referred to teams made up of indispensable general partner executives. This was the institutionalisation that Abraaj craved; turning what was perceived as the magical touch of Naqvi to the operating dynamic of the team. And yet, interestingly, when APEF VI was imminently about to do its first close, a source told me that it was the new investors, that made up Abraaj 2.0, who were insisting on the key man clause being amended to reflect Naqvi's centrality as the key man; it seems they wanted the best of both worlds. Moreover, the Abraaj 2.0 investors were either large US institutional investors or quasi-government entities from Europe. They did not have the scope to use their judgement about reciprocity in the future; they had to follow rules. Nor could they fail to meet their legal obligations at the time of a drawdown, because they were publicly accountable. For these bodies, the entity in which they were investing was not the broad entity of 'Abraaj' in the same way as it was for the legacy investors but the specific part of the elephant that they had in front of them; and frankly, from correspondence I have reviewed, that is all they seemed to be concerned about. Indeed, many of the familiar faces they had worked with before seemed to be being pushed out if they had not already gone. The innate conservatism of the bureaucrats rebelled against this change and looked for reasons to attack Abraaj in turn. The LPAs provided the pretext. The Abraaj team interpreted and based their actions on a reading of the LPAs that allowed them considerable flexibility in the use of the funds since they were available on a demand deposit basis if the funds required them in order to be invested in the portfolio companies. In this case the intricacies of movements of funds and commingling are irrelevant. Internally, if anyone in the group entities or funds owed money it was the responsibility of the parent to ensure that funds were made available; an inherent guarantee. Regional creditors to the parent company and the funds understood that management was focused on ensuring that no debt anywhere remained unpaid when funds were made available. It was actually the way the company had grown up, and it was its modus operandi.

Houlihan Lokey, after a thorough research process, concluded that the balance sheet had sufficient assets to pay back all liabilities, so long as the process was orderly and the fund management business continued to operate, which raises the question, when is a company balance sheet insolvent and when is it cash-flow insolvent? If assets exceed liabilities on the balance sheet, as any expert on liquidation would say, then you are not balance sheet insolvent, and if you have access to funds on a continuing basis, irrespective of whether the cash sits amongst the company's assets, is available on demand or relates to fresh borrowings because a bank considers you creditworthy, as Abraaj proved during the critical month of December 2017, then you are not cash-flow insolvent. Insolvency occurs when you can no longer repay your obligations as and when they become due. In other words, insolvency was only *triggered* by the actions of creditors. To make matters worse, insolvency experts have explained to me that when seeking to restructure a business run on a consolidated basis as one entity where assets can be sold to extinguish liabilities at different constituent parts of the group, breaking it into separate liquidation processes for constituent parts ensures the crystallisation of mismatched assets and liabilities and inevitably leads to a headlong dive into oblivion.

There was also an overriding requirement that each fund could show at the time of audit at year end that funds drawn down, but not yet invested, were present in the accounts for those funds. No one is disputing in any of the litigation that there was ever an occasion on which funds were not present in the right amount and at the appropriate time; the question becomes whether Abraaj, as AIML, the manager, under the respective LPAs for each of the funds in the spotlight – namely APEF IV and AGHF – had the right to move the funds around and substitute them with funds from other sources at year end; in other words, what I understand to be the accounting differences between cash and demand deposits, which accountants have assured me does not exist. Finally, there were regular general partner reports to limited partners on the progress that was being made in the operation of the funds. Abraaj executives maintain that its reporting requirements were that it showed that funds were present on a demand deposit basis or aggregated within current fund assets and that explanations were given for the spend and volume of investments that had been made from the funds available. There is a clear dispute between six out of the 400 parties to these agreements on the content, regularity and quality of reporting by the general partners to the limited partners with respect to issues like the disbursement of funds from the sale of portfolio companies invested in by the funds. But this dispute was not general, and it is not the case that all or even most of the limited partners had a problem with the way in which the reporting was handled. In fact, of all the investors across all three of the funds mentioned in the indictments – APEF IV, AGHF and APEF VI – only six raised these issues initially or indicated there were any problems with the way in which Abraaj was running its funds, and it was only four, all US-based, which took further action. Two of this group of six US investors were only provoked to ask questions by the reporting of the issues raised by the other US investors. None of the questions raised concerned missing funds or lack of returns on investment. But once questions had been asked the towers started burning, many joined the fireworks party, if for nothing else, to get seats at the table. Interestingly, I learnt that in a critical conversation in February when Hamilton Lane started applying maximum pressure on Abraaj, Andrea Kramer, head of fund investments, and Hartley Rogers, the chairman, requested Naqvi to resolve the issues by quietly stepping up personally and to provide the funds necessary to make APEF IV 'whole' because he was clearly wealthy and nobody wanted to have any more noise and that their own reputation was on the line. When Naqvi protested that he had already done so and had no more assets to deploy threats were made about regulatory visits by the SEC if APEF VI were not dissolved.

These and many other technical legal matters will be decided in the courts. The discovery process has not even commenced, and I am sure much more audio and written evidence will be presented by both sides that has not yet seen the light of day, which will leave many more people squirming. But the implications should be clear enough. The movement of funds and their deployment as far as it was originally disputed by a small minority of investors, some of whom are important in terms of symbolism, was in no way an attempt to defraud anyone. Emails seen by me seem to indicate that the actions of the Abraaj team were taken in good faith, based on extensive precedent and, in their honest view and in the view of their lawyers and their auditors at the time and prior to any litigation, entirely legal and covered by the terms and conditions of the LPAs. On many occasions in the past, they had supported the funds in question when they were in danger of defaulting; and if the funds had excess liquidity available and the LPAs permitted it, they felt that their backstop guarantee as a group was sufficient for them to deal with these 'demand deposits' as they saw fit, especially at a time of severe liquidity constraints, which appeared to have a runway for resolution if the firm were left alone to achieve its objectives.

That is the general picture and the general conclusion. The specific context of the cash crunch from 2016 when the Karachi Electric deal was first done to the endgame of mid-2018 emerged because Abraaj had accumulated over $1 billion of receivables in the AHL balance sheet. If any one of the outstanding receivables were resolved, most critically the K-Electric sale to SEP, the deficiencies would have been corrected and Abraaj would have resumed its rising trajectory. Instead, 2017 was dominated by Abraaj managing its cash flow whilst trying to close APEF VI and the sale of Karachi Electric.

So how did the cash crunch occur at Abraaj in the first place? The initial euphoria of having sold Karachi Electric in 2016 had largely waned when, a year later, there appeared to be no sign of a breakthrough in getting the NSCC or a satisfactory tariff regime for the next seven-year term.

The NSCC for the Chinese buyers of Karachi Electric was reportedly finally granted on 27 September 2017 but this did not move the deal forward as much as expected.[1] The tariff issue remained outstanding and SEP continued playing their long game, but the sale was halted yet again by bureaucrats who took issue with the settlement of accounts between the state-owned gas supplier and K-Electric as a new issue introduced at the last minute. SEP said it would be more than willing to inherit the issue, but the Pakistani bureaucrats viewed this as an insurmountable obstacle to the deal's completion. If the buyer and seller are in agreement and it is shares that are being transferred in a functional operating entity rather than a sale of assets, the settlement of accounts is an issue overcome in the normal course of business; why would bureaucrats impose its settlement as a condition? What was even more perplexing was that the bureaucrats appeared to be supporting a creditor claim by Sui Southern, the supplier of natural gas to K-Electric and another listed entity but under governmental control, and that more than 80 per cent of the debt related to interest payments on overdue debt, which in itself was outstanding due to a dispute between Sui Southern and K-Electric. At the same time, K-Electric was being told that its own receivables from other government entities could not attract interest. Unless they thought that it would be easier to twist Abraaj's arm, which was operating in crisis mode, rather than that of the incoming buyer. The Karachi Electric sale was in limbo, which meant that the cash-flow issue would continue and get worse.

Meanwhile, the take-down operation had begun in earnest in September 2017 and combined events in Dubai with events in Pakistan. A week before, on 20 September 2017, an anonymous email was sent to prospective investors in APEF VI[2] – which was lining up for what looked like a very successful first close – who were primarily based in the US and China, and the existing limited partners of AGHF. This coincided with progress being made in Pakistan when the NSCC that would move the completion of the Karachi Electric deal forwards was finally granted after intense efforts by Naqvi shuttling back and forth to Islamabad and the media was reporting that a deal was imminent. The positive impact of the NSCC coming through and being communicated to investors as a breakthrough was immediately undermined by the coverage that then appeared in the anonymous email that was sent to the same investors who had received the good news about the NSCC.

An internal Abraaj report on the source of the email was sought by Naqvi, and he commissioned Pradeep Ramamurthy, who was the main Abraaj liaison for US clients and had a security and intelligence background, to use a well-regarded US counter-intelligence firm Nardello. Nardello found that the email came via Russian Yandex servers through multiple virtual private networks and the email address was self-destructing.[3] When this was discovered, it became clear that only an extremely sophisticated and well-financed actor could have delivered such a complex system to cover its tracks. It is not clear why the company does not seem to have investigated the email further or made a greater effort to discover its source beyond this investigation. If they did, they have kept their conclusions secret. In hindsight, the entire email leak was clearly a carefully orchestrated exercise meant to discredit Abraaj and derail the imminent first close of APEF VI, whilst also generating negative media cycles in Pakistan to undermine confidence in Abraaj there. The whistle-blower was therefore nothing of the sort but an economic hitman from either inside Abraaj or working with a source inside the firm. The email had the subject line 'Abraaj Fund 6 Warning' and began: 'Some friendly advice. Before committing to the new Fund 6, do your diligence properly and do not believe what you are told by the partners or what you see on the slides. It is all show.' The anonymous email focused on highlighting a number of concerns, including unrealised gain valuations, problems with certain existing investments, the misuse of LP drawdowns and exit proceeds.

Tarang Katira, an employee of Hamilton Lane, forwarded the email to Naqvi and Mark Bourgeois: 'Gents ... got this email overnight. Not sure if anyone else has forwarded it to you already. Sending it so that you're aware it's out there and clearly targeting LPs. Should we chat?' The tone and syntax structure of the email made it seem as if a low-level employee, whose first language was not English, had sent it, but the timing and the content suggested it was from someone very senior in Abraaj who understood that the impact this kind of message would have was likely to be incendiary.[4]

Internally, news of the anonymous email spread as rumours like a wildfire. Certain senior members of the Abraaj team were already disgruntled with the move to the single unified fund structure of APEF VI because it would weaken and then replace the regional hubs, and the attempt to promote younger members was seen as a challenge to some of the senior incumbents. Discussions with Abraaj employees validated the fact that the November 2017 town hall meeting was rife with discontent from senior management, with rumours swirling that some were threatening to leave, activating key man triggers in the various Gen-5 funds that would leave Abraaj in a vulnerable position. Some partners were more threatened by the growth of US influence in the management group, which had advanced steadily since Mark Bourgeois had formally joined Abraaj in 2016, because it would underwrite the move to the single global fund.

Elsewhere in Abraaj, the simmering discontent on the part of the four investors in AGHF continued to gnaw away at the confidence of employees; although Naqvi had requested that knowledge of the dispute be limited to a few managers, the information was being widely disseminated internally. At the end of November 2017, an email on behalf of four of the LPs in AGHF, who were also on the AGHF limited partner advisory committee, namely BMGF, IFC, CDC and Proparco, continued to probe AIML to provide AGHF statements showing all transactions in and out of the accounts. The investors were questioning the way in which funds had been used.

By the start of December 2017, it was clear that the resolution of problems with the four disgruntled members of the LPAC could not be delayed. The Abraaj team decided rather than force investors to stick to the letter of their LPAs or have that argument with them in court, they would instead address the matter once and for all and return all monies that had been drawn down but not yet invested, aiming to restore all funds with their correct cash balances by 31 December and ensuring that there was sufficient cash to repay short-term borrowings coming due. This meant that in that month, Abraaj had to restructure its balance sheet by urgently selling some assets and rescheduling some loans that were coming due to ensure that it managed to square off its books by the end of the year.

With the Karachi Electric sale in stasis in 2017, Abraaj had engaged JPMorgan to value its shares and, based on their tentative and preliminary valuation, they sold two blocks valued at $50 million each in December from the treasury shares in AHL held by them through AE2L – to Thomas Schmidheiny from Switzerland, who was on the board of Abraaj, and Sri Prakash Lohia from the UK, who was the founder of Indorama and a partner of Abraaj in Nigeria's largest fertiliser business. This established both the marketability of these blocks of shares (Abraaj had another six similarly sized blocks it could sell from the significant amount of shares that it held as treasury shares through AE2L) and the validation of the price. Naqvi then approached Mohammad Al Gergawi, who was the UAE Minister for Cabinet Affairs and the most powerful non-royal in the country, to seek UAE government assistance. Abraaj's success had been intimately connected to Dubai and so Naqvi pitched that it was in Dubai's best interest to support the company as the reputational damage it would be subject to if it was unable to repay the limited partners would tarnish Dubai's image. Gergawi had been Naqvi's friend for decades so agreed to ask the executive chairman of the largest state-owned bank in Dubai, NBD, to lend Abraaj $250 million to help cover the shortfall.[5]

However, over time Emirates NBD appeared reluctant to help; many days were lost in establishing the security package and the term sheet when received was onerous in the extreme. It required not just charges on all available Abraaj assets, but a variety of personal guarantees from Naqvi himself against the loan, giving him the impression that the funds were viewed as a personal loan and favour to him rather than as assistance to Abraaj. This was the first of a number of occasions in the frenzied moves that followed in which Naqvi's personal position and the position of Abraaj were confused. For now, Naqvi decided to stall on accepting the facility because of the guarantees that were being demanded of him personally.

In parallel, Naqvi had also approached a long-standing Abraaj investor and founding board member, Hamid Jafar, whose son Badr had succeeded him on the Abraaj board. Jafar immediately agreed to lend Naqvi $100 million personally, which he accepted gratefully. Since this was apparently based on their personal relationship, no documentation and no security were required; believe it or not, this is still the way things often work in the Middle East. Naqvi confided to Badr Jafar that the negotiations with Emirates NBD had stalled. Badr agreed to provide Abraaj directly with an additional $200 million, emphasising that Emirates NBD's onerous terms should be rejected; but for this additional amount, the Jafars asked for collateral of the treasury shares of AHL held at AE2L. As Badr was a board member he would have been aware of the value of Abraaj, its issues with AGHF and the recent transactions involving the sale of shares in AHL – moreover, in the event that for any reason the loans were not repaid, this enforcement against shares pledged to them with their pre-existing holdings would potentially give effective control of Abraaj to the Jafars.[6] Jafar also requested that Abraaj issue three post-dated security cheques dated 28 February 2018, by which time the issues in the funds would be resolved, the shares sold and the crisis would have been averted and the company re-established on its trajectory. Naqvi was extremely grateful to Jafar for having resolved a critical issue for Abraaj.

Naqvi then also secured an additional $75 million loan from Air

Arabia based on the long-standing arrangement that had been used numerous times between 2013 and 2017, whereby Abraaj's short-term liquidity requirements would be met by the airline in return for a higher rate of interest than most commercial loans. Along with the various loans and the receipt of fees and disbursements from a number of transactions and the value from the sale of shares, Abraaj was able to settle all external and fund liabilities that were required by 31 December 2017. The details may sound like immense amounts of money moving around but, in the context of the size of the funds and overall numbers Abraaj dealt in, these were 'normal' flows.

The cash was found and the crisis averted; it seemed that Abraaj's short-term cash-flow issues had been dealt with. However, Abraaj was not out of the water yet. January was to be the month in which the remaining treasury shares and excess inventory in funds, held by AHL, were to be sold to ensure the repayment of the short-term loans from Jafar taken in December. The approach of settling AGHF cash by returning it to limited partners appears not to have been done as an acknowledgement of wrongdoing; it looks like this was done in an attempt to maintain trust with investors. *This was the first big mistake.*

If you were touching a certain part of the elephant and this was all you could see, then this was a strategic blunder by Abraaj; the first in a series of three big mistakes that fed into the hands of the predator. If what Abraaj had done was covered by LPAs and this was now being challenged, the company should have stuck by their actions. This was not the same as dealing with the legacy investors from the Middle East, Abraaj was now dealing with large-scale US institutional investors who had signed agreements that Abraaj felt justified the way in which the funds had been used, but by returning all the funds with interest made it appear that there was something to hide. It also meant Abraaj had to raise sufficient funds to cover the shortfall. The way in which those funds were put together hastily in December 2017, the 'security package' involving post-dated security cheques, to ensure that the acquired funds could be returned to the investors rapidly was complex and as it turned out, highly risky. The details of the various sources and uses of the funds received and disbursed in December, the frenzied speed at which it was completed and the intensity of the workload meant that only the chief financial officer, the chief operating officer and Naqvi himself (with their respective teams) were involved in the execution. There was no time or attempt made to brief the other senior partners; these partners just saw that somehow Naqvi had solved the problem, paid back the AGHF investors, replaced internal borrowings and deferred impending liabilities.

These senior partners felt that a sleight of hand, a piece of magic, a dubious deal must have happened; how else was it pulled off? Many had assumed it was game over by the start of December, some hedged their bets and stayed on the side lines, whilst two tendered their resignations. The senior team was already feeling profoundly insecure after the new key man clause was introduced into the APEF VI first close at the insistence of the limited partners. When the collapse did not happen, their disbelief turned into hostility. They had cried abandon ship at the November town hall meeting and then the ship had not sunk. Misinformation deliberately started circulating amongst the senior partners with rumours abounding internally that Naqvi had pledged their carried interest to the banks and he had sold his shares and was getting ready to leave; some deception must have occurred.

As the further sale of shares was the major source for the repayment to Hamid Jafar against his advanced funds, $200 million of the liability to him was recorded within AE2L and the AHL shares held by it were pledged to him, pending their sale and his consequent repayment, with the balance being the $100 million owed to him directly by Naqvi. This became a source of disagreement between Jafar and Abraaj over 'who' the money had been lent to in March 2018: was it to AHL, AE2L, AIML or all of it to Naqvi himself? In effect, by cashing the security cheques and pushing for the liquidation of both AIML and AHL, Jafar pursued the return of his funds from all parties as he was legally entitled to do.

Abraaj also had a substantial position in excess inventory in the funds it managed held on its balance sheet that could be sold to buyers of secondary stakes; there was a globally established marketplace for such products. By January 2018, Abraaj had a provisional deal with HarbourVest that was due to be executed in early February 2018, but this was also stopped by the media reports released at the beginning of February 2018, with HarbourVest preferring to pause the decision at a time of uncertainty.[7]

The speediest key to resolving the liquidity issue was to release capital from the balance sheet. In internal partner meetings at the time, Naqvi said that in combination with the final close of APEF VI, a further sale of the inventory of shares held by AE2L and the excess inventory would solve Abraaj's cash-flow issues even if the Karachi Electric sale continued to be delayed and, had it not been for the curated crisis in AGHF continuing and the carefully timed media firestorm, this would have all been completed by early February 2018. This was no secret either; Naqvi had widely shared his strategy internally and with board members, with the many takers for the six remaining individual $50 million blocks of treasury shares and in the 'done deal' for the excess inventory, there were no secrets there. Somebody did not want that to happen and the plan never got executed because at each stage when there was a spectre of hope; it was dashed by carefully timed counter moves.

Once the money was returned in December, the four AGHF investors (by now, joined by OPIC as a lender to the fund) switched their attack by refusing to honour any future drawdowns until Abraaj agreed to an investigative audit into the fund's operation, contrary to what they had agreed before the funds had been returned to them, and the letter sent by the AGHF investors and OPIC was almost simultaneously leaked to the *Wall Street Journal* and the *New York Times*. This created a cycle of negative media coinciding with the proposed sale of shares as well as the excess inventory and effectively blocked any possibility of those deals going ahead.

To proceed with the sale of shares in Abraaj owned by AE2L was impossible within the toxic media environment and the agreed sale of excess inventory with HarbourVest was also cancelled in response to the news stories. The failure to sell the shares held by AE2L and the excess inventory held by AHL as a result of the media onslaught left Abraaj in a difficult position as the team felt that going back to market after the damaging media coverage and the widely circulated anonymous emails would result in a significant dilution of price and value accompanied by reputational damage.

The *New York Times* and *Wall Street Journal* published virtually identical stories on 2 February 2018, condemning Abraaj for misusing investor funds; the first time that an accusation of this kind had been levelled against the company. The *Wall Street Journal* had been pursuing Abraaj throughout January prior to this publication. Both papers seem to have based their stories on the same dossier of material that had been supplied to them.[8] These reports were incredibly damaging as in the world of private equity, an accusation of misusing or misappropriating funds could permanently damage a firm's reputation. There was no doubt by this point that the concerted moves over the preceding six months were bound to undermine Abraaj and the common US thread was apparent. The *New York Times* piece was more balanced than the shrill *Wall Street Journal* piece and, amidst the negativity around the AGHF, also reported that:

> The Abraaj Group has a reputation as one of the developing world's largest and most influential investors … Now some of those investors are claiming that The Abraaj Group and its founder, Arif Naqvi, misused funds, according to people who are familiar with the allegations but not authorized to speak publicly … The continuing dispute has arisen at a time of flux for the development community. The World Bank president, Jim Yong Kim, and Bill Gates have been promoting the idea

that private-sector investors need to take on a larger role in risky projects in the developing world.

In the past, governments and foundations led the way, via direct loans and grants. But over the past year, Mr Kim and Mr Gates have argued that it is possible for large pools of capital – such as private equity funds, insurance companies and pension funds – to score big profits by, for example, investing in hospitals in Pakistan and Nigeria. Mr Kim recently has singled out Abraaj and Mr Naqvi for praise.[9]

The appearance of these articles transformed the situation. From the issue being the concerns of four US investors who took a different view of the working of the LPAs, the sensationalist articles prompted all investors to start asking questions. Now everyone wanted to know what was happening, and with hundreds of investors across its various funds, almost 100 partner companies and numerous stakeholders, an avalanche of literally thousands of calls besieged the Abraaj management team; US limited partners led by Hamilton Lane became vociferous and militant as they moved to protect their own reputations. An adviser told me that with fewer than a dozen left in his team to help formulate strategy, the weight of management was beginning to become unsustainable for Naqvi.

When the damaging stories appeared, Abraaj had denied the reports, which it said in a statement on its website were linked to its AGHF: 'All capital that was drawn from AGHF investors was for approved Fund investments ... Some capital was not used as quickly as anticipated due to unforeseen political and regulatory developments in several of the Fund's operating markets.' It said that it had also hired KPMG to 'verify all receipts and payments made by the Fund'. Abraaj went to the Dubai Financial Services Authority and handed over all relevant documents pertaining to AGHF and were assured that the current media storm was not a serious concern for the authority. On 8 February, Abraaj announced that KPMG found no misuse of money.

Under pressure, Abraaj agreed to the AGHF request for an alternative investigative audit. Abraaj requested this be done by one of the big four accountancy firms. The four investors, led by the BMGF and OPIC, pushed for Ankura Consulting to conduct the audit instead.[10] Ankura was virtually unknown to Abraaj and an internet search by Abraaj executives revealed that it was staffed by many former US government employees and advisors, including former director of the Defence Intelligence Agency and senior financial advisor to the SEC and the DoJ, and that it was partially owned by a US private equity firm, Madison Dearborn and, surprisingly or unsurprisingly, was headquartered in Washington DC.[11] Abraaj told the Ankura consultants in February 2018 that the reassigned money was for 'temporary investments', as permitted in the LPAs and provided them with the opinion from Freshfields, which confirmed that Abraaj had been entitled to use the cash in ways that it had in accordance with the terms of the LPAs. Abraaj never received Ankura's findings and the DoJ indictment cited February 2018 as the beginning of its investigation. This could be a coincidence or it could be linked, we will probably never know. It is worth stressing that of the several occasions on which the Abraaj team opened their books fully to external scrutiny, this was the only time they were reluctant to do so; Ankura just didn't feel 'right' to them, it was too small, too unknown, too niche and they would have preferred and indeed welcomed another firm. They had already been scrutinised by their law firms and by the DFSA, KPMG and Deloitte. This was hardly the behaviour of people who felt they had something to hide.

In short, the newspaper reports caused panic amongst the investor base. Vettivetpillai, who was closest to the DFIs having previously worked for CDC and been CEO of Aureos until it was acquired by Abraaj, acting as an apparent spokesman for the DFIs, told Naqvi that the CDC believed that Abraaj's problems would be solved if Naqvi personally stepped away from AIML and the fund management business and volunteered to step in himself to fill Naqvi's shoes. He was supported in this by Abdel-Wadood and, for a while, it looked like the warring competitors for the top slot at Abraaj after Naqvi, who had never seen eye-to-eye with one another, were now united in getting Naqvi out, whatever it took; this despite the fact that both had theoretically resigned in December in view of what they had seemingly perceived to be an impending collapse. Naqvi authorised Vettivetpillai and Abdel-Wadood to conclude an agreement with the DFIs and the BMGF, believing that they were being propelled to step forward by loyalty to Abraaj. The proposal was that Naqvi would step away from running the fund management business in exchange for an end to the ongoing dispute and it was clearly hoped that this would be enough to enable Abraaj to get back to an even keel; Naqvi would after all remain the CEO of The Abraaj Group and chair of the global investment committee, which was where he wanted to eventually transition to anyway ahead of an IPO. Nobody disputed his commercial acumen, but it was apparent to him that the DFIs wanted to distance themselves from any potential conflict of interest issues between AHL and AIML and, being bureaucrats, they wanted to avoid getting involved in the media hysteria that had started. This advice was echoed by Abraaj's PR firm Finsbury and legal advisers Freshfields, who both heavily pushed for it. Each of the six managing partners at Abraaj pushed forward to be appointed CEO of AIML and the situation became ridiculous with all of the senior team nakedly making a power grab for themselves individually. On 25 February, as part of a restructuring process, Naqvi bypassed the managing partners and appointed two regional partners as co-CEO of AIML and announced he would give up control of the fund management business, AIML, whilst remaining the CEO of AHL. *This was the second big mistake.*

Beyond the AGHF news leaks, the media reports of Naqvi stepping aside now became even more slanted towards an anti-Naqvi rhetoric and implied that he alone was the issue. With various media outlets competing for airtime on the story rumours abounded. Naqvi had intended it to be a separation of activities and potential future conflicts of interest, but the media hyped it as a resignation; the clear implication in the presented narrative was that this was some kind of admission of wrongdoing. This caused even more panic amongst the limited partners in other Abraaj funds, many of whom felt that without Naqvi managing the funds their future performance was in jeopardy, whilst others asked for details of what the four investors knew that they did not. It was clearly perceived to be a signal of weakness to the market; the opposite of what Abraaj had intended. Hamilton Lane demanded that Abraaj make a gesture to relieve the pressure it was receiving from its own clients to whom it had recommended participation in Abraaj funds, with Mark Bourgeois, in emails seen by me, adding his internal weight to accede to their demands. Bourgeois's relationship with Hamilton Lane was a few decades old and understandably important to him. The Hamilton Lane team may have been feeling exposed and, having recently been listed on the New York Stock Exchange and given the US media coverage of Abraaj, they naturally needed to defend their reputation. There was an immediate effect on their share price. A JPMorgan analyst downgraded them to neutral on the Abraaj news and their stock fell 13 per cent.[12] To remedy concerns and to try to maintain these relationships in the long-run and under pressure from Andrea Kramer and Hartley Rogers at Hamilton Lane that they would complain to the SEC if Abraaj did not release investors that same day, which was a Friday when banks and businesses in Dubai were closed, Abraaj announced that it had released all APEF VI investors from their commitments and stopped fundraising.[13] *This was the third big mistake.*

Abraaj was now in free fall and the endgame was now in motion. The last of the three big mistakes was the most immediately disastrous. Abraaj had drawn down $75 million from a loan facility of $150 million, which was secured against the limited partnership commitments of the institutions that would be the investors in the first close of APEF VI and had been provided by the French bank, Société Générale. This is a common practice in private equity as funding initial acquisitions with debt at low rates of interest improves the overall internal rate of return at the end of the investment time frame. The bank naturally objected to Abraaj's decision to release investors as this was the basis of the security of their loan and they froze all Abraaj's accounts, effectively taking control of $45 million of the firm's money that was within the system ostensibly as working capital.[14] Halting APEF VI was a key development in undermining Abraaj's ability to operate in the future, particularly regarding working with Chinese capital, as they had been the biggest potential investors. Indeed, the Hong Kong Monetary Authority even sent an email to Abraaj, requesting it to stand firm and weather the media storm. I specifically asked Naqvi why he took these three decisions and in response he said, 'Bad call, bad advice, bad actors, bad timing and bad luck.' He then recounted a conversation he had with President Trump's then close friend Tom Barrack of Colony Capital in which Barrack questioned why Abraaj would ever release investors from commitments once they had been received and called it pure folly to have done so.

Naqvi also apparently received clear messages of what was actually expected of him now that the take-down was in full swing. A senior adviser to Abraaj at the time told me that these messages came from both internal and external routes and Naqvi asked his small circle repeatedly to help decipher their rationale. An external message came in a meeting with Naqvi when the founder of a major US private equity firm offered him $1 for Abraaj. If this were accepted, the individual promised that all the negative media surrounding Abraaj would cease. I believe it was around the end of February that Naqvi realised for the first time, with what can be seen as clarity in hindsight, that he was facing a concerted attack from US interests; what he could not figure out was whether this was individual or institutional. Was it a BMGF- and IFC-incited firestorm into which Hamilton Lane had jumped in? Or was OPIC leading a geopolitically inspired Trumpian exercise? Or had the leviathan of the US government decided that Naqvi was no longer needed? This interpretation and confusion as to the source of the attacks was reinforced by a conversation Naqvi had with a senior UAE royal who served as a government minister. This individual had close links to Pakistan, had invested in Abraaj funds and was a friend of Naqvi. He told him:

> Arif, your crime is that you gatecrashed a party that you were not invited to, and that you will be forced out of existence in the same way that other businesses have been toppled by the US; I know because I have seen it happen with another company, decades before you, and how it was taken apart.

Internally, the message came from Hamid and Badr Jafar. After the media articles appeared, sources with knowledge of the meetings allege that Badr Jafar assumed a more assertive role in the AHL board, which began with multiple phone meetings every week to try to stay abreast of the unfolding crisis. Badr and Hamid Jafar told Naqvi during these months that these outstanding loan payments could be resolved by transferring the control and equity position of Karachi Electric to them. The attempt to recover their debt was executed with clinical efficiency.

Towards the end of February, Naqvi met with the Jafars, their banker and their lawyer to discuss the cheques that had been signed back in December 2017. As a direct result of the media coverage and the continuing blocking of progress on the Karachi Electric sale, Abraaj had been unable to recover any more of the receivables that would have ameliorated its cash-flow issues and ensured the repayment to Jafar. These issues were compounded by demands from Société Générale in the wake of the decision to suspend APEF VI and release limited partners from their commitments. The tone of the meeting was distinctly hostile, with the Jafars essentially claiming that Abraaj now effectively belonged to them and that they were entitled to all of its assets – primarily Karachi

Electric – and that there was an unwritten guarantee that Naqvi would stand behind all obligations personally if their debt were not repaid by Abraaj.

Naqvi immediately reported the meeting blow-by-blow to Freshfields and on their advice personally engaged a law firm, Addleshaw Goddard, to advise him. The bouncing of corporate cheques (if proven to have been in bad faith) is a criminal act in Dubai. Naqvi believed that the spirit of the agreement in which the cheques had been given was that the cheques would never be cashed. The Jafars were perfectly legally entitled to cash the cheques whatever Naqvi's understanding or common practice in the UAE might be. Since Naqvi owed $100 million personally to Hamid Jafar from the amounts the Jafars had advanced, on the written advice of the CEO of the Bank of Sharjah, who had been present at the meeting, he immediately paid $33 million from his personal account to cover a portion of this amount (this was later stated by the Jafars to be payment for the fees and penal interest for the entire $300 million), whilst the $200 million lent to Abraaj remained under discussion, with Abraaj proposing that it would ensure repayment by 31 May 2018 at the latest. This was based on the assurances from Pakistan, including then Prime Minister Abbasi, that the Karachi Electric deal would be authorised before he left office at the end of May.

Whilst Naqvi's authority in the firm was being undermined from within by his missteps and by the media reporting, which began to focus more on him personally, his separation from having any influence over strategy and fund operations had fuelled the perception that Abraaj was in free fall. The new co-CEOs of AIML appointed by him, Selcuk Yorgancioglu and Omar Lodhi, were keen to establish their writ and there was also a physical separation of office spaces; Naqvi left with only six to eight professionals to help him navigate Abraaj out of crisis, whilst the rest of the Abraaj machine resided outside his control on different floors of the Abraaj building to which he no longer had automatic access. At the same time, the co-CEOs fired 15 per cent of the staff globally as their opening gambit, creating another cycle of stories about panic and disintegration at Abraaj.[15] On 29 March, the *Wall Street Journal* reported that the IFC and CDC were broadening their investigation into Abraaj. They were both conducting audits of the company's other managed funds to see if any funds had been misused.[16] Both were using the same, no longer little-known, firm, Ankura.

Naqvi now realised that his ability to control the situation had passed and the only way to generate cash was to engage with a number of potential buyers interested in acquiring AIML. After the separation of AIML from AHL in February 2018, AIML remained an attractive fund management entity as the main Abraaj asset management platform and it had no liabilities, other than cross collateralisation and guarantees that are normal in commercial borrowing practices; these quite properly were housed in AHL, which was also the group's repository of its asset wealth. AIML had an excellent market presence. Despite being valued at close to $1.2 billion in 2017 by JPMorgan for the asset management platform, initial offers in February and March 2018 were around $500 million (that is at book value) – in hindsight that is fifty times more than what was in the end paid for AIML after the liquidation process by Deloitte. AHL received interest from Mubadala, KBBO, the Saudi PIF and SoftBank, but each in turn pulled out at the last minute, citing more or less the same message: 'Uncertainty about what the US would do next, and we don't want to be the ones to deal with them.'[17]

This left just two major private equity investment firms interested in buying AIML: Cerberus Capital Management and Colony Capital, who had appeared out of nowhere and neither appeared to have the relevant emerging market experience to manage the complex Abraaj operation. The founder of Cerberus, Stephen Feinberg, was a major Republican donor and close friend of Trump who donated nearly $1.5 million to Trump's political action committees and was appointed as chairman of the President's Intelligence Advisory Board,[18] a body that advises the President on the quality and adequacy of intelligence collection.

Colony Capital was even closer to Trump: founder Tom Barrack had been a close friend and confidant for thirty years. Barrack was chair of Trump's inaugural committee, but the two fell out over allegations of corruption during Trump's inauguration in August 2018.[19] On 26 March, reports were published about Abraaj contemplating the sale of a stake in its fund management business to raise much needed capital. Abraaj received non-binding offers from both parties, Cerberus and Colony, in the first ten days of April 2018, between $250 to $300 million, with additional commitments to acquire the underlying stakes in the funds held by AHL.[20]

Towards the end of March, it was agreed by the AHL board, which was by now meeting in crisis mode at least weekly, that Abraaj needed external financial advice to help develop a strategy to alleviate its ongoing cash-flow issues and to help in the sale negotiations. People familiar with the board deliberations at the time told me that Badr Jafar suggested that the board retain Houlihan Lokey, a globally renowned restructuring and investment banking financial services company based in the US. Houlihan Lokey had spent the previous six months working closely with Dana Gas, a public company primarily owned and controlled by the Jafars.[21] Interestingly, the Jafars again re-appointed Houlihan Lokey as their financial advisers in July 2020 on an entirely separate matter.[22] Although some senior Abraaj executives have told me that they were uncomfortable because they felt that Houlihan might be communicating with the Jafars outside the AHL boardroom, Naqvi welcomed Houlihan's involvement because it represented 'feet on the ground' and intellectual muscle; something he had been cut off from within Abraaj. Houlihan's team was thorough in their diligence exercise of verifying the asset and liability positions on the balance sheet and agreed a standstill with the secured creditors whilst they evaluated restructuring options and protective measures; Houlihan was keen that Abraaj file for Chapter 11 bankruptcy protection in the US as opposed to Freshfields and then the Allen & Overy legal teams, who felt that seeking protection in the

Cayman Islands was more appropriate. As Naqvi learnt about these processes, it became clear that Chapter 11 would have resulted in control passing to unsecured creditors: Jafar and the PIFSS.

Through April the media tumult was vociferous. All fundraising and investment activity by Abraaj had been ceased. AIML and AHL had separated, the DFSA was by now actively investigating Abraaj, buyers were circling and Naqvi was attempting to construct a viable sale for the private equity platform. In this context, Cerberus appeared as an attractive potential buyer despite having virtually no international presence and no directly relevant private equity experience. Its main business was acquiring distressed debt, but it also owned businesses like DynCorp, a major national security contractor for the US government, and the Cerberus chairman, Steve Feinberg, and CEO, Frank Bruno, were directly overseeing the interest in Abraaj, which showed that the transaction was highly political and that as a result the approach required senior attention.[23]

In April, Naqvi faced renewed pressure to sign a single agreement between Jafar and AHL and AIML accepting liability with himself as an additional guarantor. The official Abraaj board position was that the borrowers were AE2L and Naqvi personally. Naqvi agreed to sign on the condition that he would be signing two distinct documents: one on behalf of himself and one on behalf of Abraaj. Hamid Jafar told him this would not work and that he was writing to the AHL board to inform them that his position was that the money was owed by the group directly, rather than AE2L or AIML. A board meeting was arranged on 2 May to discuss the security package that could be offered by Abraaj directly to Hamid Jafar. Meanwhile, a threatening letter was sent from Hamid Jafar seeking immediate full repayment of all $300 million plus penal interest as outstanding amounts from Abraaj directly and asserting that he was ready to present the security cheques for payment, but omitting to mention the $33 million repayment that Naqvi had already made to reduce his personal liability portion earlier in March.[24]

Jafar ought to have known that the cheques would bounce because Naqvi had already paid him back all he could from his own assets but he had every legal right to cash them.[25] If the cheques were cashed and could not be honoured it was inevitable, because of the way in which the law of the UAE works with respect to bounced cheques both personal and company, that criminal proceedings would commence. It was also inevitable, if this course of action were followed, that debt would be ascribed to AIML, which up to this point had not had any debt ascribed to it because the cheques were company cheques. In the UAE, if a company cheque bounces immediate legal proceedings are initiated. This is not as fast as if a personal cheque bounces but it is nevertheless inevitable. It is impossible to know why the Jafars acted in this way but it is possible to see the negative consequences of their actions for what they logically could have been trying to achieve. It could be, as Simeon Kerr wrote in the *Financial Times*, that they were just desperate to get their money back somehow. Though if this were the case, their actions made it less likely that they would get their money back.[26]

Abraaj became effectively insolvent and filed for voluntary creditor protection in the Cayman Islands.[27] At this point Abraaj's assets still exceeded its liabilities despite the cash-flow issues, but some of the debt began to be duplicated on both sets of entities (e.g. Jafar had filed his claims at both AH and AIML).

As reported in the *Financial Times*, it was at this point that the PIFSS and Hamid Jafar pushed for a separate liquidation process,[28] which effectively resulted in splitting AHL and AIML into two because the debt to the Jafars was ascribed to AIML.[29]

The cheques were presented to the Commercial Bank of Dubai on 3 May and were not honoured; the matter was now in the public domain and instantly reported by the *Wall Street Journal*, Bloomberg and Reuters. It was one thing to have allegations of impropriety that were being contested; it was quite another not to be able to honour payments. Abraaj was besieged by creditors, suppliers and investors; all demanding their money be returned. This was now the proverbial 'run on the bank'. This was the tipping point in the relationship between Naqvi and the Jafars. Prior to the presentation of the cheques, Naqvi seems to have assumed that, despite their disagreements, the Jafars wanted to recover the money Abraaj owed them. Cashing the cheques (including one that covered Naqvi's personal liability) looks on the face of it unduly aggressive and also on the face of it detrimental to the Jafars' own commercial interests. If it could be proven in court that Naqvi had written the cheques in bad faith then this would place Naqvi in the centre of a criminal case. That would not only do serious reputational damage to Naqvi personally; it would also, if there was a conviction, lead to virtually all of Abraaj's LPAs being cancelled across all funds. Within all the LPAs across the whole industry there are clauses that ensure that individuals who have criminal convictions cannot be 'key men' in the operating funds. Naqvi was the key man in virtually all Abraaj funds operating, so a conviction would bring chaos to the firm and mean that new key men would have to be appointed to the funds. This would have to be someone who was acceptable to the limited partners, which would have needed complex negotiations at a time of crisis. It remains a mystery as to why the Jafars behaved in this way and seemingly against their own interests.

The Jafar approach was echoed by the behaviour of the PIFSS. Naqvi's back was truly against the wall; attempting to ensure the completion of the Karachi Electric deal and selling the asset management platform to the highest bidder was now the only option. Even at the throwaway values – compared with their real worth – that were being discussed at this time, the proceeds from these deals would have been sufficient to meet all outstanding liabilities.

Throughout May, the AHL board had been obsessed with structuring a security package for Hamid Jafar to the complete dismay of the secured banking creditors, who independently refused to allow Jafar to assume any security whatsoever.[30] On 19 May, media reports highlighted that two separate examinations into the alleged commingling of money at Abraaj had found potential operational irregularities beyond the healthcare fund but without any allegations of any funds missing.[31] The media claimed that the Ankura audit commissioned by the four AGHF investors had suggested that money from the healthcare fund had been diverted elsewhere although that report was never made available to Abraaj; just selectively leaked to the press. Preliminary findings from a separate review by Deloitte at Abraaj's request also threw up potential discrepancies in the accounting of some of the other funds but did not report that any money was missing. Separately, to quell at least one fire at a general meeting of AGHF in May, the AIML team collectively agreed to reduce their exposure to criticism and so handed the fund over to AlixPartners, a US advisory firm, who later sold it to TPG, a large private equity firm based in the US.[32]

Naqvi and Houlihan Lokey now put forward a restructuring plan, which was worked on by a number of industry experts, who not only considered it viable but also endorsed it. This plan outlined a clear roadmap to the return of 100 per cent of both secured and unsecured liabilities with the support of the secured banking consortium. However, given that the PIFSS made up a significant portion of the unsecured creditor pool, it had enough blocking power to ensure that creditors would not receive even a fraction of their money back by blocking both the sale to Cerberus or Colony and the rescue package proposed by Naqvi and the outside experts.[33]

*Forbes* described the behaviour of the PIFSS in the following way:

> Many creditors who are owed a combined $1 billion agreed to explore a restructuring deal in early May. But the ... PIFSS, an unsecured lender, demanded liquidation proceedings following a default this summer on $100 million in debt plus $7 million in interest. The loan was part of a $200 million five-year lending deal signed in 2013. The Kuwaitis fast-forwarded the crisis at Abraaj, which was trying to sell some of its assets to private

equity firms, like Cerberus Capital Management in the US. Cerberus walked away as a potential buyer this summer when it became clear that PIFSS wanted to force a bankruptcy. Such a move would cheapen the value of the assets a buyer was acquiring. As a lender, the Kuwaitis were the most aggressive … Abraaj held numerous meetings with the Kuwaitis and other lenders starting in the second quarter. At the time people working on the Abraaj firm's restructuring wondered why an unsecured lender would do such a thing, because unsecured lenders are the last lenders to be paid.[34]

Hence, simultaneously with the Jafar assault, the final element in the seemingly orchestrated process of bringing down Abraaj was played by the PIFSS. This led some to conclude that the return of capital or acting on its fiduciary responsibilities seemed to be less important for the PIFSS than bringing down Abraaj. A very senior banker remarked at the time, 'This is the State of Kuwait vs Arif Naqvi.'[35] If Abraaj went into liquidation, the PIFSS would be the last to be paid and it was in their interests for that not to happen. Logically therefore, the PIFSS should have been heavily involved in all discussions and negotiations that might have prevented liquidation, rather than actively seeking the Abraaj liquidation themselves. Instead, it was largely absent from the discussions about restructuring or simply would not engage and regularly sent junior representatives to meetings who could not make decisions.[36] Reuters reported that:

'The secured creditors are expected to imminently conclude a standstill which will provide Abraaj the ability to meet its obligations in an orderly fashion,' Abraaj said in a statement after a meeting with lenders, shareholders, and other parties to discuss the restructuring of the firm. Most of the creditors agreed to the standstill, which would see Abraaj's debt frozen

for around ninety to 120 days, two sources said, estimating
Abraaj's total debt at around $1 billion. But the sources said that
in order for the sale of its business [*sic*] investment management
business to go ahead, Abraaj needs the support of all lenders,
including unsecured creditors. A potential obstacle to that deal
emerged when … PIFSS … an unsecured creditor, refused to
agree to the standstill, the sources said.[37]

The culmination of the PIFSS's stance came on 25 May, two weeks before
its loan was due for repayment, when Abraaj learnt that the PIFSS had
filed a winding-up petition against AHL in the Cayman Islands in
regard to its 2013 loan. The law in Cayman requires that in response to a
winding-up petition a company either consents or itself files for what is
called a joint provisional liquidation (JPL) process, effectively a protected
restructuring under the guidance of the court. This filing also torpedoed
the attempt to sell Abraaj as a coherent entity with value as it led to Colony
Capital backing away from the deal on 31 May leaving only Cerberus at
the table, who continued to pursue the acquisition by gradually offering
less and less. The Abraaj board had to make a decision and the creditors
had to be consulted. As both Reuters and *Forbes* reported, the approach
and behaviour of the PIFSS was noted to be strange by the broader
creditor group, especially given the number of viable options that were
on the table; each of which would have ensured that all creditors, both
secured and unsecured, got their money back.[38]

Naqvi now returned to his continued attempt to execute the Karachi
Electric deal because its completion was the only alternative that would
solve all Abraaj's issues. He was due to fly to Islamabad later that same
evening but, to his shock, he was detained at the airport as there was a
warrant out for his arrest in Dubai. However, a rare lack of coordination
between the police and immigration systems meant that he was eventually
allowed to board, mistakenly as far as the police were concerned.
According to a fellow Abraaj stakeholder who was an eyewitness present

at the airport, Naqvi called Badr Jafar before he boarded. This witness alleges that Naqvi told them immediately after the call that Badr Jafar said that Naqvi should have known better than to have picked the fight that he had. Since that date, Naqvi has never returned to Dubai. The deck was stacked against him and his known adversary was powerful; he had no idea how powerful his unknown adversary was but he was soon to find out. Lawyers in the UAE told me that they would normally consider it impossible for the claimant at that stage of the proceedings to have obtained an arrest warrant or have a criminal complaint filed. When a corporate cheque is issued, the law requires a court to find that the signatories who signed the cheque did so dishonestly without assurance that funds would be in place to honour an eventual presentation; at that stage there had been no time for a case to have been filed let alone heard.

On 4 June, following a meeting with all creditors the day before, the AHL board with the agreement of all secured and unsecured creditors (except the Jafars and the PIFSS) agreed to appoint PwC as joint provisional liquidators to pursue the potential restructuring of Abraaj, whilst also agreeing to sign a letter of intent with Cerberus to acquire AIML.[39] Almost immediately though, Cerberus withdrew its written offer and came back with a much lower offer to acquire AIML for $5 million, which the board rejected.[40] During these negotiations, the Cerberus executives made it clear to Naqvi that what they really wanted was the IGCF fund and Karachi Electric.[41]

The endgame was swift and unstoppable and was reported blow by blow in the media. The *Wall Street Journal* and Bloomberg were reporting events often before Naqvi or the senior management team at AIML knew what was happening. It was like reality TV for the participants; they felt like they were being led to a destination rather than having any ability to influence what was happening. Sources with knowledge of the events have confirmed that Jafar had hired a PR agency based in the UAE, who were having daily confidential briefings with key journalists and presumably directing a strategic communications campaign against Naqvi and his reputation in Dubai.[42]

On 7 June, Naqvi asked Waqar Siddique to come to Islamabad and assist on the Karachi Electric transaction; Siddique was still chairman of Karachi Electric and also Naqvi's brother-in-law. When attempting to leave Dubai, Siddique was told that he was banned from travelling but no reason was given. In the case of Naqvi, it appeared that whatever legal process existed had been thwarted by making sure that the criminal arrest warrant was in place even before a civil case for dishonouring corporate cheques had been filed. Siddique however was utterly unconnected with the cheques and the ongoing discussion with the creditors; however, this forced Naqvi to the table. If somebody was preventing him from leaving, as sources close to these events have alleged, then anonymously pulling the levers of state power is a powerful tool to have in your arsenal, and very few have it. Allen & Overy and Dr Habib Al-Mulla, chairman of eminent law firm Baker & McKenzie Habib Al Mulla and former chairman of the DFSA, made enquiries but there was no record in the system that indicated that any arm of the UAE government was involved in keeping Siddique in Dubai, and yet, although he tried repeatedly, he could not leave.

On 10 June, Deloitte's review found that Abraaj had commingled about $95 million between funds managed by it and the company's own accounts, according to Bloomberg.[43] Abraaj continued to maintain that money had been commingled between funds, but this was not in breach of the LPAs and was thus perfectly legitimate behaviour according to the legal opinion provided to them by Freshfields in relation to AGHF. On Monday 11 June, following marathon talks between Naqvi and Addleshaw Goddard with Hamid Jafar and his team over the removal of all travel bans, which had lasted uninterrupted since 8 June, an agreement appeared to have been reached; however, Naqvi received a call from the Cayman Islands informing him that the Jafars had already filed for liquidation in the jurisdiction against AIML on the Friday before.

This accelerated the restructuring plans and forced Abraaj into action. The Naqvi and Houlihan Lokey restructuring plans from May were updated, PwC were engaged in London to oversee the protective JPL process in the Cayman Islands and, on 12 June, the AHL board announced that it planned to file for provisional liquidation in the Caymans.

The co-CEOs of AIML now threw a spanner into the works and informed the board of AHL that they had decided to independently file for a JPL process despite the fact that Houlihan, the board, Naqvi, Colony Capital, Allen & Overy and PwC all insisted that they were making a mistake. Yorgancioglu and Lodhi had developed aspirations of their own to buy the asset management platform that they had been given to manage or, at the very least, strike their own deals with an incoming buyer; they, and their newly promoted management team of Bisher Barazi, Peter Brady, Giles Montgomery-Swann, Matt McGuire and Paul Blessing, proved suspicious of every move made by AHL. These five had risen to the top because many of the Abraaj stars had left. Going forward, as going concerns the two entities could theoretically operate independently but the overhead structure was too large for AIML to manage from the fees that were being generated and they needed continuous support from AHL, which led to unwise decisions made to cut costs that contributed to the media frenzy. But in a restructuring process involving historical records and assets, it was crucial to treat the group as one integrated entity since it had operated that way since inception and it was impossible to reallocate the balance sheet assets; after all, they belonged to the shareholders, who also shouldered all the liabilities. Holistically, AHL was where the external assets and investments of the group sat, in addition to all liabilities, both secured and unsecured. AIML was essentially a captive entity that could only operate on its own if it was sold for consideration and under the ambit of a new buyer with patience and deep pockets. AIML was the fund management entity and owned the GPs of the various funds, but the value was nominal; its main operating activity was to receive management fees from all the funds and spend it in the operations of the group, with shortfalls being financed by AHL. Separated, it would only have liabilities to suppliers and be insolvent from the outset since that was how it had historically evolved and it relied on AHL to fund it. However, AIML's new management had its own interests to guard and seemed unwilling to listen; they appointed Deloitte as JPL for AIML and petitioned the Cayman Islands court to give them a hearing at the same time as AHL. The task of managing such a complex business and keeping all the individual pieces going without what appears to have been, in the opinion of some observers in the industry, either sufficient prior experience or management skills, which meant that mistakes may have been compounded by inexperience.

On 14 June, after the announcement of a provisional liquidation process being initiated, Colony returned to the table to engage with AHL (having cited the liquidation petition by the PIFSS as the reason for having walked away two weeks earlier) and presented a comprehensive deal to acquire a significant proportion of the AIML business in an offer worth almost $500 million – excluding the Asian funds (ASEAF II, APEF IV and IGCF) – which would have enabled Abraaj to settle with the majority of its creditors. The nature of the offer itself brought clarity and at this point it became clear to Naqvi, Houlihan and the board why AIML had insisted on filing its own JPL application. The new offer by Colony specifically excluded Omar Lodhi, one of the AIML co-CEOs, because of the exclusion of the Asian funds. It now emerged that the co-CEOs had differences amongst themselves as well; Lodhi was determined to work with Cerberus, whilst Yorgancioglu wanted to work with Colony. Unbeknownst to Naqvi and the board, Lodhi and Yorgancioglu must have been negotiating with both bidders on a parallel track. According to sources close to the events, Colony allegedly did not want to take on Lodhi and the Asia business but was willing to deal with Yorgancioglu because he led one of the geographies, Turkey, that interested them. This meant that Lodhi went to New York to pursue the Cerberus option. Sources close to these discussions allege that Cerberus advised him to pursue the separated liquidation processes for AHL and for AIML. Hindsight suggests that all Cerberus was really interested in acquiring was IGCF, which owned Karachi Electric. The evidence of contemporaneous reporting suggests that these actions and the commencement of the two separate processes was partly a product of the competition between the joint-CEOs or their ambitions, but the division between the two entities, which Houlihan Lokey and others and argued strongly against, accentuated the problems. The entire value destruction in the Abraaj estate and the actions that followed can be traced to the separation of the company into two parts and then to the commencement of these two separate processes.

Naqvi wanted cash and a sale to cushion the JPL process and to allow a restructuring and therefore agreed the deal with Colony. His interests were clear, if perhaps selfish. He wanted the carving up of the Abraaj estate outside the public eye and within a protective JPL process because, by this stage, with an offer on the table, the incentive was no longer to save or restructure the business; it was to minimise the reputational damage, keep the accumulated carried interest for all the employees intact (not to mention his own substantial portion, which, in the restructuring plan that he submitted later in August, he proposed to contribute into Abraaj, alongside his contractual claims, in an effort to ensure that creditors would be fully repaid) and repay the creditors so that he could pursue new interests without being branded a failure. Central to his thinking was the need for a successful sale process of Karachi Electric, not only to release the cash for the estate creditors, but also because it would ensure that his reputation in Pakistan would be improved. The Colony offer, which he accepted with alacrity, and convinced PwC as the JPLs of the AHL estate to accept as well, was favoured because Colony seemed less volatile and more reliable than Cerberus.

The deal was reported in the media: 'Abraaj Group inks a pact with New York-listed Colony Capital, Inc., reaching an agreement for the sale and purchase of the Group's Latin America, Sub Saharan Africa, North Africa and Turkey Funds management business and the group's limited partnership interests in the underlying funds.'[44] This 'done' deal was completed just before the hearing to appoint the provisional liquidators in the Caymans, and needed to be completed under the care of the PwC JPL and, having consulted with them throughout the negotiations, PwC had also agreed to the transaction in advance. Cerberus and Lodhi had been outmanoeuvred but at that point Cerberus did something very curious: it made an offer to the board to take over *only* the legacy funds, which effectively comprised APEF IV, IGCF and ASEAF II. The rationale of doing so appeared to be to gain control over the sale process of Karachi Electric and for Omar Lodhi to oversee it.

On 18 June, a Cayman Islands court[45] approved the appointment of PwC as joint liquidators for AHL, whilst Deloitte were appointed for AIML despite the objections of AHL.[46]

The Cayman Islands court must have been like Piccadilly Circus that day. Separate QCs, separate legal firms, separate insolvency practitioners and separate provisional liquidators were representing AHL and AIML, the board, Hamid Jafar and the PIFSS; but unsolicited and without an apparent role to play, APEF IV, IGCF, AGHF, Hamilton Lane, CDC, the IFC and the BMGF all sent legal representatives to ensure that they had a voice at the table as well. The fee-fest had started and there was a feeding frenzy as service providers lined up for a bite at the carcass of Abraaj.

With the JPLs appointed, Naqvi returned his focus on getting Siddique out of Dubai. The pressure within the family was intense because Naqvi knew that although he was safe from the application of the medieval law which imprisoned debtors, his brother-in-law seemed unlikely to be able to leave until he had dealt with the Jafar liability personally and signed over personal assets and wealth. Apart from the $33 million Naqvi had transferred to Hamid Jafar in March, known to the creditor banks at the time, Naqvi apparently handed over personal assets which had been agreed by both parties at the time to be worth approximately an incremental $150 million. A source with direct knowledge of those discussions said that, in the process, Naqvi signed over virtually all his personal and family assets, emptying trust structures and taking on the balance of the corporate liability personally. Despite this, Jafar also asserted claims in the creditor estates of both AHL and AIML, according to Cayman Islands court records, to which he might have been entitled in terms of debt but the consequences of which, as we have seen, was to allocate debt to these companies and thereby force them into their own liquidation. Strangely, very soon thereafter, the criminal case in Sharjah against Naqvi was dropped. Siddique also became free to travel out of Dubai at the same time.

The trauma from this episode for Naqvi's entire family was considerable but more was to follow. What Naqvi did not realise was that having depleted himself of his assets and his ability to fight the battles that lay ahead, he was tying both of his hands behind his back when it came to dealing with the myriad issues he now faced. In the world of insolvency and restructuring, Naqvi was a fish out of water. His lack of experience proved to be damning.

# 11

# Liquidations and betrayals

AIML had historically been responsible for managing the funds as well as holding the nominal equity interest in all the GPs operated by Abraaj. AHL made the investments for the group into those funds in addition to other investments alongside the funds and was also primarily responsible for injecting capital into the growth of the platform: it was a firm that grew beyond its management fee income's ability to match its cost base during the growth and consolidation years. This was done in order to grow further and build its defensible advantage in the emerging market space – with the eventual idea that Abraaj's presence would grow to a stage where it did not need to increase its cost base and continue raising funds and adding assets under management to its books, which would lead to an immediate increase in profitability.

So to illustrate the point, Abraaj had a cost base that exceeded its fee income annually by approximately $25 million but the raising of APEF VI would have had two concurrent effects; the cost base would have gone down through office closures and the exit of senior personnel and cost reductions approximating that deficit, since the firm would no longer need regional silos and replicated functions; whilst, at the same time, the expected annual fee income would go straight towards the bottom line of approximately $120 million and completely transform

231

the economics of the firm. There was much at stake which explains the relentless drive to raise APEF VI; it was like the launch of a new iPhone for Abraaj. As described earlier, in some ways Abraaj had behaved like a tech start-up to this point. Like Amazon or Facebook, Abraaj developed over a long period without immediate profits to plough that money back in to grow the company so that there would be the security of greater profits over a longer term through an eventual IPO. These companies grow and burn capital to build moats. But this Abraaj fund platform, which was eventually sold through the mismanaged liquidation process by Deloitte, was sold in aggregate value for a fraction of its true worth, not really to pay creditors given the quantum collected, but to settle fees.

As JPL of the AIML estate, Deloitte immediately realised that there were no assets and that AIML was an entity that could exist only with support from its parent entity. However, Deloitte demanded a seat at the table with Colony and the disruption this caused probably led to the deal falling through. That left the $5 million deal with Cerberus as the only option, which was patently unreasonable and was rejected. Instead, Deloitte commenced a disastrous process to sell the asset management platform piece by piece and fund by fund.[1] The $1 billion AGHF was taken over by TPG's growth platform for free, renaming it Evercare Health Fund[2] and Colony Capital acquired the Latin America private equity platform, including its $300 million Latin America Fund II.[3] Franklin Templeton was reported to have acquired the $526 million Abraaj Turkey Fund.[4] UK-based Actis acquired five of Abraaj's Africa funds, including the $990 million Africa Fund III and the $375 million North Africa Fund II.[5] The Abraaj art collection was also sold off for a fraction of its value.[6]

The decision to separate the company in the liquidation process was highly detrimental to the recovery of funds. With Abraaj Holdings and AIML separated, each liquidator proceeded to claim that various assets belonged to their component. It's a type of dance that is always performed in liquidations and the only beneficiary is inevitably the fee-earners, not the creditors; the argument is created to ensure involvement. Each liquidator demanded and asserted proprietary claims on one another's estate. Into this mix entered a third party that had nothing to do with the creditors of the group, whose interests the liquidators were meant to serve and protect. This third party was actually at least a dozen additional separate parties, including the larger limited partner advisory committees of the various funds, with the common thread being the assertiveness of the IFC, Bank of America Merrill Lynch and Hamilton Lane, along with the BMGF (i.e. US-based investors). They all wanted a say in deciding who the next asset managers were going to be and Deloitte obliged them. There is an argument I have heard that says that by doing so Deloitte did not act in the interests of the parties it was meant to represent, namely the creditors. However, I am no lawyer and do not profess expertise in the nuances of the liquidation process except to say that it appears there will be many more parties suing each other in the years to come. That is just the way this particular dance plays out.

It is not my intent in writing this book to chronicle what happened next; the liquidation will be a long and costly process with no winners except the fee-earners. Up to the point at which the liquidators were appointed, I have pulled the narrative together such that it shows me clearly that the sequence of events and the changes in attitudes of key individuals had inevitable consequences because they accentuated the demise of the firm's standing and hindered its capacity to do business in the future. The business lay in ruins and, as a final twist of the sword, Naqvi was sent a message with an attached photograph by Paul Blessing, a junior employee, of the vacated Abraaj offices in Dubai which looked like a train wreck; boxes, files, overturned tables, paper everywhere, a complete disaster, with the words: 'Look what happened to your empire.'

How should we understand the actions and the reactions of the key players in this drama during the take-down? Many of the Abraaj team suffered from hubris and a sense of invulnerability, which was not actually as naive or foolish as it appears at first glance. Imagine for a

233

moment that the most powerful state in the world was dead set against allowing the one thing you needed to happen, to save your bacon, from happening. Imagine further that successive Prime Ministers of the country in which that event was taking place were telling you that it would be properly resolved imminently. You would, in those circumstances, have a clear choice. Either to stop dead, assume a foetal position and wait for the shit to get kicked out of you, or keep running as hard you can towards the finishing line not looking down but looking ahead. If you had paused to look down, you would have seen a series of trip wires had been laid across your path. There is no such thing as perfect knowledge outside the abstract models of econometrics; the human condition is imperfect knowledge driven by hope.

The senior management team of Abraaj was also a house divided against itself. That division was partly a product of founder's syndrome. This happens so often in charisma-based leadership models that it should not come as any surprise that it happened at Abraaj. Arif Naqvi had built a global company in part by the sheer force of his personality. He knew he had to bring big beasts into that company and take a step or two back if it was going to move to the next stage of its development. A former board member of AHL told me that Naqvi often discussed succession plans with the board without other executives present; and that the collective view was that none of the others had any hope of succeeding him and all board members knew that a successor would have to be brought in from the outside once APEF VI had been completed and the path to the IPO opened. But knowing something and having sufficient control of your ego to let it happen are two very different things. When things are going well it is perhaps easier for the founder to step back. When things start going wrong, this is your baby that is being attacked and you will fight to the death to defend it.

If it had not been a leviathan they were up against, that might have worked. But Naqvi and his team faced the United States and for a long stretch of their battle they did not even know the identity of their real adversary. When the BMGF insisted on the appointment of Ankura as auditors of AGHF, their report was never submitted to Abraaj, but whilst it was being completed the DoJ had already commenced a parallel investigation. Wiretaps were employed, people were given immunity and others were likely coerced. Regulators fed each other and the DFSA was surely put under pressure by the SEC and the DoJ to follow rather than lead, and to attempt to recover lost ground by imposing fines on companies already in liquidation seemed like a feeble attempt to join the US bandwagon; this was confirmed during a conversation that a UK barrister had with a senior DFSA official in Dubai. Abraaj's email system was hacked and emails were leaked. What those emails showed is profoundly contested by all sides; remember that in this story each blind man holds a different part of the elephant. For the Dubai Financial Services Authority, this meant that Abraaj should pay a fine. For the DoJ this meant that Arif Naqvi should spend 291 years in jail. In the end, the courts will decide those issues. For now, we will take another look at what happened. The sequence of events is quite clear. Abraaj was desperately running to get to the point at which the money from the sale of Karachi Electric would arrive. It requested and accepted credit from long-time associates and board members: the Jafar family. The team asked long-term creditors, the PIFSS, for an extension on a loan. They attempted to sell shares and move other assets off their balance sheet to generate liquidity. At each point, exactly the worst possible thing that could happen then happened. Emails that had all the hallmarks and technical attributes that indicated they had been crafted by an intelligence agency or by an individual with such a background and expertise raised questions about Abraaj's probity, which ensured that the Karachi Electric transaction kept being delayed. The Jafars tried to force the issue allegedly to gain control of Karachi Electric and used legal processes in the UAE against Naqvi for bouncing cheques. Internal and external actors briefed the media on the inner workings of Abraaj, and US private equity firms came in to pick up the pieces at bargain basement prices. Hacked or leaked data was then delivered to the *Wall Street Journal*, which allowed them to feed the story at critical moments. Or were they provided with this information in a curated form as an element of the overall strategy? Indeed, if we consider the articles in the *Wall Street Journal*, we also come back to these central 'why' questions.

Before considering the specific role of the *Wall Street Journal*, we should consider the four main questions raised by the bonfire of Abraaj and the liquidation process itself:

1. Why has the Karachi Electric deal not concluded five years after it was signed?
2. If Abraaj itself was an organised criminal conspiracy what exactly was stolen?
3. Who has ultimately benefited from the closing of The Abraaj Group?
4. Why were there so many overt acts against Abraaj in concentrated periods of time and by both internal and external actors and were they linked in any way?

There are two plausible explanations and answers to these questions. Neither of which support the contentions of the DoJ that the group of executives named in the original indictment were conducting a criminal conspiracy and racketeering. The DoJ explanation does not work because of the multiple material and factual flaws in the indictment. I repeatedly attempted to get Naqvi to talk about the indictment or even the charges in an abstract form, but he refused on his lawyer's strict advice; he seemed to be more intimidated by his lawyers than the charges. However, he did share the fact that the series of WhatsApp messages quoted in the indictment were taken totally out of context and constructed to present a particular narrative; the selected messages were often weeks apart and intervening messages were not shown in the indictment, which would have shown that innocent actions appeared to be guilty actions thereby helping to build a self-serving and specific narrative.

The Abraaj Group was not hollowed out of cash leading to its liquidation and collapse. It became insolvent because of the actions of a range of malign actors. The real answer to the four key questions will perhaps never be known but it is in this interconnection of the internal and the external forces that the answer will lie. Following his diagnosis with cancer in December 2014, Naqvi was a man in even more of a hurry than he had been before. Rather than going for an IPO by 2023, he wanted it done by 2018 when the Pakistani national elections were scheduled to be held so that he could then go into full-time politics in a government under Imran Khan in Pakistan. That meant the movement to the single global fund, APEF VI, had to be sped up and that the regional hubs would no longer be the engine driving the company; a centralised business would be so much easier to manage by an outsider brought in to replace him, who was fit for purpose – Naqvi even knew who that person was and had preliminary conversations with them. Senior partners knew and were directly threatened by this development. Much of the senior team had a future in Abraaj so long as the legacy funds, like APEF IV and the other Gen-5 funds, had a life. After that point they would be out. This created a window of opportunity for them to take control of these funds themselves or negotiate exits from Abraaj to other private equity firms to be replaced by the rising stars in the firm who saw the potential of APEF VI and wanted to seize it. But other individuals must have understood that Naqvi's style, overstretch and political ambitions were vulnerable to attack in relation to his drawings and current account arrangements. Even if this was operated strictly in line with the letter of the board's policy it would not look that way to outsiders. I return to my fundamental question: if Naqvi had substantial drawings, was he entitled to them? Were the amounts drawn in line with what he should have been paid as per his contractual employment agreement? And when he took drawings, and before the amounts were reconciled as debits and credits, were the accounting entries made that reflected him having a liability? If these questions are answered there may have been a cash shortfall, but there was certainly no way to allege that money was missing or fraud involved.

Senior employees must also have understood that there was a fundamental difference between the legacy investors and the newer institutional investors from the US. Both these things could be exploited if done cleverly. They might also have understood that the change in the methodology for the valuation of assets could be easily misrepresented. In turn, several members of the Abraaj board must have understood that the liquidity problems created by the delay in the Karachi Electric sale made Naqvi uniquely vulnerable. At a specific point in time a white knight could be used to bridge the gap until either the Karachi Electric deal came through, APEF VI closed or assets were sold. With Abraaj in a vulnerable position, the Jafars stepped in. Perhaps they wanted to save the company. Perhaps they saw an opportunity to gain control over Karachi Electric. Or maybe given the weakness of Naqvi and Abraaj's position they saw the opportunity of salvaging something with their chosen bidders: Cerberus. There are a number of possible logical explanations to their actions. But their post-facto push for perfected documentation in respect of their loans perversely reduced their ability to recoup their funds, and the imposition of debt to AIML through encashing security cheques at the same time that the PIFSS filed a winding-up order forced the company onto the path to liquidation. They were far too savvy as global businesspeople not to have known that or not to have factored it in into their thinking.

The Jafars were not alone in acting in ways that appear to be against their own interests. The other seemingly irrational actor in all this appears to be the PIFSS. Again, they might have acted this way because of their own local difficulties or problems with their previous director, who had been removed for disputed allegations of corruption but had overseen the granting of the original loan to Abraaj.

Perhaps the Jafars and the PIFSS played their parts in the bringing down of Abraaj because of individual feuds with Arif Naqvi and key senior staff acted against the group by leaking to the press information that was then misrepresented. Perhaps also when all of this information was given to the DoJ it spontaneously decided on the basis of its well-established judicial activism in the financial field to open an investigation, despite the absence of US creditors at the AHL level. Then, given the number of players in Abraaj with well-established intelligence backgrounds and the others who were preparing to quit to avoid being made redundant, it was not difficult to find people prepared to become witnesses to ensure that they had immunity. At that point, they clearly had an interest in shifting blame and painting pictures of events and processes in the most dramatic light possible to cast shade on Arif Naqvi.

The SDNY team who launched the prosecution and unsealed the indictment has their own colourful history of highly politicised cases.[7] For one example, look at the case of Premium Point Investments co-founder Anilesh Ahuja, who was convicted of securities fraud and given fifty months in prison in 2018. He and his co-defendant would later allege that federal prosecutors added the statement 'I knew what I was doing was wrong' to his own words given in cooperation with the court, and that this was not disclosed to him until June 2020. Other differences included an expansion of the timeline when the asset mismarking took place and the added mention of Jeremy Shor, his co-defendant.[8] A second case following on the heels Ahuja was that of Ali Sadr Hashemi Nejad, who faced similar accusations of politicised sharp practice. The man in question, an Iranian national, was indicted on charges of conspiracy to defraud the United States, conspiracy to violate the International Emergency Economic Powers Act, bank fraud and money laundering offences in 2018, and found guilty on five counts in March 2020. After trial, Sadr moved a motion for a new trial and the federal government asked the district court to vacate its verdict and drop all charges. The reason given for this was for similar failures of the prosecution, failures of disclosure, of misconduct around government handling of search warrants and the hiding of exculpatory evidence.[9] This is a department that has faced multiple judicial rebukes over its proceedings.[10] Despite this, however, the relentless momentum of the US justice system pushes ever forward, and once the indictment was unsealed the lives of the accused were effectively placed in stasis.

Each defendant then entered the Kafkaesque world and each became the other's potential nemesis. The entire system of plea bargaining and deal making is designed to concentrate guilt on specific targets if they do not play ball. In multiple other cases in which the operation of financial institutions has been questioned it has been left to the regulator to deal with the matter. Or if the issue came to court for there to be fines to pay. It is only in a few highly selective prosecutions that the decision is made to throw the book at the accused. If the sale of Karachi Electric had concluded in a timely manner or if the sale of AHL's balance sheet assets had not been scuppered by leaks to the press, we would not be reading this story. You might be able to explain the careful spoon-feeding of material to the willing recipients at the *Wall Street Journal* by the initial actions of senior Abraaj team members on their way out. So, there could be an individual explanation for all of these things. But even if all of these developments are explained in this way the fact remains that no money was stolen since all transfers were recorded as either an asset or an expense and approved by the policy of the board. Changes in valuation were standard practice and no evidence for bribery was offered or charges made. There is no case to answer, which raises the question: why did the case arise and why has the prosecution and extradition process taken place?

The answer can only be geopolitical rather than judicial.

Once this kind of process begins it is impossible or very difficult to stop it until it comes before a judge. If Trump had been re-elected in 2021, then the case would have been directly in line with his administration's China policy. In fact, that policy has not altered significantly with Biden. Preventing Karachi Electric being sold to the Chinese, keeping Chinese private equity investments out of emerging markets and keeping Pakistan dependent on IMF loans for liquidity remain the policy of the United States.

Consider the far more publicised case of US opposition to Nord Stream 2 that has been playing out in 2021 involving Germany, Russia, Ukraine and the US in geopolitics and the remarkable similarity to the Karachi Electric sale and geopolitics involving Pakistan, China, India and the US. Nord Stream 2 is seen as a threat to US national interests and Gazprom as a threat to US energy companies and Russia needs to be curtailed. The sale of Karachi Electric is seen as a threat to US national interests and Abraaj as a threat to US private equity firms and China needs to be curtailed. There is a Ukrainian man facing judicial overreach on the 'energy' rights of the US in the broader elements of the first case; and there is a Pakistani man facing judicial overreach on the 'energy' rights of the US in the second case; both are desperately fighting extradition in jurisdictions that cower before the leviathan. Both individuals in these cases were meant to be rich, but it turns out that one used almost all his money trying to save his company with the facts he had at that time; but if Naqvi was so connected, how could this have happened?

Arif Naqvi might have survived being a problem for the United States if he had been an obstacle in just one of the respects identified above, but being an obstacle in all of them proved fatal. Even after a change of administration it remains in the interests of the US for Naqvi to go down and if his co-defendants do not cooperate with the DoJ and agree to testify for the SDNY then they can go down as well. It is important for the tattered reputation of the SDNY team that Naqvi is not vindicated and that his case does not collapse or get tossed out. If it does collapse Naqvi could be propelled back into the politics of Pakistan. This case will be allowed to collapse only after either the break-up and sale of the Karachi Electric monopoly has been achieved, with US firms picking up some part of what is sold, or the sale to Chinese interests falls away. Once this is achieved there will be little point in pursuing the case, which is highly unlikely to succeed anyway. The indictment has, in that sense, already achieved its wider geopolitical objective, with much personal collateral damage.

# 12

# The *Wall Street Journal* and the death of Abraaj

*The press does not tell you what to think,*
*it tells you what to think about.*

Stanley Baran

The *Wall Street Journal* reporters who authored *The Key Man* say that they got much of their material by reviewing the indictments and SEC claims; but many of the indictments and SEC claims also appear to mirror much of what the *Wall Street Journal* had been reporting sequentially in the fourteen months leading up to the indictment being unsealed. Who was the cart and who was the horse?

At the beginning of the take-down operation in the winter of 2017/18, the *Wall Street Journal* began to bombard Abraaj's PR team with a series of questions, sometimes sending emails at 8 p.m. or 10 p.m. and demanding responses the next day. From that time until August 2018, Abraaj and the PR firm Finsbury and thereafter Naqvi and his lawyers and PR advisers, Simkins and Project Associates, provided a series of detailed on-the-record and off-the-record responses as quickly as they could. Simon Clark and a range of his colleagues at the *Wall Street Journal* then wrote a major article and follow-up pieces, which reproduced almost all the allegations with varying accounts and details before the indictment came out, but with very little coverage of the responses. A former member of the Abraaj PR team told me that Naqvi gave a two- or three-hour recorded telephone interview with Simon Clark as well as an in-person interview with the *Wall Street Journal* Dubai correspondent almost immediately after the initial article was published. Nothing, this source claims, that Naqvi said was reported. Nothing. The articles were based on either leaked or hacked emails from Abraaj's servers. Without seeing the entire email chains from which the content has been selected it is impossible to know how accurate the journalist's interpretations of the contents of the messages are or how selective they have been. Indeed, without seeing the entire archive it is impossible to say how selective the leaker or hacker has been. For the same reason it is impossible to entirely judge how accurate Abraaj or Naqvi's responses were. But given the overall context presented so far in this book it is not hard to see what the source was trying to achieve and the extent to which the *Wall Street Journal* wittingly or unwittingly helped them hit every target they shot for.

All the questions raised reflect the issues in the subsequent DFSA report or those in the DoJ or SEC indictments. We know from other evidence that elements of the allegations are repeated there and that they are all profoundly contested; a dispute that will be decided by courts. A deeper question is: who or what was the source for all of these leaked documents? And why did they surface when they did? Their purpose was all too obvious.

Naqvi appeared to have provided responses to the questions he was asked. Clark persisted in sending more questions over the course of a number of months, sometimes adding in new questions or repeating the same questions with slightly different wording. As so little of these responses made it into the published articles, it is not clear why he was so persistent aside perhaps from the need to satisfy his editors that he was not just reproducing his quotes from the leaked material uncritically.

The on-the-record responses from Naqvi were clear and unambiguous in his denial of the claims that were to appear in the *Wall Street Journal* articles. As at the time of writing he has not made any public statement, these replies are the only public record of Naqvi's response to the allegations against him. They therefore deserve to be seen at length:

> The allegations against me are entirely false and vehemently denied. They are premised on isolated extracts from illegally obtained documents taken out of context. It appears that unidentified individuals who are unfairly biased against me and Abraaj are seeking to undermine the sale of K-Electric, damage my and Abraaj's reputation, and thereby prejudice the creditors of The Abraaj Group.
>
> I have never contemplated, directed, authorised, or paid any bribes with respect to the K-Electric sale. I am a patriot of Pakistan and the sale was and remains in the best interest of the country.
>
> It is also untrue that I either inflated the value of the funds' assets or otherwise misled investors or regulators. I was and still remain an advocate of proper marking of investments even when that entailed mark downs in some instances as is reflected in the illegally obtained emails in the *Wall Street Journal*'s possession. Valuation principles were actively debated by senior management and discussed with key external investors before being adopted across the Group to determine individual asset values.
>
> In respect of any allegations about my use of Abraaj funds, I confirm that I have neither misused nor misappropriated any Abraaj funds. There was nothing untoward about my requests for transfers of Abraaj Group funds to me or my family, or for

my personal investments or obligations. In drawing down funds from Abraaj, I acted in accordance with the arrangements put in place by The Abraaj Group. All drawdowns were properly recorded and accounted for, as were the set offs of compensation owed to me and transfers from me to Abraaj or for its benefit.

Abraaj sought and received independent legal advice as to whether it was permissible for it to use money from the health-care fund for Abraaj's general corporate purposes. Subsequently, two international audit firms confirmed that all uninvested monies were accounted for and returned to investors in the healthcare fund with interest as of 31 December 2017.

On the general question of commingling of funds, the Naqvi response, contained in letters to Clark from his lawyers, was that 'substantial monies were also transferred in the opposite direction as well. Some amounts were transferred to Abraaj to settle intercompany balances and bridge positions that Abraaj had taken on behalf of those funds. All transfers were properly recorded and accounted for.'

On the more specific allegations, Naqvi's lawyers maintained that

money from the healthcare fund was used by Abraaj on a temporary basis for general corporate purposes and was always available to the healthcare fund on a demand deposit basis as required to complete investment activity on time. Abraaj did not transfer any loans from Air Arabia into the healthcare fund to conceal money missing from the fund since money was always available to the fund on a demand deposit basis. Proper written arrangements were in place with Air Arabia to utilise short-term funding needs for Abraaj on a demand deposit basis and all transfers were done in accordance with accepted procedures prevalent in the Group at the time. Two international audit firms confirmed that all uninvested monies

were accounted for and returned to investors in the healthcare
fund with interest as of 31 December 2017.

These answers contain all the key elements of Naqvi's response to the
allegations about his conduct and the way Abraaj allegedly operated.
Firstly, that the funds were moved around and could have been returned
at any time since they were treated as demand deposits. Secondly, that
all actions were done as part of 'accepted procedures', which refers, presumably, to the terms of the limited partner agreements. The issue is
if the LPAs allowed the use of funds for temporary investments and in
turn if the term 'temporary investments' covered the use of these funds
for general corporate purposes, or whether this use was not specifically
allowed by other clauses in the agreements. Thirdly, that all the transactions were properly recorded. This was also a central feature of the
response to the allegations concerning the payments that were made
to Naqvi's family, their companies and to personal investments made by
Naqvi in a company called The Modist. The *Wall Street Journal* levelled
this allegation in a variety of ways, for example: 'More than US$200
million flowed from Abraaj accounts to Mr Naqvi and people close to
him, including his sons. Or on another occasion: Abraaj money was
also sent to Axil Advisers and to Silverline,' (two companies controlled
by family and friends). In another email: 'What was the total amount
Abraaj sent to Axil Advisers? Mr Naqvi said Abraaj sent US$400,000
directly to his sons, but emails and documents show Abraaj also sent
millions of dollars to their company, Axil Advisers.' Also, in an email
not seen by this author: 'Can you confirm that in Email 3 above you
ask Rafique Lakhani to send US$300,000 to your son and US$300,000
to The Modist from Abraaj's bank accounts? Do you accept this email
shows you are spending Abraaj money effectively as if it were your own
money, and on personal matters?'

Naqvi's response each time was the same and made it clear that if he
was paid then it was from Abraaj treasury accounts and not from funds

or investors and that it was following a process agreed and documented by the board of directors and recorded in the books that had been reviewed by auditors:

> Mr Naqvi rejects any implication that there was anything untoward about any transfers from Abraaj to the persons named. In fact, only one payment was sent from Abraaj to each of Mr Naqvi's sons personally (totalling approximately US$400,000), which is in line with Mr Naqvi's entitlements. No payments were made at all by Mr Naqvi to Ms [Ghizlan] Guenez personally. In drawing down funds from Abraaj, Mr Naqvi acted in accordance with the arrangements put in place by The Abraaj Group. Mr. Naqvi was perfectly entitled to direct where all such drawdowns were to be paid, including for his personal investment in The Modist. As stated above, drawdowns, set offs and transfers were properly recorded and accounted for. Given that all payments were made and recorded as Mr Naqvi's personal liability to the company, onward payments are a matter for him alone.
>
> All payments were properly made in accordance with the practice approved by the Board of advancing Abraaj monies to Mr Naqvi to be offset against outstanding monies owed to Mr Naqvi by Abraaj under his contract. All such transfers were properly recorded as Mr Naqvi's personal liability towards Abraaj.
>
> This does not show Mr Naqvi spending Abraaj money as if it was his own. Mr Naqvi has not drawn down funds from The Abraaj Group other than in accordance with the permission of the Board of Directors (including by the relevant Compensation Committee of the Board) and as permitted under his contract with Abraaj. The relevant committee of the Board of Directors for The Abraaj Group passed a resolution that allowed Mr Naqvi to drawdown sums from time to time. Such drawdowns were properly recorded in the books as being a personal liability

repayable by Mr Naqvi or to be offset by Abraaj's obligations to Mr Naqvi. At no stage was any of the money that Mr Naqvi drew down or paid on his behalf taken from underlying investor funds. Every transaction was properly accounted for.

The most damaging allegation made by the *Wall Street Journal* was also put to Naqvi on several different occasions with a range of different wording: 'Mr Naqvi recruited Navaid Malik to secure the cooperation of former Pakistan Prime Minister Nawaz Sharif and his brother Shehbaz for the sale of K-Electric. A $20 million contract was prepared for Mr Malik to show to the Sharif brothers.' And on another occasion: 'Omar Lodhi wrote in an email to Mr Naqvi that Mr Malik said the Sharif brothers would inform you how to distribute money, such as a portion to charity and a portion to the election fund kitty.' Naqvi's lawyer's response began by questioning the source of this information:

It appears that malicious individuals have illegally leaked selected documents in a misconceived attempt to undermine the sale of K-Electric. Mr Naqvi is a patriot of Pakistan and this sale is in the best interest of the country. Mr Malik was not recruited to secure the cooperation of the Sharif brothers. It was public knowledge that Mr Malik worked for Abraaj as an adviser in connection with a variety of activities, including subsequently assisting with the sale of K-Electric.

The emails seen by the *Wall Street Journal* are part of a lengthy discussion as to the terms of Mr Malik's advisory agreement. Abraaj wanted to make sure that there were no conflicts of interest and Mr Malik did not have any potential conflicting roles.

Then they set out to explain the payment as part of an ongoing negotiation:

Mr Malik wanted to have a document which he could use to demonstrate that he had Abraaj's authority to act. In due course, a properly documented engagement letter was agreed with Mr Malik. This was fully disclosed to the shareholders of KES Power and board of Abraaj. That contract has now lapsed, and no fees were paid.

Mr Naqvi has not at any time contemplated, directed, authorised, or paid any bribes in respect of the sale of K-Electric and he categorically denies being part of any conversation express or implied that involved a payment to anyone in political office for purposes of facilitating the sale of K-Electric. He is not the author of this email and as far as he is aware, Mr Lodhi was simply reporting Mr Malik's comments, or his interpretation of them. These emails do not give a full or clear picture of the trail of communication from which they have been selected. They are a small part of a long sequence of the meetings, conversations, and other communications over many months as part of complex commercial negotiations which culminated in the signing of an agreement that ensured that no conflict of interest would occur and in fact no fees were paid.

Finally, that Mr Naqvi described the $20 million contract for Mr Malik as 'explosive'. To which Naqvi and his team replied that it would be explosive because it would expose the fact that K-Electric, a listed and highly politically significant entity, was going to be sold as early as October 2015 when in fact the transaction was consummated a year later. The journalist described his many questions as coming from 'key chunks of text' from emails in his possession. It is not clear if this meant that he had the full emails and had quoted from them selectively or that he had been leaked selected text from a much larger set of emails that had been hacked from Abraaj servers. Naqvi's lawyers responded:

It is unclear how and when Mr Clark came to be in possession of these emails and other material which he refers to. It appears the emails have been improperly and unlawfully obtained and distributed by whoever has provided the emails to Mr Clark and the *Wall Street Journal* must be aware they are seeking to rely on illegally obtained documents. It also appears that information has been selectively leaked to Mr Clark by one or more individuals with the intention of causing harm to Mr Naqvi and Abraaj.

The quoted extracts from the emails obviously do not tell the whole story of any of these actions or events. As the *Wall Street Journal* reproduced so little of Naqvi's responses in its original articles, I have included the responses here to provide some greater context to the way the articles appeared. Readers can make up their own minds, as courts will do, but what is very clear is that whoever gave this material to the *Wall Street Journal* team knew what they were doing and must have known the degree of harm they would inflict at the most damaging moments beginning in February 2018. The *Wall Street Journal* team in turn, wittingly or unwittingly, obliged 'whoever' in that they did not print a single thing from Naqvi aside from his blanket denial.

There are a number of major areas of wrongdoing alleged in the articles and articulated in the questions sent to Naqvi that he responded to through his lawyers. These four claims created the foundations for the accusation that Naqvi was the key man in the fall of Abraaj, that he was personally corrupt and that it was his actions and greed that led to the firm's collapse.

First, that Naqvi was paid substantial sums by Abraaj and that he transferred some of these funds from Abraaj accounts to companies owned or controlled by members of his family and close associates. The sums alleged to have been paid totalled $200 million from 2013 to 2018 – so perhaps $20 million a year, with discretionary bonuses of

$46 million in 2015 and $14 million in 2016, notwithstanding what he would take home in carried interest with performance of the Gen-5 funds once they started a divestment process, in addition to his shareholding position in the firm. Significant amounts of his compensation were left unpaid to keep cash in Abraaj when needed, but these are still obscenely high levels of renumeration by normal standards. They are quite ordinary levels of remuneration in private equity. Abraaj's executive team was well paid, but this was on par with the rest of the industry, and Naqvi himself was paid less than other founders of private equity companies.[1] In 2016, when Naqvi made $36 million, Stephen Schwarzman, the CEO and a co-founder of the Blackstone Group, received just under $800 million, up from $689 million the year before. Hamilton James, Blackstone's president, received $233 million in 2015, whilst their real estate chief, Jonathan Gray, earned $249 million. In 2013, Leon Black, the head of Apollo Global Management, was paid $543 million. In 2015, Henry Kravis and George Roberts, co-heads of Kohlberg Kravis Roberts & Company, made a combined $356 million.[2] These immense numbers are derived primarily from the carried interest from investments. Typically, founders will keep 80 to 90 per cent of the firm's share of carried interest. Naqvi agreed with the board when the company was founded to keep 75 per cent for himself, and codified this in a manner where he initially kept half (i.e. 37.5 per cent) for himself and divided the balance amongst other senior team members at his discretion. This changed with the Gen-5 funds. For these funds and all the legacy funds that were in operation as of 2012 (except the pre-2012 Aureos funds) the regional teams that did the transactions and had oversight of them until exit took 37.5 per cent of the carry. The central team was allocated 37.5 per cent. Naqvi got 50 per cent of the central pool, so his carried interest entitlement was approximately 20 per cent of the overall total, which is very different to other private equity firms. The other interesting fact to note is that between 2012 and 2018 no carried interest was disbursed on any of the Gen-5 funds because the exit cycle had just commenced when Abraaj was brought down. Therefore, from the $2.5 billion raised in Gen-5 funds, there was no carried interest paid out on businesses that later exited at substantially strong values that would have generated strong returns for the firm and its team members.

Second, that the commingling of funds took place between AIML and its individual fund accounts and AHL 'treasury' accounts. This is discussed at length elsewhere, and it will form the heart of the case against Naqvi and his co-defendants if the DoJ indictment ever comes to court. The success of this argument will rest on the meaning of the LPAs. The issue hinges on whether the practice of drawing down unused funds for 'general corporate purposes' as against actual 'temporary investments' will be accepted. As a result of following this approach, no investor actually lost any money or any interest from any funds that were managed by Abraaj.

Third, that a bribe was channelled through a Pakistani fixer to Pakistan Prime Minister Nawaz Sharif to facilitate the sale of K-Electric to a Chinese company. The full responses to this are covered above, but a covering letter from one of Naqvi's legal team stated:

> The fee negotiated with Mr Malik in respect of the separate advisory agreement was based on the complexities involved in obtaining the relevant consents and approvals, which were numerous and for which he would need to play a full-time role.
>
> The complexities of the proposed K-Electric sale are reflected in the fact that the consents and approvals have still not been obtained and certainly were not obtained during the tenure of Mr Sharif, as Prime Minister. This very fact is plainly inconsistent with the allegation that Mr Sharif was bribed to facilitate the deal. The agreement with Mr Malik is no longer operative and no fee was due or paid to him in relation to the proposed sale.

The DoJ indictment mentions these allegations but does not proceed to charge any of the defendants under the Foreign Corrupt Practices

Act on this matter as part of its sixteen counts and given the political sensitivities of the K-Electric deal, it would be surprising if legitimate contributions had not been made to political parties in the highly polarised political market of Pakistan. Other political markets had seen similar increases in political donations, in particular the US. The top thirty private equity firms contributed $68.7 million to federal elections and candidates from 2007 to 2018, with 54 per cent of the donations going to Republicans and 46 per cent to Democrats.[3] To put that number in perspective, private equity donations dwarfed the tobacco industry's political spending of $52.6 million since 2000; about a third more money in half the time. And the federal campaign spending has rapidly accelerated and jumped seven-fold from the 2010 to 2018 election cycles according to research by the Center for Popular Democracy. These record levels of spending were then smashed in the 2020 election when employees of private equity and other investment firms, excluding hedge funds, contributed $132 million to candidates, parties, political action committees and outside groups up to 30 September 2020, according to the Center for Responsive Politics.

That sum is the most the industry has ever spent on an election cycle, exceeding the $117.4 million spent on the 2016 race.

It is striking that when the story of Abraaj broke in Pakistan it was denied by both the government and the opposition, and media outlets that initially covered the story later retracted their articles.[4] There is no evidence that a bribe was paid through Malik to Nawaz and Shehbaz Sharif. Political contributions could well have been made, although this would have seen Naqvi backing both sides because he is also alleged to have been a major financial backer of Imran Khan and to have facilitated financial support for Khan from expats in the UAE – which at best would demonstrate irrational behaviour by him.[5] There are no allegations or counts against Naqvi relating to the Sharif brothers contained in the indictments.

This also raises a much more basic question: if you were going to pay a bribe to the Prime Minister of the country with the largest CIA station outside of the US, would you really put that in an email? The more general issue is if there is any other evidence that Abraaj contradicted the entire *raison d'être* of its own mission in emerging markets – to prove that the rule of law was sufficient for private equity to do business – by using bribery to solve their problems. If they did this in Pakistan, then why not elsewhere? As countless cases have demonstrated, the payment of bribes is a central feature of capitalism and sadly a series of banks have been found guilty of this but they continue to operate after paying fines.[6] There is even a global league table for those countries that are perceived to be the most corrupt in the world – the Corruption Perception Index. Abraaj had major problems with projects that were held up in Kenya and Nigeria, which prevented AGHF from progressing in those places. In 2016, the crunch year for so much of what happened to Abraaj, New Zealand was seen as the least corrupt country and ranked first out of 176 countries and Pakistan was 116th. Nigeria was 136th and Kenya was 145th; both were perceived to be more open to corruption than Pakistan.[7] There were never any other allegations made against Abraaj in this regard, in fact the opposite applied to the company and its approach for every single other deal, transaction and geography. One line that was quoted out of context from a long email chain does not constitute evidence that is substantial enough for any kind of charge to be made, but it is more than enough for a newspaper headline.

The fourth claim against Abraaj and Naqvi was that there were a range of other issues with the way funds were managed and the way investor funds were used at times. Much of this has been described in the previous chapters and is derived from the same sources used by the DFSA to compile their report and the SEC and the DoJ in their indictments. As Naqvi's lawyers had made clear, two independent audits by KPMG and Deloitte signed off on all of the transactions that were called into question. On the issue of the commingling, Freshfields had endorsed the practice under the LPAs over the operation of AGHF. The deeper question remains: why was this material leaked to the *Wall Street Journal* and why was it leaked and released when it was? The reality is that the *Wall Street Journal* was played like a violin. The only mystery is: who was playing them? In February 2018, the *Wall Street Journal* and the *New York Times* both covered the story detailing the anonymous email that was sent to Abraaj's investors. It is not known if that email came from an internal Abraaj source or an external agency. The technology used to access Abraaj's investor contact details and send an email to them suggests a state actor. The content of the email, however, suggests that it was, or was made to look like, a very well-informed internal source at a high level in Abraaj who was threatened by the development of the APEF VI single fund model and/or was trying to break off one of the funds to control it themselves. In other words, someone who was opposing Arif Naqvi's strategy to get to an IPO by 2018. The stories that appeared in the press in February were timed to destroy the equilibrium in the firm that had been achieved by the end of December 2017 and would have been consolidated by the sale of treasury shares in AHL itself – the stories stopped the sale. Still, Naqvi did not give up and tried to manage an orderly and successful liquidation restructuring process. In October 2018, Deloitte, as the liquidators of AIML under considerable pressure from the investors in the deal, including the LPAC of IGCF and their advisers, conceded that only Naqvi had the respect and gravitas needed in Pakistan to move the Karachi Electric deal forward and agreed that he would be brought back to lead that process, despite intense lobbying by Omar Lodhi, Tabish Gauhar and Wahid Hamid to take that role, according to a source involved directly in those discussions at that time. At exactly this moment another wave of negative stories emerged in the *Wall Street Journal* making baseless allegations that Abraaj had bribed the former Prime Minister, but both the government and opposition in Pakistan dismissed the story and considerable progress was made in moving the transaction forward. When it was days away from completion Naqvi was arrested, but even after his release from prison on bail after the chairman of KES Power and the CEO of Karachi Electric submitted affidavits and pleaded with the court to release him because he was crucial to the ongoing negotiations, Deloitte took Naqvi off the Karachi Electric deal and it stalled again. This continuous undermining of Abraaj in the media also gave the PIFSS a pretext to oppose the restructuring plan that Naqvi had put forward. The *Wall Street Journal* played its part in the destruction of The Abraaj Group to perfection.

# PART V

# DENOUEMENT

# 13

# Legacy

In 2017, The Abraaj Group was on the verge of achieving its revolution in private equity in emerging markets. Arif Naqvi's big idea was coming of age and Abraaj was hosting conferences and events on the side lines of the UN General Assembly week. The global fund APEF VI was aimed at a 'pipeline' of deals worth up to $39 billion; it would have transformed the firm and the sector.[1] This was a stratospheric leap in ambition, but one that was rooted in what had been achieved since 2002. To paraphrase Naqvi, Abraaj was no longer an emerging company, impact investment was no longer an emerging concept and emerging markets themselves needed to be redefined as global growth markets; all three had come into their own as growth areas of private equity. The end goal was that once the previous generation of funds, Gen-5, were closed and invested and APEF VI had been successfully raised, the firm would be in a position to run an IPO process in 2018 in London. This was not to be done at the expense of impact investing; rather, it was to be done to prove the methodology of impact investing could work at this scale. Abraaj in January 2018 was a firm with no false modesty about its ambition or what it believed it could achieve, and Naqvi was looking for an exit that would catapult him into politics.

The Gen-5 funds, which had some overlap in terms of investors with

APEF VI but were mainly from DFIs and Abraaj 1.0 investors illustrate that, even under the old model, Abraaj was already making impact work. There were five Gen-5 funds targeted regionally and one legacy fund, APEF IV, which acted as a global feeder fund; a recognition of the firm's enhanced capacity to act globally but still within its established structure.[2] These were collectively worth $2.6 billion,[3] and aggregated had a track record of 27.5 per cent gross IRR and 17.7 per cent net adjusted (after accounting for fees and expenses of the fund) IRR; out-performing the private equity industry benchmark for success by 3 to 5 per cent.[4] Of successful deals, 77 per cent had been actively managed and only 23 per cent passively. As we have seen, the norm for the private equity industry was passive or negative management rather than active positive management. These types of deal-level interventions that are necessary in emerging markets had resulted in 25.2 per cent and 9.4 per cent gross IRR. This disparity suggests Abraaj had a methodology that was replicable across emerging markets and was reflected in returns. The success of the model, and the overperformance of the funds and the resultant capital brought in was a clear signpost that Abraaj could successfully become a global firm generating wealth, jobs, public good and a growing middle class across all emerging markets.[5]

The five Gen-5 funds were organised regionally and focused on the four key sectors in which Abraaj claimed focus and expertise: consumer goods and services; financial services; healthcare and education; and industrials, materials and logistics.[6] A look at the three case studies below shows how structurally and within the model itself the firm had developed and what might have come in the future:

- The North Africa Hospital Holdings Group (NAHHG), Egypt and Tunisia.[7] The NAHHG was formed in 2014 as a hospital operator with four hospitals active in Egypt and three in Tunisia. Abraaj took an 80 per cent stake in Tunisia and a 99.99 per cent stake in Egypt in July 2014, with combined capital worth $179.8 million. In countries with fragmented healthcare markets that are growing at an average rate of 9 per cent per year, the result is a dire shortage of hospital beds and an inability to treat non-communicable diseases. Abraaj sought to leverage economies of scale to tackle supply issues, upgrade facilities, equipment and training, and looked to buy failing hospitals in the cities to expand, as well as set up outpatient centres to lighten the immediate weight of demand on them. On the operational side of things, it looked to enhance efficiency by engaging qualified management teams and upgrading the management information systems in hospitals.

- Singapore International Group of Schools (SIS).[8] SIS is a private school operator with eight schools and 3,000 students across five cities in Indonesia, based on the Singapore, Cambridge and International Baccalaureate curriculums tailored to Indonesian students. Their pupils came from a wide income range of families, and Abraaj identified that the context of low-quality state education, rising incomes and demographic growth mean that affordable high-quality private education was a feasible investment opportunity. Abraaj entered the deal in October 2015 with $32.5 million, buying a 77 per cent stake in SIS. It upgraded the schools' IT infrastructure, brought in new academic hires, secured long-term funding through an IFC loan and aimed to open new schools in the under-served cities of Surabaya, Bandung and Makassar. On a wider scale, the endpoint of the investment was to create a regional K-12 school platform – something which would have required a deep level of collaboration with the Indonesian government.
- Selina, Latin America.[9] Founded in 2015 as a 'lifestyle hospitality' business, Selina is Latin America's fastest growing tech-enabled hostel platform and currently operates twenty properties across Colombia, Mexico, Panama, Costa Rica, Guatemala and Nicaragua. Abraaj invested $50 million in January 2018, making it one of its most recent investments, and took control of a 16.4 per cent stake in

the company. Selina is explicitly marketed at tech-savvy millennial tourists, is based on an asset-light and scalable business model and a staffed by a team with international experience. Abraaj planned to help Selina expand both further in Latin America and into Asia, push its technological component even further and formalise and institutionalise corporate structures – at time of investment Selina did not have a board.

All three investments have factors in common. There is a significant focus on digital and information technology and its applications, even in fields like healthcare where it would not be obvious at first glance, particularly in emerging markets, but also where it can be vital to bypass normal steps of development. There is also more of a focus on the bigger picture, on increasing the scale of single investments; of Abraaj realising it had weight it could throw about. From this, the transition to the single global fund had the logic of creating impact behind it.

Below we discuss the refinement of Abraaj's philosophy and model, but it should be borne in mind that there was always a solid bedrock of financial success behind the firm's evolution. As a single global mega fund, APEF VI focused in on four key industry sectors that were seen as critical to Abraaj's mission of creating impact, but the firm saw success across the board. At a time of overlap between the legacy funds, the Gen-5 funds and the beginnings of APEF VI, Abraaj had made 160 active investments worth a collective $6.12 billion. In the sectors APEF VI was designed to invest in it had a gross IRR of 34.5 per cent, which is to say the initial return had a profit of over a third of the original investment. The four target sectors were financial services, industrials, materials and logistics, consumer goods and services and healthcare and education. In terms of track record, there was compelling evidence to further push all the eggs into the mega fund basket, and it remains a true adage that success and not failure should be reinforced. Quite whether this was enough to undertake such a fundamental restructuring as the firm attempted is another matter, but this record of success validated the impact investment hypothesis that progress did not have to hurt the balance sheet. Additionally, the growing sentiment and theme towards technology enablement in emerging markets meant that with a partner like Abraaj that could put substantial growth capital into businesses, companies could leapfrog and sometimes surpass their developed market rivals. This was the case when the Middle Eastern ride-hailing company Careem was bought by Uber for $3.1 billion in a move to acquire its local advantage and infrastructure, much of which had been developed during the Abraaj period of making an investment in Careem.

Based on the internal documents in the Abraaj archive as well as publicly available Abraaj marketing materials, it seems that the most fundamental change Abraaj saw with the launch of APEF VI was structural. The firm's philosophy had become more refined and codified, which together with its track record could soothe potential investors' fears and prejudices about emerging markets, but the real change came in organisation. APEF VI was structured far more vertically than previous Abraaj funds; a statement of its global intent and a shift away from being seen simply as good people to know in a specific region. At the head was the global investment committee, which managed the risk of each deal, optimised deal choice and put its '135 years of experience' into judging each investment. Below this, sat both the sector groups, who identified opportunities and provided access to a network of expert professionals in their respective sectors, and the local operating and investment professionals (LOIPs), who were responsible for local sourcing, due diligence to be reported upwards and with managing partner company relationships through the course of each deal. The LOIPs were geographically dispersed, based in global capitals in all the continents Abraaj was operating in.[10] Coupled to this was the growth of an explicit 'One Firm' approach, which rejected a franchise operation in favour of looking to ensure connectivity between all branches of the firm; sharing knowledge and expertise and making sure that the philosophy always remained the same. As part of this, all deals, regardless of geographical location, were subject to a global portfolio review committee and the group held an annual 'town hall' meeting in Dubai, bringing together the entire firm 'from receptionist to partner', to 'unite a diverse organisation to a common purpose'.[11] In a sense, the firm had become the fund and vice versa, but if this was a gamble it was one which had good odds as a result of past success. Naqvi was juggling both US investors engagement with this fund and Chinese investors desire for scale and projection into these markets.

The evolution of the philosophy of impact investing was also a signifier of the way things were heading for Abraaj. In the company materials the team felt confident enough to describe themselves as the only 'institutional investor'[12] in emerging markets, and they had codified their focus into a 'disaggregated' model of the future of the global economy, to better identify where to invest. This was named the 'Three Cs'. The first 'C' was a focus on cities as markets in which rates of consumption and GDP trended towards being multiples of the national average;[13] an old favourite of Naqvi's evangelism for globalisation. The second 'C' was those emerging markets that were consumer-driven with growth coming through the long-term trends that Abraaj had always identified as the future. The third 'C' was those markets that were commodity-dependant, with resultant cyclical growth and currency risks, which Abraaj generally avoided. Underpinning this, a fourth 'C' was China, which Abraaj argued should not be viewed as a proxy for all emerging markets and needed its own distinct strategy, which was fast bearing fruit. This refinement of Abraaj's philosophy seemed a natural progression that was in line with the shift towards one large central fund and away from a regional focus. There was also an increased focus on risk management through the team's knowledge of emerging markets. Abraaj made a big deal in the fundraising for APEF VI that risk is not where investors traditionally think it is in these markets, highlighting that deals failed with bad underwriting, poor partner and sector selection, inadequate control rights on the part of the investor, over-paying and the failure to see things through.[14]

Left not-so-unsaid in all of this was that Abraaj would never make those mistakes. The firm's stated failure rate of less than 3 per cent makes it seem a justified position for the firm to have held. It is tempting to attribute all the changes Abraaj underwent to the endpoint of the IPO, but that is both too retrospective a justification and a disservice to its mission of impact investment. Naqvi's rhetoric in his messages to the firm was clearly pushing the company towards being ready to undergo this evolution and Abraaj's track record would have provided confidence in the path forward – indeed, the $3 billion committed by investors to APEF VI also supported this rhetoric, until they were released from their commitments and all fundraising was halted as a result of the media furore.

Abraaj's insolvency was not the insolvency of its funds. Abraaj worked as an impact-based private equity firm. The underlying funds themselves continue to operate under new management and continue to support businesses and implement principles of impact investment and ESG through the Abraaj model, which is now the standard throughout the sector and the number of funds that target growth markets and articulate a methodology of impact investment is growing all the time. Abraaj will not be present in the post-Covid-19 'build back a better world', but its values and approach will be in those underlying legacy funds and the way those companies are managed.

Irrespective of what happens to any individual who forms part of this story, what also matters are the broader lessons about the lengths that states will go to protect their interests, disrupt the objectives of other states and reward their own players. These things will also be part of the legacy of this story. As the world attempts to rebuild after Covid-19 and the US re-engages with the world after the Trump administration's isolationism, nationalism and proto-fascism, there will be a pressing need to rebuild the movements allowed by globalisation and the more open economies that the reforms of the 1990s set us on the road towards. Economic nationalism has to be challenged in the interests of growing the world economy based on free trade for all. If that means challenges to the energy and the economic policy and narrowly defined national interests of the US, then that has to be allowed to run its course. If China buys Karachi Electric, it will be the fault of US isolationists for overstretching at this point. That they took down Abraaj to stop it happening will either be a dark chapter of a dark age from which we have emerged or a harbinger of what is to come as the competition for economic recovery after Covid-19 reinforces the protectionist forces that Trump unleashed. Either way, when the history of private equity comes to be critically and fairly written for this period, the real story of Abraaj and its destruction will be central to the transformation of an industry by the mainstreaming of a methodology of impact investment.

Why does this matter? Why should we care? In the ordinary course of events the fact that a small group of individuals have been arrested and charged would not be much of a cause for concern for those other than their immediate family and friends. In the hierarchy of the world's victims, these characters would, after all, come at or near the bottom of the list of things we should care about today. I get that. I did not initially make the connection between Abraaj and Arif Naqvi. I had been aware of Abraaj as being the most successful advocate of impact investing and the promise to utilise private investment to help address poverty and inequality because states and their development agencies had failed in this task for so long. I had studied the way in which the international development industry had failed in its modernisation projects over many decades and wrote an academic paper on the broader failure of state-led modernisation projects, going as far as to compare them to the projects of Hitler and Stalin in their blindness to human need.[15] But charity had also failed to address the problems of development and compassion fatigue and the limits of charitable reach would also limit its ability to deal with structural problems of inequality. The state is still central to the answer and regional cooperation between states is still vital because if everyone paid their fair share of tax and shared their access to water then many of our most fundamental problems of inequality would disappear. But in the end, it is capitalism which works, not liberalism, not socialism and certainly not communism. As forms of government, they endure, but what each of them shares is the same system for the production, distribution and exchange of goods and services: a market-based one, either openly in non-socialist or communist countries or covertly in command economy systems. It is always mitigated by varying degrees of state provision, by cooperation, by bartering, but it has not been replaced in any system entirely. The profit motive in which individuals maximise their own utility has been proved to work, but it must be managed by a socially conscious state. In the same way that the state mitigates the distribution of public goods through intervention, so the distribution of private capital can be mitigated by the way in which the investors behave, by socially conscious corporations. That was the revolution of which Abraaj was a key part and for which Arif Naqvi was *the* key global advocate. Aside from the obvious injustice that Naqvi and his fellow defendants are being subjected to, this is why we should care and care urgently about this case.

The Abraaj Group mattered because of the impact investment it practised and the audacity with which it was on the verge, with APEF VI, of breaking through to the big time. In development terms, Abraaj was the vanguard that was en route to winning the arguments that could have seen $7 trillion released from private sources alongside some state funds, to invest in emerging markets, which included some of the poorest and most unequal on earth. Its story also matters because it is geopolitics that has prevented this from taking place. If the US can only beat China in the struggle for influence in emerging markets by taking down private equity firms, then the war has already been lost.

# 14

# Reckoning

*Pakistanis cannot be my partners; Pakistanis
are meant to bring in the tea.*

Inchcape local partner company owner, 1999

It all comes down to this: did The Abraaj Group commit suicide because of the dishonesty of its founder? Or was Abraaj murdered because it got in the way of geopolitics?

The suicide explanation – indeed, it is really a suicide-pact explanation, because it relies on there being an evil genius masterminding the theft of hundreds of millions of dollars with willing accomplices – has been pushed hard, as we have seen, by the *Wall Street Journal*. It is also supported by the narrative in the DoJ's 'Al Capone' indictment.[1] There are fatal flaws in this explanation. There is no substance in the way the actions of the players are described.

These are conspirators who do not conspire. They have large meetings and discussions about cash flow. These conspirators then throw open their books to multiple investigations in which all transactions are faithfully recorded. There are fraudsters who do not commit fraud. A small number of US investors questioned the management of a fund and, rather than assert their own legal rights, Abraaj returns everyone's money with interest because it fully intended to carry on working with those investors in the future. There are thieves who do not take their full legal entitlement for salary and carried interest. Thieves who were so good at what they do that investors are still making money from their investments today and no money ever went missing. These racketeers who, at the moment their company was liquidated, had not left a hollowed-out shell but a company with assets that were worth more than the claimed liabilities. All working for an evil genius who used the money he had not already given away through his philanthropy and all his energy and ingenuity to first try to save the company and then get the creditors paid back. The *Key Man* account includes details of the millionaire lifestyle Naqvi led and innuendos about his personal life and that of his colleagues in terms of their extravagant behaviour; their lifestyles, cars, vacations and assets. It is the tabloid version of this story and, whilst it is entertaining, it does not really address the key issue. These private equity professionals were incentivised by fat pay cheques, but their investments were based on impact and they chose to focus on this space and these geographies rather than others. $7 billion was ready to be deployed across AGHF and APEF VI. It is certainly worth debating if these people deserved these rewards for what they did but as a proportion of the total that was being invested. If we are serious about addressing poverty and the delivery of health and education in these geographies, then we need private capital to do it and to get private capital these rewards need to be offered. The thesis in *The Key Man* is in essence a fall guy thesis, which just does not stand up to scrutiny. This was not a suicide pact; it was an assassination.

Private equity is a sector which likes to draw on the blood of others and when there is a wound the victims are left to bleed out. At key moments in this story, actors from the private equity industry both inside and outside Abraaj made decisions that accelerated the company towards oblivion – some unwitting and some acting intentionally. People on the inside took actions that reflected the interests of state actors by selectively leaking information from within the company and others seemed to panic, which added to the confusion. It is not clear how aware they were of the consequences of their actions or the extent to which they were being guided by external forces to act as they did. The job of a good intelligence agency is, after all, to achieve an outcome but leave nothing that can be traced back to their intervention so that on the face of it the information may not have been leaked and may have been hacked. People on the outside, like the leading US private equity player quoted at the beginning of this book, took the actions they did because they sought to gain control of what Abraaj had created in the service of both their own self-interest and their ideological commitment to Trump's China policy. But these private equity actors operated as facilitators and schemers; what was needed was an actor with agency that could coalesce unstoppable forces and multiple captive states into action to do Caesar's bidding – and that is the wider geopolitical story at play.

Human error and failures in strategic leadership, desperation to save the legacy of what they had created, self-interests and national interests all collide in this story, but the only realistic explanation for the speed and orchestration of the destruction of Abraaj is that state actors were involved. States were acting negatively against the company to ensure that it was taken down. Other states, or parts of states that wanted to defend Abraaj, lost out to those who wanted the firm destroyed. It had to be destroyed if it could not be controlled. This story encompasses actions and inactions by entities controlled or influenced by the states of Pakistan, UAE and Kuwait, amongst others, but also superpowers pursing their geopolitical interests through the Belt and Road Initiative, the string of pearls ports and the desire to 'Make America Great Again'. As we have seen, the US and China have been competing for political influence in Pakistan for decades and both enjoy strong political relationships with different groups within the Pakistani state and military. Pakistan is seen as a geopolitically strategic asset and Karachi Electric a vital asset in Pakistan. This company is emblematic of the struggle for influence between these two superpowers. For such a vital asset to be unsold despite a deal supported by three successive Pakistani governments having been signed five years ago suggests that neither side is winning in that struggle. The deal did not stall on its own or by accident but neither has an alternative to the deal won through. Abraaj was a pawn in a much bigger and longer-term strategic power play in which the fate of a single company, ordinarily something that barely registers in the grand scheme of the great game, appeared vital enough to inspire actions of state. That moment passed, but the processes set in motion by the geopolitical needs of the United States are still being played out in the streets of Karachi and in the courtrooms of London and New York.

Arif Naqvi and his fellow defendants who have not been granted immunity are subject to a political prosecution based on furthering the geopolitical interests of the US and the economic interests of the US private equity industry in relation to the threat of and competition from China. The evidence for this conclusion is based on both the sequence of events and the inherent weaknesses of the DoJ indictment. There were multiple reasons for Abraaj to be taken down but they all, in the end, required the obliteration of Arif Naqvi. If Naqvi had abandoned the deal to sell Karachi Electric and found a more suitable buyer, this assault would not have taken place. But not only did he persist with the deal he also opened up APEF VI to a significant volume of Chinese investment, continued to work hard to secure the deal to sell Karachi Electric and spoke both against the possibility of a Trump regime before the 2016 election and in favour of the BRI throughout 2017. On top of all that, he was advising the government of Imran Khan in its talks with the IMF and was helping develop an economic policy for the PTI government, which would have allowed it to navigate a path that was more independent of the US. He was acting against the interests of the United States and against the interests of the US lobby in Pakistan.

It is also important to remember that the UAE was having a honey-moon period with the Trump administration, from similarly held views on Iran to the sale of the most sophisticated weaponry in the US arsenal.[2] Ambassador Yousef Al Otaiba was referred to as the most influential foreign ambassador in DC, and the UAE was a massive employer of lobbyists, often known as the 'Beltway bandits'.[3] The two countries were too close for them to have not coordinated their approaches to the Abraaj issues that were raised in 2018. It is also striking that aside from agreeing but then stalling the granting of a loan of $250 million to Abraaj at a key moment – with extremely arduous security provisions – no state entity in the UAE stepped in to assist the firm during the crisis and no other state, many of which had been interested in the firm in the past, stepped in to help. Moreover, Middle Eastern funds that expressed an interest in buying the firm pulled out when the interests of the US private firms were made clear.

The behaviour of key Abraaj executives in relation to the US private equity firms that were trying to take over the firm and the motives for these firms making their bids are also contributing factors and was also linked directly to geopolitics.

Finally, the February 2018 media coverage of Abraaj prevented Naqvi joining the incoming government of Imran Khan until such time as he could resolve the crisis in Dubai; he was now 'damaged goods'. The October 2018 articles made it even more difficult for him to assume a formal role, but he continued to play an important informal role in the IMF talks, a role which was only finally ended by his arrest at Heathrow airport and the unsealing of the SDNY indictment. These events, when taken together and in sequence, demonstrate the way in which Abraaj was taken down. It did not collapse and the way in which it took strike after strike to finally stop Naqvi trying to save the company is dramatically telling. To understand this fully it is necessary to delve into the detail of the DoJ criminal indictment.

There are many structural and logical flaws in the indictment that when taken together should in my opinion lead to a judge deciding that there is no case to answer. There are also blatant misrepresentations. At the highest level, as discussed in detail in Chapter 9, almost everything contained in the DoJ indictment rests on the differences in the interpretation of the limited partner agreements between Abraaj on one side, and a tiny but influential group of five investors and one creditor representing 1 per cent of the number of affected investors on the other.[4] In industry terms, LPAs do not give significant influence or grant many rights to the limited partners themselves, they are designed to give maximum flexibility to the general partners to get on with running the fund. If Abraaj is proved correct, then almost everything described in the indictment will fall away immediately because it was all authorised by these agreements. (There seems a strong case for restructuring this system in favour of limited partners and reforming the carried interest system, as Ludovic Phalippou has argued in his ongoing critique of the private equity industry,[5] but at the time Abraaj was operating this was the norm.) Even if the 1 per cent are proved correct in their view, they have had all their funds returned and with interest. No money is missing so there is no criminal case to answer but only one concerning potential regulatory breaches, and arguably that has already been dealt with by the DFSA. Moreover, at the point of liquidation the assets of Abraaj exceeded the claimed liabilities from creditors in the professional judgement of the leading US firm in the business of restructuring so the value of Abraaj had largely remained intact despite the hammer blows delivered up to that point. For the logic of the indictment to hold the value of the company should have been hollowed out. This was also the case throughout the period between 2016 and 2018. It only stopped being the case after the fund management firm AIML and the holding company AHL were separated and one of the creditors forced AIML to assume debt, by presenting security cheques for encashment, at which point the board had no option in law other than to file for liquidation.

These are not the actions of a group of conspirators. Indeed, there was no conspiracy. The selectively quoted documents cited in the indictment describe the operation of a complex international firm with multiple moving parts and not a group of gangsters plotting to defraud anyone. Documents are clearly quoted out of context and in ways that set out to change their meaning and distort the record. Assessing the cash-flow situation across the multiple funds in multiple jurisdictions in which there were flows in and out looks like a normal process of cash management rather than a conspiracy to commit wire fraud. Changing the methodology of the valuation of assets in line with the development of the new single global fund APEF VI was an aggressive move by Abraaj in comparison with its more traditional conservative investment approach, but this reflected best practice in the industry. This methodology was introduced and adopted by Abraaj at the instigation of Mark Bourgeois and Hamilton Lane. Bourgeois is clearly identifiable in the indictment as a key witness, which raises an interesting question. Given that the DoJ felt it right to take no action against Mark Bourgeois and were satisfied as to his explanation of his role in the matter, the question must arise as to why the others were indicted. The argument would then become what role did he play. As his career had been built as a fundraiser, persuading people to come into funds as investors and his pay was based on the success of this, then it would have been in his interests to have Abraaj enhance their valuation methodology. He was in charge of fundraising for APEF VI so he was therefore central to the valuation process. He was the central witness because he has intimate knowledge of what happened. It is unclear on what terms he cooperated with the DoJ, but if they were satisfied with his explanation of his role in the matter, then by extension therefore the other defendants did not commit crimes, at least with respect to the counts in the indictment concerning valuation. He then took the bonuses from APEF VI's closure at $3 billion, to which he was entitled, and then began to support Hamilton Lane's demands to dissolve the fund. Shortly thereafter the collapse took place.

Arif Naqvi and his sons repeatedly refused to answer any questions relating to the indictment that I could not find explanations for in the public domain. But Naqvi did make one very pointed response when it came to a discussion of his WhatsApp messages that appear in a number of places in the indictment. Where, for example, the indictment quoted him saying that dealing with Deutsche Bank in a negotiation was a 'bit like playing poker', he noted that this is an accurate description of deal making rather than an illustration of a conspiracy; the context in which he and a colleague were discussing negotiations at the time on a particular deal involving Deutsche Bank had absolutely nothing to do with any kind of conspiracy. But quoting just that message in the indictment when it had no relevance helped to paint him in a negative light.

Or how in another instance, he mentioned how a WhatsApp message exchange was stitched together to appear as part of a continuous conversation when actually the two messages shown were sent weeks apart and easily explainable by providing the context of the two distinct topics being discussed. Then he stopped talking, refused to elaborate further and the meeting ended.

There are several disturbing things about this glimpse into the inner workings of the indictment. The purpose of the indictment was to persuade a grand jury that there was a case to answer and then to persuade the UK government that the individual should be extradited. In neither of these instances do you require the same standard of proof or disclosure of the evidence that you require when the case comes to court after years of document disclosure by both sides in the case.

The US penal code states: 'The Federal or District Attorney may order the person ... to be tried' if the reasonable suspicion test is met. The indictment is trying to win an argument, not win the case. It is trying to win an argument with the grand jury that there is sufficient wrongdoing to justify arrests and charges. It is trying to win an argument with the UK government that there are real crimes underlying the indictment and that they primarily took place in the United States of America. In other words, the indictment documents are designed to be as sensational as they can possibly be and to leave as little room for a common sense challenge from a grand jury member or an administrative challenge or process opening for the UK court to refuse the extradition. They are also based on the information that the investigation has at that moment so they have to make the best use of this information and present the accused in the worst possible light. But they have to be based on the truth.[6]

These brief comments were sufficiently interesting for me, though. My understanding of just this brief exchange shows me that wilful misrepresentation goes beyond simply constructing a case for the prosecution, it is designed to both destroy the reputation of those charged and frighten others into providing the most damning interpretation of the actions of others that they possibly can. I am not a lawyer or a judge, but a close reading of the indictment suggests that the payments made to Naqvi are presented as some kind of theft from managed funds, but, as outlined in Naqvi's responses to the *Wall Street Journal*, none of the money mentioned was paid from managed funds but from AIML on behalf of the holding company AHL; I would assume that this is what AIML did in respect of most of the transactions it processed as it was the expense management entity of the group. Similarly, Naqvi told the *Wall Street Journal* that payments were fully recorded, shared with multiple auditors and law firms and made in line with the policy of the remuneration committee of the board. An element of confidentiality was preserved, but few private entities publish the remuneration details of founders and chief executives, especially when they are entitled to a large amount of pay in comparison with the majority of their employees. We have seen that Naqvi's renumeration was not excessive by the standards of the private equity industry. He had not taken the full level of payment to which he was entitled, had deferred the receipt of his non-discretionary bonus so that the firm's annual accounts did not reflect adversely and had cut his entitlement to carried interest to

20 per cent when the industry standard for founders of private equity firms was 80 to 90 per cent. This all seems to highlight places in the indictment where there was a clear attempt to misrepresent.

At an even more fundamental level, there was no conspiracy because there was no attempt to hide anything. The dishonest presentation of the WhatsApp message sequences in which time lapses between messages were omitted was designed to misrepresent the events. No documents were moved or destroyed to prevent their review. In fact KPMG, Deloitte, Freshfields, the DFSA, Allen & Overy and Ankura had access to all the information they required. To have the case argued in the media before an indictment is presented is a technique that was perfected by Rudi Giuliani as a way to use the media within a system that is bent on success at all costs. Here I must reiterate my earlier conviction: there is no way a fair trial is going to happen in this case.

I do not know whether there was a CIA case officer or an individual economic hitman who was given the job of setting fire to the towers of Abraaj with the actions described above and by providing information to the DoJ for the indictment. We may never know unless there is another WikiLeaks release. All we can do from the outside is look at the sequence of events and dispassionately repeat the questions I posed in Chapter 1 and 11: who benefited and who suffered from the slowing and stopping of the sale of Karachi Electric to Shanghai Electric? If Abraaj was an organised criminal conspiracy what exactly was stolen? Who benefited and who suffered from the collapse of Abraaj? Who picked up the pieces of investments in the emerging and growth markets where Abraaj was dominant and who paid the price? And finally, how did the different actors in this story behave?

The underlying power play that destroyed Arif Naqvi, his co-defendant colleagues and his company was also intended to capture and control the idea of impact investment in emerging markets so that it could be implemented in ways that benefited US companies and investors rather than Chinese companies and investors. To achieve that objective, judicial activism was mobilised when everything else more subtle had failed. It does not really matter to those who instigated it whether the prosecution succeeds or is dismissed by the first judge who considers it on its merits. The prosecution has already done its job because it stopped Naqvi in his tracks and stopped the global impact fund, APEF VI, from closing.

The blocking of APEF VI was a key element in capturing the idea of impact investment and stopping Chinese capital from breaking further into this space through Abraaj funds. It was important to capture this idea in this way on multiple commercial and geopolitical levels. It mattered because Abraaj was not just selling Karachi Electric to the Chinese, Abraaj was building a broader set of connections with Chinese capital that would have opened the door of key emerging market geographies in Africa and Latin America, for example, to that Chinese capital and thus further extend the reach of the BRI around the world. It would have also answered one of the major criticisms of the BRI because Chinese capital would have made a profit from these investments, but that profit would not have depended on the use of Chinese firms or the parachuting-in of Chinese labour. The money would have been put to work in portfolio companies in emerging markets. The profit would have been extracted at exit, but the value would have been left in the entity. For all these reasons, the sophisticated operation that was launched to destroy Naqvi, his colleagues and his company was also an operation to capture and retool an idea so that US capital rather than Chinese capital could move into these markets and ensuring that US private equity firms would benefit. There are too many elements working together for this to have been an accident. Moreover, the normal run of an inquiry did not occur. The DFSA in the UAE is Abraaj's local regulator and it would normally have been the body to deal with allegations of corporate malpractice such as those in this case. The DFSA investigated and reported and Abraaj was given a record fine but only after liquidation proceedings had commenced and there was no realistic expectation of payment by anyone; there are loud whispers in Dubai that the DFSA was simply told to step aside. For an entity like the DFSA, which is seeking to establish its global relevance, this approach can only hurt it overall; corporations wish to be regulated in jurisdictions that can be seen to be impartial and not represent the interests or diktat of states. I am sure that the DFSA will announce individual sanctions – much as the SEC has already done in Abdel-Wadood's case in the United States – but their efforts will be made in an attempt to close the loop and move on, rather than any real attempt to bring the issue home and deal with it properly. Abraaj did not have an opportunity to contest the fine imposed by the DFSA because the DoJ stepped in with its prosecution and a series of attacks had already forced the company into liquidation. The selective and politicised prosecution of Abraaj is evident in the scope and substance of the DoJ's indictment. The indictment paints a picture of an organised criminal conspiracy based on racketeering, but the cast of characters is drawn very tightly and precisely. The critical target is Arif Naqvi. There is a very small circle around him that has been implicated because not even in the fevered imagination of the US attorney at the SDNY office could Naqvi have acted alone. The circle has been drawn, however, to exclude all the senior US citizens involved.

As I laid out at the beginning of this book, there are also more invidious and deeper prejudices at work here.

The elite aligned to give Abraaj and Naqvi the support and the platforms – Davos, the World Economic Forum and the media – they needed and craved to promote themselves and their philosophy of capitalism. In turn, it is as if the global elite were happy to have found one of 'them', in this case a Pakistani, that they could have as a poster boy for a new kind of capitalism. The poster boy could be invited into The Giving Pledge and they could even indulge the Gulf a little to let Dubai get some important meetings and conferences. Deep down, however, perhaps the Davos set shared the view of the Gulf company owner, who after being told he would be partnering with Cupola decades earlier, stated:

'Pakistanis cannot be my partners; Pakistanis are meant to bring in the tea.'[7] But Abraaj proved to be a bit too good at the impact investing game and Dubai was becoming a bit too attractive as a destination for financial service companies. The idea worked so long as it did not directly challenge the profound interests of capital. When it did, in the context of a shift in political power within the US elite, Abraaj had to be removed. Abraaj was not big enough to save or sustain itself. And, as I have argued, the people who ran Abraaj were not like other private equity executives and the companies they invested in were not Silicon Valley start-ups. For the global elite they were not 'people like us'. They were, therefore, not white enough to save because they came from the Middle East, Asia and Africa. Naqvi and his colleagues were attempting to be the global citizens that Davos rhetoric had told them would be the economic players of the globalised future. In this imagined future the power of nation states was withering away. Their problem was that the power of nation states was not withering but waiting. The nation state struck back with the force of Make America Great Again and the Belt and Road Initiative. In the end one of Abraaj's problems was that it was not tied to a nation state. It believed it could somehow operate above nation states with its own corporate foreign policy because world opinion leaders were saying that it could. For fifteen years it succeeded in doing just that. But when the superpower nation state began to strike back, Abraaj had nowhere to turn.

New forms of colonialism and imperialism sit at the heart of the Chinese economic model as much as they do in the hopefully fading ideology of Make America Great Again. The rear-guard action under Trump to try to regain imperial and colonial initiative had some successes but often resembled the old-style power play of firing the bows and arrows at the castle walls of mega infrastructure projects. Both superpowers have interests deployed in this conflict. Shanghai Electric, American private equity companies, the *Wall Street Journal*, all are instruments of nation state power, which, in the end, is the moral of this tale. The explanation for why Abraaj was left to burn lies in these power relations, social relations of capital, race, ethnicity and ultimately in what has turned out to be the myth of globalisation. It is a complex story. It is not a simple tale of an individual who came like a thief in the night and stole hundreds of millions from global financial institutions and individuals. A power play took place, nation states fought over the corpse of Abraaj to the benefit of their respective commercial interests and in the service of their geopolitical and strategic interests. The craven and naked greed of service providers competing against each other for the fee pot fanned the flames and made the fire more combustible and difficult to manage, even for those who lit it in the first place; the process of destruction acquired a life of its own. But that is OK, because virtually all of the service providers were 'people like us'. The towers of Abraaj were torched by those acting in the interests of the United States and were left to burn because state power remains dominant over globalisation. For many in Abraaj, globalisation felt like a lived reality, but in the end it proved to be a myth they lived and finally died by.

It is now two years since Arif Naqvi entered into the stasis of modern purgatory both physically and figuratively. Frozen by judicial activism based on the application of a highly selective strategy of prosecution. In this world of financial crime there is no equality before the law. The imposition of the condition of stasis has destroyed not just the life of an individual but those of his family members and those people closest to him as well as the lives of his associates and their families and others dependent on them, which is unjust and an indictment itself of the operation of US politicised judiciary. But it has also set back an idea that literally had the capacity to change the world for the better and that is a tragedy. The idea that private capital can be unleashed into the poorest places in the world to build a new middle class that would lift entire societies out of poverty is a vision that is too important to be lost.

Naqvi describes feeling like his life had been frozen when he understood that he was being arrested. His brain seemed to stop. At Heathrow he was moved to a holding cell at the airport and then to prison. He was initially refused bail. His cellmate was a Hungarian. Naqvi prayed each day and the Hungarian watched him pray. Finally, his cellmate asked Naqvi if he could help him. He said he had not been a good man but that since he had been born a Muslim, he wanted to learn how to pray. Naqvi said this lifted him, it gave him a purpose and his brain began to thaw. Naqvi taught the man to pray and his life in prison acquired a purpose.

If Arif Naqvi ever asks me again, 'So, what do you think I am?' I will say, 'You are human and flawed, you indulged yourself and you were clever, but you are not a crook.' But his is a complicated story. He was guilty of hubris. He should have seen it coming. But he deserves his day in court and to have his name cleared. With the forces aligned against him – a superpower, other states, the media and the US private equity industry – that now seems highly unlikely. If the justice system betrays him further, natural justice will ensure that his idea, impact investment, will make a difference in this world and give purpose to the people who put it into practice.

# Postscript

## Abraaj and private equity; private equity and Abraaj

This postscript is designed for readers who are not familiar with private equity or who know the field but want to know what made Abraaj different.

It is important that you keep two things in your mind when you read about the story of The Abraaj Group. Firstly, the end of the company was not an inevitable result of its character or the character of the people who ran it, worked for it, invested with it or owned or worked in its portfolio companies. The manner of its demise should not be the sum of its place in history. Indeed, the overwhelming evidence about the company from its foundation in 2002, and with its precursor Cupola in 1994 to 2002, up to the end, is that it was an outstanding corporate citizen. Secondly, Abraaj should be assessed in exactly the opposite way to how you might ordinarily assess a private equity company; the bottom line is not all that matters. Of course, profit mattered to Abraaj. The people who ran Abraaj were capitalists: they believed in the bottom line and, to an extent at least, they lived and died by it. But they did not operate a company in which that was the only metric; Naqvi argued that the idea of necessary financial trade-offs between impact and profit is a myth – and that instead it was a 'trade-on'. There is also a fundamentally different approach to successful private equity elsewhere in the world that had to be taken as a consequence of operating in emerging markets that, frankly, cannot be judged purely on the same criteria as Western markets. Abraaj can of course be looked at through profit and loss, earnings before interest, taxation, depreciation and amortisation (EBITDA) figures, fund sizes and the glittering prizes. The financial sector is second only to the film and advertising industries in its love for awarding each other accolades. Abraaj won more than its fair share and it made a great deal of money for itself, its limited partner investors and for the portfolio companies its funds invested in. But it was not just another private equity company run by a charismatic founder who spotted how to identify value and liked the sound of his own voice.

The initial home base of Abraaj, which later fanned out to five regional hubs, was in a very particular part of the world. It called its region – the Middle East, North Africa and South Asia – MENASA. In fact, Abraaj coined the term, much as it would go on to re-engineer the term 'emerging markets' as its platform grew into new 'global growth markets'.[1]

Abraaj was based in Dubai within this region, and it grew as Dubai grew as a financial centre. The company can be read as an early adopter, a pioneer of private equity in this region.

The kind of private equity Abraaj set out to do was impact investing in the emerging markets of MENASA. It defined its impact investing by the geographies in which it invested. It also defined impact investment by the way in which it invested.

Abraaj wanted to have an impact, both in the way it performed and in the way the companies in which it invested behaved. It did so by bringing to the portfolio companies an elaborate and well-articulated architecture of corporate social responsibility and environment, social and governance principles. This process took a step change when Abraaj bought Aureos Capital[2] and incorporated a cadre of development professionals with government development finance institution backgrounds. What had kept most of the private equity industry out of the emerging market sectors before Abraaj was a fear of doing business in places in which theoretically, and often in practice, the so-called normal rules did not apply. Abraaj's answer was to write the rules for the companies it invested in so that they could see that using professional services, following rules of governance and providing global standards in health, safety and conditions for staff wherever possible contributed to the bottom line no matter where in the world you happened to be. Abraaj's ESG programme was known as Abraaj Sustainability and Stakeholder Engagement Track (ASSET) and was run by Frederic Sicre, who joined Abraaj in 2005 as a partner from the World Economic Forum, where he had been a managing director. If companies did not show a willingness to engage with ASSET it would be increasingly difficult for them to attract capital from Abraaj – and as the firm grew, getting investment from it became a kind of stamp of approval for companies in its target markets. In turn, Abraaj took its position in its region seriously by both engaging in geopolitical investing in areas such as food security in the Gulf and power generation in Karachi, whilst also wanting to be a good corporate citizen itself, which meant strategic philanthropy and stakeholder and community engagement through thought leadership, charity foundations and art prizes.

Abraaj did not emerge into the world fully formed, operating across all these dimensions at once, nor did things always go smoothly. But this was the kind of company that evolved over time and to understand it we must read across each of these six dimensions – profit-driven private equity, the emerging markets of MENASA, impact investing, stakeholder engagement, geopolitical investing and ESG-led change programmes – together.[3] Each of these elements are laden with political implications that changed over the time that Abraaj operated from 2002 to 2018. To an extent, Abraaj's story can be read as a company breaking through a series of glass ceilings. Reaching the first $1 billion fund from the Middle East. Doing a public–private–public play with its first Abraaj investment – Aramex – which was the first time this had happened in the region. Dual listing a hospital and healthcare group, IHH, across novel exchanges like Singapore and Malaysia and going on to become one of the largest IPOs in the world that year (beaten only by the likes of Facebook). Developing its own metrics, enhanced by the 2012 acquisition of Aureus, for impact, sustainability and governance. Navigating through the 2008 financial crash intact but not unscathed and emerging from that crisis to embrace a wider range of complex geographies in which to invest. Utilising significant amounts of balance sheet capital – the raising of which was in itself unheard of at the time – to bolster companies managed by it but owned by its funds, in effect as what some Abraaj employees have called, rightly or wrongly, a 'lender of last resort'. Using early adopter status in the Middle East to hold off traditional firms trying to soak up investors and opportunities from across that region and keeping its nerve and encouraging others to do so during and after the Arab Spring. But, as mentioned above, perhaps Abraaj's greatest coup was to take advantage of market timing and raise its own share capital to $1.5 billion between 2006 and 2009 starting from a mere $10 million, which gave it the firepower to grow, acquire, consolidate and invest in a manner and quantum never seen before in emerging markets. Growth was not constrained by management fees or timely investor drawdowns, but it became a function of market opportunity and the availability of talent. Deal flow, local knowledge and understanding the ability to navigate these markets were critical elements for talent acquisition at any level: inverting the structure of the deployment of private equity teams so that local, contingent and geographical knowledge was prized over connections in the Western financial centres of London and New York.[4]

From a purely private equity perspective, what makes emerging market investing both separate from traditional models in the West and more receptive to the long-term focus on impact is the comparative lack of information available. Access to information is critical in all stages across a private equity transaction, from sourcing to preliminary analysis and due diligence, post-acquisition value creation, company reporting and obviously disclosure to potential buyers on exit. Because of the lack of sophistication in emerging markets, companies do not track the general metrics on an ongoing basis in the same way that Western companies routinely would. This can be for a few reasons:

1. Managing the dynamics of largely family-owned businesses in those environments where institutional capital partnerships had not been common practice.
2. A general lack of information gathering from the companies themselves because of an inability to gather (firms had to quickly pull macro-level figures, like jobs reports, GDP growth and economic forecasting, together to pass the investment committee).
3. A lack of sophistication around reporting 'standards' (compared with Western standards); or
4. A simple inability to provide the information because it does not form part of the bigger picture for many companies and individuals – for example, in order to avoid taxes.

Therefore, the ability of an investor to be able to effectively track valuation on a monthly or quarterly basis in an accurate format is skewed. This creates a need to rely on the methodologies employed by the firm in question to produce a valuation which makes sense for that business in that market. That valuation is only as good as itself, given the subjective nature of valuation which comes into play specifically in emerging markets.

Abraaj had a history of quite conservative valuation methodologies by the standards of the industry, partly because it was based on more subjectivity in analysis and fewer hard numbers. This also allowed Abraaj to shape the conception of value in its investments towards a more impact-oriented position, and once it had tasted success this allowed it to hold up its methodologies as proof that emerging markets were not inherently too volatile for investment. Much of the valuation methodology was based on an understanding of the local market, with the underlying macro conditions in a valuation, such as long-term trends in a particular market, playing a large role. Understanding these conditions thoroughly, therefore, was key. This arose because of the perceived general volatility of emerging markets in comparison to the developed world where sovereign risk is generally priced and stays at that level. The yo-yo effect, therefore, is a big factor in what someone is willing to pay for a product; as is scarcity value.[5] Abraaj's approach overcame this by hiring an extensive on-the-ground presence and building infrastructure and framework in local markets to be able to make both a local and institutionally informed decision around the trajectory of a business. It was also central to Abraaj's approach to formalise the structures and practices of the markets through ESG and CSR to bring them in line with norms more acceptable to Western investors. This all applied to Abraaj's general approach – more specific elements of the company's modification of standard private equity practice is examined below – but what can be taken right from the start is that Abraaj's methodology aimed at overcoming the central limitation of emerging markets – access to information – by filling that role themselves.

In the early years and in the foundation of the company, Naqvi was the central dealmaker, but it is obvious from the annual reports and the press coverage of the firm that the team was evolving. The senior management team and the board of first Cupola and then Abraaj were a critical cross-section of the GCC's elite players, with an increasing sprinkling of international experts. The management team had grown by 2006, at the time at which it did its capital increase, to 115 financial professionals who knew their regions intimately.

The initial senior management team had also been working in the region and some had worked together since the late 1990s when they founded Cupola, but as the firm grew, new world-class talent was also recruited. There were star dealmakers and thought leaders coming in from Pakistan, the Gulf, the Levant, Turkey, India and all were complemented by the balanced European sensitivities of dealmakers from the UK and Europe, who were more familiar with the cut-throat financial ways of private equity growth and financial markets in general but embraced the Abraaj approach as the returns continued to grow. The absence of US nationals in the team pre-2012 is quite striking, but there was no absence of talent; the top team included people like Tom Speechley, Matteo Stefanel, Ahmed Badreldin, Selcuk Yorgancioglu and Mustafa Abdel-Wadood. It was these things taken together that provided the immense ballast of early adoption in these emerging markets and this was gradually complemented by people who knew other geographies and other larger investors. It was also in this interaction between the companies that were invested in and the local teams doing the investing and managing such relationships, that Abraaj really added value.

This added value improved the performance and profitability of the target companies, often through introducing better training, and in turn this created more jobs and increased disposable income in the communities in which they were based and from which the workforces were drawn.[6] These communities were often much poorer than the middle-class customers in the wine bars Abraaj also invested in, or the foreign tourists on safari in one of the travel firms backed by Abraaj. Improved wages and more jobs in these communities had an obvious knock-on effect thanks to the money spent by these new workers and the taxes paid by them and the firms they worked for. These investments then influenced the overall economy in classic Keynesian ways but with private sector money at its root.

This sounds very micro level in terms of contributing to economic development, but in aggregate across all activities in specific markets the hundreds of millions of dollars invested in this way did make a difference, and in turn heavily influenced the way in which other private equity firms went about their engagements in these geographies. Abraaj was a key player in mainstreaming impact investment across the private equity industry, but being a 'first mover' in emerging markets inevitably came with some costs. Market expansion enabled the firm to grow globally, and it was widely known that Abraaj's employees were paid well. The pool of local talent available with meaningful international private equity, asset management or operational experience was very limited and therefore to reverse the brain drain, local nationals were often repatriated with a salary and bonus structure that was well above the local (and sometimes international) benchmarks. There was a constant need to incentivise world-class talent and Abraaj staff were paid the same salary at a given designation level irrespective of where they were based. By intentionally choosing to take the lead in building a 'next-generation' business model, Abraaj laid much of the groundwork so that those who followed did not have to. One example are the costs of developing a local office network across twenty-five cities, supported centrally in a hub-and-spoke model. As local offices became more dispersed and the business grew geographically, the hidden costs of doing business increased. For example, there are a limited number of direct flights from central hubs to Lagos, Lima, or Tunis, which makes flights invariably more expensive, especially when there is a need for a growing number of professionals to travel back and forth between the hubs and local markets. In isolation this may seem trivial, but given the fact that local infrastructure, support and visibility are critical to emerging market deal sourcing and due diligence processes, which are generally more arduous, time-consuming, lengthy and require in-person discussions, there is always a consequential knock-on cost implication compared with doing similar deals in the developed world. Added to this were large investments into a common technology and knowledge management platform that gave Abraaj offices a competitive edge in evaluation compared with local peers.

The following section provides a basic overview of the way in which private equity usually works, which is important if we are to understand how and why Abraaj was different. In the jargon of the private equity world, Abraaj made a difference through 'deal-level abnormal performance', rather than simply picking the right sector or clever financial management and presentation – particularly challenging given the above-mentioned costs of operating as a trailblazer in emerging markets.

Deals are at the heart of how private equity works. The reputation of a private equity fund depends on its ability to identify companies to invest in or buy outright, so that they can increase the value of the business, or at any rate extract value from it, and then exit either by selling it to another company or through a stock market flotation, returning a handsome profit to the investors who backed the fund. In the West, for a long time these funds were rightly seen as predators, buying companies to strip out costs (and frequently jobs), sell assets, finance special dividends to themselves by burdening the business with debt and eventually exiting a hollowed-out husk that had been sucked dry of value – the investment world's vampires.[7] Of course, there are occasions when such companies actually invest to build up a business, creating jobs, but this tends to take longer and requires greater effort, and these people are often in a hurry and are impatient for fast returns. For the most part the private equity world is hard-nosed, cynical and brutal; ruthless sharks preying on targets that for whatever reason find themselves in a situation of weakness. Paramount skills are an ability to 'manage' the numbers – financial engineering – and a single-minded focus on value extraction regardless of the human cost.

The private equity firm is built around the reputation of its founder or group of founders and their deal-making skills; in the jargon of the industry, when they raise a new fund, they are called the general partner (GP). The money that the GP of the fund invests is committed by limited partners (LPs or investors), on the basis that for a given period – usually ten years – that money can be called upon by the fund when needed for an investment and is therefore effectively committed to this cause. The investors are called limited partners as they have limited rights and liabilities, which in turn also limits their tax exposure. The private equity firm, or an entity very close to it through complex structuring, acts as the general partner or manager of the fund. The GP or manager identifies, invests in, manages and exits those investments and is ultimately responsible for the debts and obligations of the fund, but does not guarantee them or undertake an assurance of how the investments will turn out.[8] In the West, these funds are usually raised from institutional investors that have grown hand in hand with the private equity firms that prospered from the 1980s onwards. Institutional investors are usually capital owned or invested on behalf of others by investment banks or investment companies, endowments or pension funds, who employ specialised teams to evaluate investment opportunities, organisations created to perform the evaluation and recommendation tasks for discrete pools of capital (aggregators) and finally sovereign entities, such as DFIs. Their process of evaluating the past performance of private equity firms is known as 'investor due diligence', which is used to determine whether to invest and to what extent. Some high-net worth individuals or family offices can also participate in such private equity funds, but they would have to dish out the dough whenever there was a call regarding a new investment – only the super-rich need apply, with a level of 'reverse diligence' being done by the GP to ensure that the investor was indeed capable of making future drawdown commitments.

Judging how much to raise for a new fund is itself an art form. The fund needs to raise enough to cover its overheads and thus ensure its viability. It must be financially muscular enough to handle the opportunities it will uncover over the course of its lifetime, but at the same time it must not raise so much that a chunk of the fund is never invested and investors complain that the money they have committed is never actually put to work. This money is now 'committed' by the limited partner to the fund over that ten-year period – meaning, if it is called upon, it needs to be produced upon a drawdown notice being issued, typically within the time frames agreed in the limited partnership agreements. Normally, investor diligence processes in private equity are extremely rigorous, in contrast to hedge funds and other public market type funds, because those are accessible to the general mass public, whilst private equity is not. Institutional investors would tend to follow similar models. Following introductory meetings, and the initial company outline, investors would seek information pertaining to the size of the new fund, the strategy/execution plan and the general terms of the fund (e.g. management fee, carry, hurdle rate and fund life). After this analysis, a longer due diligence questionnaire would be sent across to the firm, which would require large amounts of data – and would usually be completed by a dedicated third party. Following this process – or running in parallel – a series of in-person meetings and reference checks with portfolio companies and other investors would be conducted. A private placement memorandum (PPM) would then be issued to the prospective limited partner encapsulating all the likely risks, conflicts of interest and taxation issues that the investor could encounter by participating in the fund; a sort of final 'buyer beware' document that distinguishes sophisticated investors making reasoned decisions and this is typically the single document which an investor would legally rely on if they wished to raise an issue with the GP. Only if this is to their satisfaction would subscription agreements and limited partner agreements be entered into by incoming investors in a new fund.

Of course, this process requires a successful marketing and fundraising campaign. If the marketing campaign meets a strong response, then the fundraising can close early. It can also be extended if it fails to meet its target. If the fund has been marketed well and positioned correctly it might be oversubscribed. All Abraaj funds underwent this process and varied in their success rates. The direction of the curve, despite the gloss of the annual reports, was never only upwards and not all funds met their targets, for example, APEF IV after the 2008 crash or ATF in 2016 given the turbulence in Turkey following the failed coup against Erdogan that year. There were reputational risks when targets were not met and private equity is all about perception, reputation and the image this creates to generate and reinforce trust. If an Abraaj fund looked like falling short AHL invariably stepped in and made up the difference in order to achieve the pre-announced 'target amount' for the fund and held that position as 'excess inventory' for eventual sell-down to newer investors or as sweeteners in subsequent transactions.[9] An example of how reputation matters is that Actis had little to no ability to enter emerging markets after some failed investments in sub-Saharan Africa and failed fundraising efforts. Ironically, today, after it has assumed two of Abraaj's larger funds, APEF IV and AAF III (Africa), it is now one of the largest investors in 'growth markets'.[10]

The money raised is then deployed in two ways: firstly, for the most part it funds the purchase of interests in companies that the firm has identified, investigated and confirmed as strong opportunities; secondly, some of the funds will go towards management fees to the GP/manager, which are typically 2 per cent of the total committed capital raised, and pay for the costs and overheads of the fund – salaries, offices, expenses, travel and so on. The investors are exited from the fund through a process involving either outright sales, stock market listings or swaps, following which if sufficient profit has been generated for investors (the so-called 'preferred return'), the private equity company will be allocated a percentage of the fund proceeds – almost always 20 per cent of the profits made on the investment, known in industry parlance as 'carried interest' or 'carry'.[11] Abraaj was in something of a difficult position in that it had different types of LPs who wanted different things. The main differences were how the investors wanted Abraaj to report to them and the type of return the investor wanted.

In relation to the first, there were a number of investors – tending to be the pre-2012 investors – many of whom would ask for very simple reporting mechanisms because they did not want to be provided with more information than they needed to digest – at least at that time. The post-2012 investors, institutional investors and DFIs needed this information for their own compliance processes. Given the fact that the quantum of investment size began to grow, and the post-2012 investors were putting in a larger majority of the capital in new funds, Abraaj ultimately decided to provide even more information than was required as part of their reporting under standard industry guidelines. With the general lack of access to information in emerging markets explained above, the responsibility for valuation fell solely on Abraaj, which was fine when it produced good results from its exits and returns but became problematic when the firm ran into difficulties.

The second issue, that of the type of return that different investors wanted, was arguably more important. There are two ways to measure the return on capital – multiple of cost and internal rate of return. The MoC is an absolute figure which measures the return based on the absolute multiple of capital returned in relation to the capital invested; IRR values the time-value of money and therefore places more onus on the private equity firm to be diligent around the time it invests and the time it exits. A friend who recently retired from a private equity firm in London explained to me that many investors, including pension funds and DFIs were solely focused on MoC: they were not concerned about when they received their capital back over the lifetime of the fund, as long as it was exponentially more than initially committed because of their need to generate funds for future liabilities to their own constituents. On the other hand, there were also many other more institutional aggregator investors, including Hamilton Lane and BofA Securities (formerly Bank of America Merrill Lynch) in the Abraaj case for example, who focused on IRR and were obsessed with the time-value of their money, because the faster the money came back, the more return they could report to investors and therefore the more money they could invest on their behalf into funds, which in turn amplified their own returns. These investors were more short-term minded and were much more active in terms of pushing the GP (Abraaj) to try to exit businesses faster than the former. An aggregator invests capital on behalf of others or directs others to invest based on their recommendation and their own returns are measured in time-value terms as their benchmark. This discrepancy in investor alignment was evident within the institutional investor base of Abraaj itself. This constant push-and-pull effect post-2012 would have created a long-running internal battle over the firm's exit strategy, but, at least in the short term, it did not seem to affect the fundamental returns.

The relationship between the limited partners and the general partner is governed by a limited partner agreement.[12] This defines what the general partner can and cannot do with the funds that are drawn down for investment. For example, something as simple as setting limits on the amounts that can be paid to the private equity firm as fees, or something as complicated as laying out in excruciating detail, the rights that limited partners have under the agreement. The term 'limited partner' is derived from the fact that investors have no role in investment decision making or investment or divestment strategy in order to maintain their tax status, and LPs generally become involved only in circumstances where the interests of the GP and the fund may diverge and this had not been addressed in the LPA. That limited partners therefore were not empowered to participate in the investment process would be the source of much controversy during the taking down of Abraaj in 2018. In the beginning, Abraaj's early investors were relaxed about the way in which things were run or how drawdowns were done in bulk, whilst the company was lenient about the late delivery of promised funds from investors and occasionally even their failure to arrive at all. In some cases, Abraaj would end up funding massive investments from its own balance sheet and collect the drawn-down capital months (sometimes years) later. This easy-going approach was consistent with the way Abraaj's investors ran their own companies and family offices. Larger US-regulated institutional investors did not take the same view.

The private equity company as the GP/manager makes decisions on the investment of the funds. In developed markets, funds usually try to purchase a majority or controlling interest in a target company or ideally buy it in its entirety – if it is a listed company, it is then taken into private ownership. Whilst over 70 per cent of private equity deals in 'developed markets' involve the purchase of majority stakes, the reverse is true in global growth markets, where over 70 per cent of private equity deals involve acquiring only a minority stake in the company. There is a greater 'reluctance of owners to part with a majority interest in promising companies' and company management want to 'raise capital for growth rather than monetarise their business, prematurely, through a sale'.[13] Abraaj would get around this at times by taking minority stakes where it still had effective control over the business through multiple shareholder agreement rights that would be inputted in (i.e. that it was impossible for the family to do anything without their approval). In some countries, for example, across the GCC, there are also laws governing the proportion of a company that can be foreign-owned. Abraaj turned this equation somewhat on its head and always sought to either have majority control or, through minority protection rights in the acquisition agreements, it sought to 'have the right to control the growth agenda' and proudly proclaimed this in the documentation it distributed at the time.

Generally speaking, private equity firms will provide their LPs with reports on a quarterly basis, with those reports being audited on an annual basis. The purpose of the GP report is to provide LP investors with a robust understanding of where the fund is positioned over certain periods of time. The report typically consists of a general update on the fund's target markets in relation to more macro conditions, underlying portfolio company performance, information related to fees and carried interest payable over the period and since the inception of the fund. This is meant to provide LPs with an information overview as per their rights in relation to the specific fund in question in which they have invested. AHL shareholders were given separate materials which were collated on an annual basis, including the audited financials of the group, which is a slightly different model than most similar private equity investment companies, but as almost all of Abraaj's shareholders were investors in one or more of the underlying funds, they would therefore gain access to the GP reports as well.

After investments are exited from the fund through sales, listings and swaps, the private equity company will be allocated a percentage of the profits – usually 20 per cent as mentioned above. This is what has made the founders of some of the famous Wall Street private equity firms fabulously wealthy because they decide how this portion of the carried interest is divided internally. Typically, the founders take roughly 80 to 90 per cent of the entitlement of the firm.[14] In the case of Abraaj, however, Naqvi as founder was entitled – as per the legal documentation – to 75 per cent of the carried interest the firm received. He brought this down to 50 per cent voluntarily in order to split more with the Abraaj team; and then subsequently brought it down again to 20 per cent. But when you think of tens of billions of dollars – 20 per cent of 20 per cent, is not so bad, especially when it adds up to the hundreds of millions if and when realised.

Most funds have a fixed maximum life span in which to achieve returns, usually ten years, with the possibility of a maximum of two, one-year extensions. The theory was that at some point in this lifespan the private equity firm sells its majority or minority stake in the companies in which it has invested. This is known as the exit. When all the portfolio of companies invested in by the fund have been sold the fund is liquidated. The investors are paid back, usually as and when exits occur, hopefully with a profit on their investment because the company has identified the right sector to invest in (sector growth), made effective use of clever debt financing to boost returns (leverage) and/or made a difference to the performance of the company (deal-level abnormal performance). In negative cases this can be done by asset stripping, selling off parts of the business, cutting costs by terminating workers or increasing prices to consumers to try to drive up margins. In most cases in developed markets the private equity fund does not get involved in the running of the company but uses leverage to enhance performance.

Abraaj challenged this tradition because it was involved in growth markets in which debt financing was challenging and risky and, more importantly, because it developed a more interventionist approach to the running of portfolio companies – something the company identified early on as operational value creation focused on both top-line and bottom-line growth; the deal-level multiplier effect that was at the heart of impact investing as described above. In positive cases, private equity makes a difference by enforcing efficiency on portfolio companies. In emerging markets, it is also possible to improve governance and employment rights. In the case of Abraaj, the fund could also bankroll further investment into portfolio companies – for example, to expand outlets or purchase competitors – thereby increasing returns. Rather than stripping assets and draining cash from investments, Abraaj set out to do the opposite, building healthier, more robust, more valuable businesses by seeking incremental 'stakeholder returns' rather than just 'investor returns', which laid the foundations for its impact investing credentials.[15]

Each of the limited partner investors are required to provide a commitment to invest a certain amount within a certain period. By way of example, if the fund is $1 billion then this might be made up of ten investors each agreeing to invest a total of $100 million. The private equity firm also tends to put its own funds into the pool. Abraaj was one of the few firms that had permanent capital available from an early stage to grow exponentially and match the rapid growth of emerging markets. Employee bonuses, stakeholder engagement costs and business development expenses for launching new businesses were all treated as capital expenditure, to be funded by capital or borrowings with short-term profitability sacrificed for hyper growth and long-term profitability.

Abraaj invested heavily into its own funds to help grow portfolio businesses, its people, its profile and future opportunities – essentially showing its skin in the game to an extent far greater than was typical because it had a significant balance sheet of its own. These 'excess inventory' stakes can also be a route for other investors to come into the fund after it has closed by buying, at a premium, the investment put into the fund by the private equity company itself in excess of its contractual requirements to retain as part of the limited partner agreements.

Further, as banks in emerging markets do not always have the capability to finance large amounts of capital, Abraaj would sometimes have to step in and act as the 'lender of last resort', in a number of instances in which its portfolio companies were not able to pay its expenses well after the equity capital was put into the company (whether because they were facing a cash-flow issue or because they were unable to repay their debt financing). In many instances in the early days, Abraaj would end up funding these shortfalls in order to keep such businesses afloat. The tradition in Western private equity is to let those portfolio companies go bankrupt if financing from banks is not available, but Abraaj deployed its substantial capital base at AHL to assist portfolio companies, especially when shepherding many of them through the 2008 financial crash.

The initial limited partners do not have to produce the money up front, but within a fixed time frame called the investment period. Conventionally, this is a legally binding commitment to provide the requisite funds defined by the LPA. However, Abraaj often allowed investors flexibility in meeting their commitments, especially in the first decade of the company's operation.[16] At the time of the financial crash of 2008, Abraaj took the extremely unusual position of releasing several investors from their obligations when they found themselves engulfed by the financial crisis; the exact opposite of what Western private equity firms were doing at the same time. Many of these investors had exposure to both Western private equity firms and their investments in Abraaj funds, which went a long way in enhancing the company's reputation in the markets in which it raised capital. As we will see later, when it attempted to do something similar in 2018 to alleviate investor concerns, the move backfired spectacularly.

The so-called 'Midas touch' with which traditional private equity firms are credited usually follows a textbook script. Normally when the private equity team is ready to invest, it will issue a drawdown notice and the investors will transfer the money to the fund so that it can be invested within a certain period of time. Imagine the fund wants to buy a company valued at $100 million.[17] The fund might issue drawdown notices for $40 million from investors. It places these into a special purpose vehicle, which is used as a bid company to acquire the target. This protects the fund investors from liability for the debt that is then incurred by the bid company itself.[18] The bid company will then borrow the $60 million needed to complete the purchase on an interest-only basis – the security for the loan being the company it is about to purchase. These loans are common across the global banking industry and are relatively easy to obtain; a 60:40 debt-to-equity ratio is considered relatively stable for an acquirer. The company is then bought and through either additional investment or more active engagement its profitability grows by say, 15 per cent per year. At some point before the end of the fund's life the company is sold, say in five years, for say $200 million. After the loan is repaid, $140 million (less the interest on the loan) will remain, which is greatly in excess of the amount originally invested and thus establishes a significant return for the investors; a return of 3.5 times the original invested capital. This is generally how private equity works and much money is made by all.

The private equity firm makes its money in several ways. Usually, it will need to invest in the fund itself, somewhere between 1 and 5 per cent of the total which is required under the terms of the LPA as a means of showing GP commitment to the LPs, but the amount allocated by the GP can be higher (the excess inventory referred to earlier), so it makes money in the same way the limited partners make money. It can also make money, as noted earlier, by selling part of its excess inventory stake to late comers to the fund for a profit – which it keeps in exchange for taking on the initial risk. A GP will also generally act as the fund manager and will take an annual management fee as well. This is usually a percentage of the investment that has been committed in aggregate by all LPs. After the end of the investment period, the charge will be a percentage of the total amount actually invested into assets acquired under the fund. These charges are paid to the GP by way of fees, usually set at 2 per cent per annum. There is also a carried interest fee (carry), which reflects the performance of the fund managers. This can be a percentage of the overall profit made by the fund or it may be conditional upon the return meeting a particular threshold level (the hurdle rate). Carried interest is usually 20 per cent of profits generated by the fund, distributed after the hurdle rate has been met and equalised through a formula contained in the LPA. The only difference between the way different funds may operate is that they may pay out carry immediately after a company has been exited and proceeds distributed to LPs (known as 'deal-by-deal' carry, or 'American-style carry') or carry is paid after investors have received back all their originally invested capital and the hurdle rate (known as 'whole-fund carry' or 'European-style carry'). Abraaj had American-style carry in its funds closed prior to 2012 and European-style carry in all funds thereafter, which is generally regarded as better for the interests of LPs and for enhancing the fund IRRs.

The final way in which private equity firms make money is through an innovation introduced by global banking institutions, called sponsor loans (the names 'private equity firm' and 'private equity sponsor' are used interchangeably in the industry). These loans are provided by the 'house banks', which is the terminology used for defining banks that have a close relationship with the GP and the individuals that comprise it. Banks are, above all, interested in 'share of wallet'; they want to lend money for portfolio investments made by funds; lend against dividend streams in the future; lend money for working capital to the portfolio companies; and provide fee-earning services, such as handling custody and administration for funds and the assets they own, foreign exchange services, hedging strategies and transfers and private banking services for high-net-worth partners. In exchange for being classified as house banks, which carry prestige for the bank the bigger its customer is, banks will help the GP and fund managers by providing sponsor loans at attractive rates of interest that enable the GP to finance its stake in the underlying funds; or lend money to the individual sponsors to finance their individual stakes in the funds; provide working capital to the GP to smooth out cash-flow issues; and finally, acquire assets that enable the firm in question to grow. Very often, these sponsor loans are provided as a legitimate form of inducement, but their purpose is clear: to gain a greater share of wallet. They bear little relationship to assets offered as security for the financings extended and, more often than not, are given to private equity firms with minimal capitalisation themselves. A senior executive in the finance team at Abraaj told me that they had sponsor loans from their three house banks: Société Générale, Commercial Bank of Dubai and Mashreq Bank and there were plenty of other banks that wanted to lend money along the way, such as Citi, Deutsche and Credit Suisse who were constantly coming to offer attractive conditions. Although Abraaj had approximately $500 million in secured borrowings and an additional $500 million in unsecured loans, they also had assets in excess of $2 billion; not a ratio that would put any business under strain, let alone one that had banks willing to continue to extend credit.

The performance of Abraaj as a private equity company in terms of the difference it made in deal-level abnormal performance is stark in comparison with its peers because profit and loss is not the only way in which a company should be read. In addition to the profit and loss metric, we need to understand the social, economic and political context in which the company was formed, developed and rapidly grew. The team who ran the company and the decisions they made are, obviously, critical in assessing the success of the company, but so too is the context in which it operated. This was not a private equity or venture capital firm making investments in high-tech start-ups in Silicon Valley. This was a private equity firm based in Dubai with an investor base of family offices of high-net-worth individuals and families, which gradually expanded that base to include more institutionalised investors making investments in emerging markets. It did not do these things in a vacuum. And it certainly was not alone in its thinking that it should do so – as it was encouraged by world-class advisers, service providers, investors and governments around the world to grow.

The support for its expansion and recognition of its contribution was hard won.

# Chronology of events

30 October 2016 – Abraaj announce the sale of Karachi Electric to Shanghai Electric Power Company.

8 November 2016 – Donald J. Trump wins the US presidential election.

19 January 2017 – Naqvi memo: 'Use your common sense... just don't shut down the business.'

15 March 2017 – Abraaj Global Healthcare Fund query, drawdown request for $115 million from the fund.

20 May 2017 – Internal email: 'We will have no funds available for the June salaries of the Group.'

21 June 2017 – Abraaj enters into an agreement with Air Arabia for a loan of $196 million.

20 September – Anonymous emails sent to existing and prospective investors warning them not to believe Abraaj's books.

27 September 2017 – Security clearances provisionally granted for Chinese buyers of Karachi Electric.

11 October 2017 – Karachi Electric's multi-year tariff is revised to Rs.12.771 kWh, significantly down from its previous rate of Rs.15.6 kWh.

4 December 2017 – Balance of Abraaj Global Healthcare Fund account is $16,185.66.

31 December 2017 – Abraaj returns all funds to investors through new borrowings and asset disposals.

January 2018 – US sovereign lender group Overseas Private Investment

Corporation enters Abraaj Global Healthcare Fund dispute with Abraaj over $65 million taken out of their loan commitment to the Health Fund.

20 January 2018 – The four main Abraaj Global Healthcare Fund investors call for an investigative audit despite existence of a KPMG report.

22 January 2018 – President Trump announces first round of tariffs on Chinese goods.

2 February 2018 – *New York Times* and *Wall Street Journal* break story accusing Abraaj of misusing investor funds.

25 February 2018 – Naqvi steps away from fund management business.

March 2018 – Abraaj Private Equity Fund VI investors released from their commitments – Société Générale freezes Abraaj accounts.

March 2018 – Senior executives leave the firm.

25 July 2018 – Imran Khan wins Pakistani elections.

5 September 2018 – Secretary of State Mike Pompeo makes first visit to Pakistan, to 'reset relations' with the new government, advises the International Monetary Fund will not fund any China–Pakistan Economic Corridor-linked infrastructure.

26 September 2018 – Abraaj staff asked to vacate the firm's Dubai offices as it is dismantled.

September 2018 to April 2019 – Naqvi focused on Abraaj restructuring liasing with creditors and working on Karachi Electric transaction.

10 to 12 April 2019 – Naqvi arrested at Heathrow airport and US Department of Justice indictments announced.

# Acknowledgements

Given the ongoing litigation involved in this story I am not listing the many people who have helped me with interviews, documents and other sources. They know who they are and they know how grateful I am to them – especially the squashed sandwich crew.

As it is mentioned at the beginning of the book, I will thank Arif Naqvi for giving me the background interviews that he did. Having known many politicians over many years of working as a contemporary historian and a biographer, I understand the difference between the image the media creates and the reality of the person in the flesh. I have never encountered a greater contrast between what I expected from the reports I had read and what I found sitting opposite me. I hope he comes out fighting one day and gives interviews and writes his memoirs because there is another side to this story and he should be able to tell it. I hope I have been fair to him in this book.

The team at Biteback – James Stephens, Olivia Beattie, James Lilford and Suzanne Sangster – have been outstanding, professional and very patient with more than the usual round of last-minute edits.

My Iraqi training partner, Ghassan Jawad, has also been patient with my slower than usual response rate whilst I completed this lockdown project – Habibi: normal service will resume shortly. My son, Max Brivati, created the referencing and support website for the book and has helped in myriad ways with the research. He is a great researcher and is available for hire at competitive rates via LinkedIn.

My wife Meg and I are used to living with books being written and books being finished. The past two times it was her study on trauma (mentioned in the Preface) and her new edited collection of Katherine Mansfield's short stories in the Macmillan classics line – available in July. So it was my turn. She has been, as always, a source of wisdom, love and support throughout the rather manic past six months. This book would not have been written without her support and the channelling of one of her many powerful mottos, with thanks to Louisa May Alcott: 'Hope and keep busy' – which, given the deadline for delivering this book, was more appropriate than ever.

My father died in 1992 but has been with me a great deal during the writing of this book – especially when I was feeling exhausted, 'Come on Titch, get your finger out!' I could hear him say, as he used to when I worked in his bakery as a kid, whilst in the background my late mother is listening to the Bach cello suites to keep me focused.

*Brian Brivati*
*London*
*June 2021*

# Notes

All the basic references are printed below. They can also be found at the website www.abraajbook.com or www.lifeanddeathofabraaj.com.

At the beginning of each chapter of references below there is a URL which will take you to the references for that chapter. The online references will, in some cases, have additional material, links and discussions. Where possible the documents cited in the references have been uploaded to the website for easy access and in case links are broken in the future. Where this is not possible for copyright reasons a link is included to the online site. The website will also contain a blog on key issues and themes from the book and in which we will include any new material that comes available after publication. If there are major new developments in the story we will also report on these via the website.

### Preface

1    Meg Jensen, *The Art and Science of Trauma and the Autobiographical: Negotiated Truths* (London: Palgrave, 2019).

### Chapter 1: Shall justice be done?
Sources available here: https://wp.me/Pd2ymq-y.

1    The full opinion and order can be found here: https://prisonology.com/wp-content/uploads/2020/11/Opinion-Nejad-Sep-16-2020.pdf.
2    *United States of America v Arif Naqvi, Waqar Siddique, Rafique Lakhani, Mustafa*

*Abdel-Wadood, Ashish Dave and Sivendran Vettivetpillai: Affidavit in support of request for the extradition of Arif Naqvi and Sivendran Vettivetpillai*, United States District Court, Southern District of New York, 3 June 2019.

3   See for example the brilliant recent study: Jed S. Rakoff, *Why the Innocent Plead Guilty and the Guilty Go Free and Other Paradoxes of our Broken Legal System* (New York: Farrar, Straus & Giroux, 2021).

4   Kelly Phillips Erb, 'Al Capone Sentenced To Prison For Tax Evasion On This Day In 1931', *Forbes*, 17 October 2018.

5   For a detailed discussion of the weaknesses in the treaty see my blog posts, especially 'Someone must have been telling lies about Joseph K', https://charlwood-review.com/2020/11/25/someone-must-have-been-telling-lies-about-joseph-k/, and 'The case of Arif Naqvi and UK–US Extradition Treaty', https://charlwood-review.com/2021/03/02/the-case-of-arif-naqvi-and-uk-us-extradition-treaty/.

6   Both documents can be accessed on my website here: https://lifeanddeathofabraaj.com/.

7   *United States of America v Arif Naqvi, Waqar Siddique, Rafique Lakhani, Mustafa Abdel-Wadood, Ashish Dave and Sivendran Vettivetpillai*.

8   Josh Lerner and Ant Bozkaya, 'Abraaj Capital', Harvard Business Publishing, July 2008. See also later citations for other work by Lerner on Abraaj and private equity.

9   Simon Clark has discussed the leaks of emails, documents and SMS messages. He stated that he still does not know who sent him the first emails. 'Abraaj Laid Bare' podcast with Ludovic Phalippou, https://pelaidbare.com/podcast/abraaj-laid-bare/.

10   Atika Rehman, 'Footprints: Arif Naqvi — the man who flew too close to the sun', *Dawn*, 1 February 2021. I am grateful for the title.

11   Tracy Alloway, Dinesh Nair and Matthew Martin, 'The Downfall of Dubai's Star Investor', Bloomberg News, 14 June 2018, https://www.bloomberg.com/news/articles/2018-06-14/the-downfall-of-arif-naqvi-s-abraaj-group-dubai-s-star-investor.

12   'Abraaj Laid Bare' podcast.

13   'Alstom Sentenced to Pay $772 Million Criminal Fine to Resolve Foreign Bribery Charges', US Department of Justice press release, 13 November 2015, https://www.justice.gov/opa/pr/alstom-sentenced-pay-772-million-criminal-fine-resolve-foreign-bribery-charges.

14   Khaleeq Kiani, 'Govt mulls over proposal to unbundle K-Electric', *Dawn*, 31 May 2021.

15   An example of this can be seen even before the birth of the APEF VI superfund in 'The Abraaj Group Corporate Video 2013'.

## Chapter 2: 'So, what do you think I am?'

Sources available here: https://wp.me/Pd2ymq-B.

1   'Abraaj collapse: What's been learned, who's charged?', *Arabian Business News*, 8 August 2019.

2   Carmela Mendoza, 'Impact investments assets break half and trillion', *Private Equity International*, 2 April 2019.

3   Melissa Gronlund, 'Fire sale of Abraaj art at auction: Million dollar work on the block starting at $66,000', The National News, 9 October, 2018, https://www.thenationalnews.com/arts-culture/art/fire-sale-of-abraaj-art-at-auction-million-dollar-work-on-the-block-starting-at-66-000-1.778917.

4   'K-Electric: the power utility at center of Abraaj debacle', TRT World, 18 October 2018, https://www.trtworld.com/asia/k-electric-the-power-utility-at-center-of-abraaj-debacle-20969; Nicholas Waller, 'Is Arif Naqvi the fall guy for Sino-Pakistan relations?', *New Europe*, 19 October 2018.

5   'Veritas', Portico Advisers Blog, 15 February 2018, https://porticoadvisers.com/2018/02/15/veritas-feb-2018/.

6   The rise of a distinctly Chinese model of consumption and doing business and the spread of it as China rises on the world stage as an economic and political power is highlighted in: Cheng Lu Wang and Xiaohua Lin, 'Migration of Chinese Consumption Values: Traditions, Modernization, and Cultural Renaissance', *Journal of Business Ethics*, Vol. 88, Supplement 3: Confucian/Chopsticks Marketing, 2009, pp. 399–409.

7   Peter Baker, 'Trump Abandons Trans-Pacific Partnership, Obama's Signature Trade Deal', *New York Times*, 23 January 2017.

8   Ana Swanson and Paul Mozur, 'Trump Mixes Economic and National Security, Plunging the US Into Multiple Fights', *New York Times*, 8 June 2019.

9   Christian Nunley, 'US warns companies to abandon work on Nord Stream 2 pipeline as Biden reportedly weighs sanctions', CNBC News, 18 March 2021, https://www.cnbc.com/2021/03/18/us-warns-companies-to-abandon-work-on-nord-stream-2-pipeline-.html.

10  Ibid., 'US State Department states Nord Stream 2 disrupts Trans-Atlantic security', 112 UA, 4 February 2021, https://112.international/politics/us-state-department-states-nord-stream-2-disrupts-transatlantic-security-58692.html, and Dave Keating, 'Trump Imposes Sanctions To Stop Nord Stream 2 – But It's Too late', *Forbes*, 21 December 2019.

11  Office of the Secretary of Defense, 'SASC Hearing on US Africa Command and US Southern Command' 28 April 2021:

GENERAL STEPHEN TOWNSEND, COMMANDER US AFRICA COMMAND: Thank you, senator. Actually we do see some backlash, as you know – you have famous – heard of the famous debt-trap diplomacy that they – the Chinese have used. That has actually worked against their efforts in a lot of African countries.

Our embassies have a very successful program where we now will review any contracts – we have an – a standing offer to review any contracts that these countries are going to undertake with China to point out the inconsistencies, the potential pitfalls. And the difference is often, we find, between the host nation language translation and the Chinese translation.

I think this is a great effort by our Department of State to help these countries make informed decisions on their own.

12  Dilawar Hussain, 'Shanghai Power committed to buying K-Electric', *Dawn*, 27 March 2018.

13  Rashid Ahmad Khan, 'Pakistan and China: cooperation in counter-terrorism', *Strategic Studies*, Vol. 32, No. 4, Winter 2012, pp. 70–78.

14  Gurpreet S. Khurana, 'China's 'String of Pearls' in the Indian Ocean and Its Security Implications', *Strategic Analysis*, Vol. 23, No. 1, 27 February 2008, pp. 1–39.

15  'Goldman Sachs to pay $3bn over 1MDB corruption scandal', BBC News, 22 October 2020, https://www.bbc.co.uk/news/business-54597256.

16  'Deutsche Bank handed $124 million in bribery fines by US court', DW.com, 8 January 2021, https://www.dw.com/en/deutsche-bank-handed-124-million-in-bribery-fines-by-us-court/a-56176485.

17  'Skeleton arguments on behalf of the respondent', In the matter of An Appeal by the Requesting State against the grant of bail, under section 1(1A) of the Bail Amendment Act 1993 between The Government of the United States of America and Arif Masood Naqvi, 3 May 2019; Simeon Kerr, 'Abraaj founder Arif Naqvi released from UK prison on bail', *Financial Times*, 29 May 2019.

18  Erik Larson, 'Abraaj's Abdel-Wadood Pleads Guilty, Will Cooperate in Probe', 28 June 2019, Bloomberg Quint, http://www.bloombergquint.com/business/abraaj-executive-abdel-wadood-pleads-guilty-to-conspiracy.

19  Rakoff, *Why the Innocent Plead Guilty and the Guilty Go Free and Other Paradoxes of our Broken Legal System*.

20  This idea has been examined and explored throughout the twentieth century. Examples include Smedley D. Butler, *War is a Racket* (New York: Round Table Press, 1935); Ruth Blakeley, *State Terrorism and Neoliberalism: The North in the South* (Abingdon and New York: Routledge, 2009); and Kevin P. Gallagher, *Ruling Capital: Emerging Markets and the Reregulation of Cross-Border Finance* (Ithaca: Cornell University Press, 2015).

21  As above, see Christian Fuchs, *Communication and Capitalism: A Critical Theory* (London: University of Westminster Press, 2020); and Mary Griffiths and Kim Barbour (eds), *Making Publics, Making Places* (Adelaide: Adelaide University Press, 2016), for examples of this idea.

### Chapter 3: The creation of a Gulf capitalist class
Sources available here: https://wp.me/Pd2ymq-F.

1   Arif M. Naqvi, Cupola Group, 13 October 1999, 'How does a company prepare

itself for corporatising and restructuring?', text from a speech delivered at the Private and Family Enterprises Seminar held by the Institute of International Research, 11 May 1997, http://web.archive.org/web/20010123204500fw_/http://cupolagroup.com/arifspeechgmr.htm.

2   Ibid.

3   Andrew C. Hess, 'Peace and Political Reform in the Gulf: The Private Sector', *Journal of International Affairs*, Vol. 49, No. 1, Summer 1995, pp. 103–22.

4   Hanieh submitted his PhD in 2009 and published his first book, *Capitalism and Class in the Gulf Arab states* (Basingstoke: Palgrave, Macmillan, 2011). Also see Simon Clark, Nicolas Parasie and William Louch, 'Private-Equity Firm Abraaj Raised Billions Pledging to Do Good – Then It Fell Apart', *Wall Street Journal*, 16 October 2018.

5   Ibid.

6   'The Infrastructure Investment Requirements of the MENASA Region', Abraaj Capital, 2015, https://www.yumpu.com/en/document/view/28179248/the-infrastructure-investment-requirements-of-the-wamdacom.

7   'Abraaj Capital US$2 billion fund targets vast infrastructure investment opportunities', Al Bawaba Business, 24 December 2006, https://www.albawaba.com/business/abraaj-capital-us2-billion-fund-targets-vast-infrastructure-investment-opportunities.

8   Adam Hanieh, *Lineages of Revolt: Issues of Contemporary Capitalism in the Middle East*, (Chicago: Haymarket Books, 2013), p. 62.

9   Ibid., p. 40.

10  Priyanka Motaparthy, 'Understanding Kafala: An archaic law at cross purposes with modern development', migrantrights.org, 11 March 2015, https://www.migrant-rights.org/2015/03/understanding-kafala-an-archaic-law-at-cross-purposes-with-modern-development/.

11  In Naqvi's speech quoted earlier, this connects with his point about 'the signing, ratifying, and implementing of GATT and WTO accords'.

12  Joel Benin, *Workers and Thieves: Labour Movements and Popular uprisings in Tunisia and Egypt*, (Stanford: Stanford University Press, 2014), pp. 55–9, 65–70.

13  Muhammad Asif Nadeem et al., 'Migration Impact on Remittances Special Focus on Gulf Countries: A Case Study of Pakistan', *North American Journal of Academic Research*, Vol. 2, Issue 8, August 2019.

14  Matthew T. Page, Jodi Vittori, 'Dubai's Role in Facilitating Corruption and Global Illicit Financial Flows', Carnegie Endowment for International Peace, 7 July 2020   https://carnegieendowment.org/2020/07/07/dubai-s-role-in-facilitating-corruption-and-global-illicit-financial-flows-pub-82180.

15  Hanieh, *Capitalism and Class in the Gulf Arab States*.

16  Karl Marx, 'Part VII. Revenues and their Sources, Chapter 48: The Trinity Formula', *Das Kapital, Volume III* (Moscow: Foreign Languages Publishing House, 1961–62).

17  Private information.

18  Imtiaz Hydari, *Leverage in the Desert: The Birth of Private Equity in the Middle East*, self-published, 2013, p. 72.

19  See for example: 'Tuning Out Politics, Abraaj Capital tries to rebuild Karachi Electrical Supply Company', 3 September 2009, https://wikileaks.org/plusd/cables/09DUBAI367_a.html.

20  'The Story of Cupola's US$130 million Inchcape acquisition', *Khaleej Times*, Tuesday 13 July 1999.

21  'Careers in Cupola Teleservices Limited', Laimoon, https://jobs.laimoon.com/uae/company/cupola-teleservices-limited.

22  Ibid.

23  Private information.

24  Imitiaz Hydari, *Leverage in the Desert*, p. 33.

25  Private information.

26  'Data Room', Divestopedia, https://www.divestopedia.com/definition/753/data-room#:~:text=A%20data%20room%20is%20a%20secure%20location%20that,also%20known%20as%20a%20due%20diligence%20data%20room.

### Chapter 4: The birth of Abraaj 1.0
Sources available here: https://wp.me/Pd2ymq-I.

1  Sara Hamdan, 'Private Equity Pioneer Looks Beyond the Unrest', *New York Times*, 27 April 2011.

2  'What is YPO?', Young Presidents' Organization, https://www.ypo.org/what-is-ypo/.

3  Fadi Ghandour, 'How I Did It: The CEO of Aramex on Turning a Failed Sale into a Huge Opportunity', *Harvard Business Review Magazine*, March 2011.

4  Ibid.

5  'ABRAAJ INVESTMENT MANAGEMENT LIMITED', Offshore Leaks Database, The International Consortium of Investigative Journalists, https://offshoreleaks.icij.org/nodes/56098759.

6  Abraaj pitch deck, 2018, p. 9.

7  In 2018 Air Arabia reported that their investment was worth $336 million. From Sarah Diaa, 'Air Arabia says investment in Abraaj valued at $336m', *Gulf News*, 20 June 2018.

8  Robert Venes, 'Abraaj closes fund II on $500m', *Private Equity International*, 31 January 2006.

9  'Abraaj Capital closes largest private equity transaction in history of Middle East and North Africa', *Albawaba News*, 3 June 2007, https://www.albawaba.com/news/abraaj-capital-closes-largest-private-equity-transaction-history-middle-east-and-north-africa.

10  'Abraaj Capital becomes first pure Private Equity company to receive licence

to operate in DIFC', press release, DIFC, 22 March 2006, https://www.difc.ae/newsroom/news/abraaj-capital-becomes-first-pure-private-equity-company-receive-licence-operate-difc/.

11  Abraaj annual report, 2007.

12  'Abraaj sells its stake in EFG-Hermes', *Arabian Business News*, 1 December 2007.

13  Helen Thomas, 'Abraaj in biggest private equity deal to date for Middle East' *Financial Times*, 7 June 2007.

14  'Insight MENA: An Overview of Trends in Select Sectors and Markets', Emerging Markets Private Equity Association, May 2009, https://www.empea.org/app/uploads/2017/03/EMPEAInsight_MENA_0509_web-2.pdf.

15  Adam Lewis, 'Actis joins growing list of PE shops pouncing on Abraaj stakes', PitchBook, 15 July 2015, https://pitchbook.com/news/articles/actis-joins-growing-list-of-pe-shops-pouncing-on-abraaj-stakes.

16  'The Abraaj Group in JV with Deutsche, Ithmaar Bank', *The Economic Times*, 24 May 2006.

17  Private information.

18  Abraaj produced annual reports from 2007 all the way up to 2016, each more glossy than the last.

19  Musharraf was also comparatively socially liberal, granting amnesty to the previously proscribed political workers of parties such as the Muttahida Qaumi Movement, and encouraging the growth of modern popular music, film, theatre and television – issuing many licences to private sector open television houses and media centres, see Pervez Musharraf, *In the Line of Fire: A Memoir*, first edition (Pakistan: Free Press, 2006), pp. 40–60.

20  Private information.

21  Private information.

22  Private information.

23  See Thomas Lynch, 'Imagining Pakistan in 2020', EastWest, 29 February 2012, https://www.eastwest.ngo/idea/imagining-pakistan-2020, *Radicalisation, Fragmentation and Reform*, p. xx.

24  'Art Dubai 2021 confirms in-person event for March', ArtForum, 23 September 2020, https://www.artforum.com/news/art-dubai-2021-confirms-in-person-event-for-march-83971#:~:text=Art%20Dubai%2C%20which%20since%20its%202007%20founding%20has,local%20economy%20in%202019%2C%20according%20to%20Arabian%20Business, and Abraaj Capital and Wamda Capital, 'The Infrastructure Investment Requirements of the MENASA Region', 2015, https://www.yumpu.com/en/document/view/28179248/the-infrastructure-investment-requirements-of-the-wamdacom.

25  Alexandra A. Seno, 'Eyes on the Prizes', *Newsweek International*, 18 January 2010.

26  The Abraaj Prize was recognised in academic analyses of art prizes globally, see Louise Wilson, 'The Turner Prize may seem out of date, but it created the UK's contemporary art scene', The Conversation, 8 December 2016,

https://theconversation.com/the-turner-prize-may-seem-out-of-date-but-it-created-the-uks-contemporary-art-scene-70148, and a review of the 2013 competition: Kaelen Wilson-Goldie, 'The Abraaj Group Art Prize names five winners', *The Daily Star*, 12 June 2013. See also, 'The Abraaj Group USD2 billion fund targets vast infrastructure investment opportunities', *Middle East Company News*, 20 December 2006, and Adam Hanieh, *Lineages of Revolt: Issues of Contemporary Capitalism in the Middle* East, (Chicago, Haymarket Books, 2013), p. 62 and p. 40.

27   Dubai Cares, https://www.dubaicares.ae/.

28   Recognition for CSR came in 2016 when Abraaj was awarded an A+ rating in the UN 'Principles for Responsible Investment Assessment', 7 December 2016.

29   'Abraaj acquires 80pc stake in MS Forgings', *Khaleej Times*, 27 November 2006.

30   'Agriculture, Region gains an appetite for Africa', *Middle East Economic Digest*, 14 November 2008.

31   'UAE investors buy Pakistan farmland', farmlandgrab.org, 11 May 2008, https://www.farmlandgrab.org/post/view/2349-uae-investors-buy-pakistan-farmland.

32   'Dubai's Abraaj interested in Pakistan agriculture', Reuters, 12 May 2008.

33   Melodena Stephens Balakrishnan and Ian Michael, 'Abraaj Capital Limited: Celebration of Entrepreneurship (CoE)', Emerald Emerging Markets Case Study, October 2011.

34   Wael Mahdi, 'Jordan finalising sale of stake in state energy firm', *Arabian Business News*, Tuesday 18 September 2007, https://www.arabianbusiness.com/jordan-finalising-sale-of-stake-in-state-energy-firm-55202.html.

35   Ibid.

36   Ibid.

37   Zubair Ahmed, 'Abraaj Group's First Investment In Pakistan: Partners with Islamabad Diagnostic Centre', PakWired, 2 March 2017 https://pakwired.com/abraaj-group-partners-with-islamabad-diagnostic-center-through-funds/.

38   Ibid.

39   Global Justice Now, 'Doing more harm than good: Why CDC must reform for people and planet', February 2020, https://www.globaljustice.org.uk/wp-content/uploads/2020/02/web_gjn_-_doing_more_harm_than_good_cdc_-_feb_2020_2.pdf, p. 20.

40   Abraaj sells its stake in EFG-Hermes, *Arabian Business News*, 1 December 2007, https://www.arabianbusiness.com/abraaj-sells-its-stake-in-efg-hermes-196614.html.

41   Video in 'Watch Barack Obama's 2009 Cairo speech on relations with the Muslim world', *The Independent*, 16 January 2017.

42   'Report from OPIC management to Board of Directors', https://www.dfc.gov/sites/default/files/2019-08/riyada_enterprise_development_fund_lp.pdf.

43   The website of the foundation still has the Abraaj logo proudly displayed: http://www.mustaqbali.org. To date they have provided 1,500 Palestinian children with educational opportunities.

44 'Economic recovery and revitalization', Middle East Strategy Task Force, The Atlantic Council, 3 February 2016, https://www.atlanticcouncil.org/in-depth-research-reports/report/economic-recovery-and-revitalization-report/.

45 Christopher Schroeder, *Startup Rising: The Entrepreneurial Revolution Remaking the Middle East* (New York City: Palgrave Macmillan, 2013).

46 Ellen Laipson, 'Seismic Shift: Understanding Change in the Middle East', Harold L Stimson Centre, May 2011, https://www.stimson.org/wp-content/files/Full_Pub-Seismic_Shift.pdf.

47 Frank Kane, 'Abraaj confident on Mena prospects despite Arab Spring', National News Business, 18 July 2011, https://www.thenationalnews.com/business/abraaj-confident-on-mena-prospects-despite-arab-spring-1.417013.

48 'Abraaj boosts Egypt investment: Chief executive' Ahram Online, 1 November 2011, https://english.ahram.org.eg/News/25691.aspx.

49 'Abraaj on North African consolidation', *Private Equity International*, 23 June 2016.

50 Abraaj Capital Annual Review, 2010.

51 Mohamed-Salah Omri, 'Tunisia: a revolution for dignity and freedom that can not be colour-coded', The Transnational Institute, 29 January 2011, https://www.tni.org/en/article/tunisia-revolution-dignity-and-freedom-can-not-be-colour-coded.

52 Abraaj Annual Review, 2016.

53 Peter Vanham, 'A brief history of globalization', World Economic Forum, 17 January 2019, https://www.weforum.org/agenda/2019/01/how-globalization-4-0-fits-into-the-history-of-globalization/.

54 Stefan Wagstyl, 'Abraaj buys Aureos: but for how much?', *Financial Times*, 20 February 2012.

55 Private information.

56 Global Justice Now, 'Doing more harm than good: Why CDC must reform for people and planet'.

57 Julia Brethenoux, 'Financing Missing Middle SMEs in Emerging Markets: Insights about Small Cap Mezzanine Finance', SME Finance Forum, 11 August 2016, https://www.smefinanceforum.org/post/financing-missing-middle-smes-in-emerging-markets-insights-about-small-cap-mezzanine-finance.

58 'Formalizing the Informal Economy', WIEGO, https://www.wiego.org/our-work-impact/themes/formalization.

59 UPDATE 3-Dubai's Abraaj buys Aureos in emerging market push', Reuters, 20 February 2012, https://www.reuters.com/article/abraaj-aureos-idUSL5E8D-K11K20120220.

60 Sustainability and Value Creation at the Abraaj Group, November 2016.

61 Ranjani Raghavan, 'Abraaj managing partner Sev Vettivetpillai to leave', VCCircle, 19 March 2018, https://www.vccircle.com/abraaj-managing-partner-sev-vettivetpillai-to-leave/.

62 'UPDATE 3-Dubai's Abraaj buys Aureos in emerging market push'.

63  For example, see Naqvi's keynote speech in 'Doing Well by Doing Good? Private Equity Investing in Emerging Markets', LSE, 30 April 2013, https://www.lse. ac.uk/finance/news/2013/doing-well-by-doing-good-private-equity-investing-in-emerging-markets. Similarly, see Naqvi's contribution to 'Rethinking Infrastructure: Voices from the Global Infrastructure Initiative', McKinsey, Vol. 2, May 2015, https://www.mckinsey.com/~/media/McKinsey/Industries/Public%20and%20Social%20Sector/Our%20Insights/The%20Global%20Infrastructure%20Initiative/Rethinking%20Infrastructure_2_%20FINAL_.pdf.

64  See for example, 'Five Ways that ESG creates value', McKinsey, October 2019, https://www.mckinsey.com/~/media/McKinsey/Business%20Functions/Strategy%20and%20Corporate%20Finance/Our%20Insights/Five%20ways%20that%20ESG%20creates%20value/Five-ways-that-ESG-creates-value.ashx.

65  The Abraaj Group 2018, pp. 47–53 – a pitch deck for potential buyers released at the time of the crisis.

66  This has become the accepted framework for the industry, see 'What You Need to Know About Impact Investing', Global Impact Investing Network, https://thegiin.org/impact-investing/need-to-know/#characteristics-of-impact-investing.

67  'Better Business, Better World: The report of the Business and Sustainable Development Commission', Business and Sustainable Development Commission, January 2017, https://sustainabledevelopment.un.org/content/documents/2399BetterBusinessBetterWorld.pdf.

68  'Introduction to The Abraaj Group: Memorandum', The Abraaj Group, May 2017, p. 27.

69  See Abraaj annual reports for 2008 to 2016.

## Chapter 5: How good was Abraaj?
Sources available here: https://wp.me/Pd2ymq-L.

1  Simon Clark and Will Louch, *The Key Man: How the Global Elite Was Duped by a Capitalist Fairy Tale* (London: Penguin, 2021).

2  Ibid.

3  Editorial reviews are commissioned by publishers from advance readers of books to place on Amazon. In this review, accessed on 27 May 2021, the reviewer wrote: 'An unbelievable true tale of greed, corruption, and manipulation among the world's financial elite and how the World Bank, Bill Gates, and the governments of the US, UK, France, Germany, Norway, the Netherlands, Sweden, and Kuwait fell victim to the world's largest private equity Ponzi scheme. This guy makes Bernie Madoff look like a saint.' – Harry Markopolos, the Bernie Madoff whistle-blower, https://www.amazon.com/Key-Man-Story-Global-Capitalist-ebook/dp/B08KQ97TDX.

4  Alex Konrad, 'Andreessen Horowitz Is Blowing Up The Venture Capital Model (Again)', *Forbes*, 2 April 2019.

5   Private information.
6   Shaka Momodu, 'Why we are passionate about investing in Nigeria', *All Africa*, 24 February 2014.
7   'Private Placement Memorandum', Abraaj Growth Health Fund, Clause 8.1 of Appendix 8: 'Conflicts of Interest'.
8   A more detailed explanation of decomposition analysis can be found here: https://wp.me/Pd2ymq-L, see also Josh Lerner and James Tighe, 'The Abraaj Group's Returns: A Decomposition Analysis', Harvard Business School and Bella Research Group, March 2015, p. iii.
9   Shourun Guo, Edith S. Hotchkiss, Weihong Song, 'Do Buyouts (Still) Create Value?' *The Journal of Finance*, Vol. 56, Issue 2, April 2011 and Viral Acharya, Oliver F. Gottschalg, Moritz Hahn, Conor Kehoe, 'Corporate Governance and Value Creation: Evidence from Private Equity', *Review of Financial Studies*, Vol. 26, Issue 2, 2013.

## Chapter 6: From Abraaj 1.0 to Abraaj 2.0
Sources available here: https://wp.me/Pd2ymq-O.

1   Former Abraaj employee, quoted in Simon Clark, Nicolas Parasie and William Louch, 'Private-Equity Firm Abraaj Raised Billions Pledging to Do Good – Then It Fell Apart', *Wall Street Journal*, 16 October 2018.
2   'Implementing SDG goals good for business', *Namibian Sun*, 16 January 2017.
3   'Ideas for action for a long-term and sustainable financial system: A paper commissioned by the Business and Sustainable Development Commission,' Business Commission on Sustainable Development, 2017, http://s3.amazonaws.com/aws-bsdc/BSDC_SustainableFinanceSystem.pdf, Abraaj had four members on the commission: Arif Naqvi, Tania Choufani, Frederic Sicre and Vinay Chawla.
4   US investors involvement with Abraaj are all outlined in detail in the judgment on the extradition request and other documents of record. See for example, 'In the matter of a request for Extradition under Part 2 of the Extradition Act 2003, *The United States Of America v Arif Masood Naqvi*'. Hamilton Lane's involvement with Abraaj is covered in multiple places, for example:

> Paragraph 30. Hamilton Lane's clients' first investment in Abraaj was in 2015 and then it invested in a total of five funds. About $175m was committed to APEF IV. Hamilton Lane's clients were overwhelmingly US based. Since early 2015, Ms Kendall says that US investors accounted for at least $340 million of the $1.6 billion of capital committed to APEF IV.

5   'The Abraaj Group, Optimism, Impact and Performance: Engagement in Africa', The Abraaj Group, 2013, https://www.altassets.net/wp-content/uploads/2013/06/africa_abraaj_altassets.pdf.

6   'The Abraaj Group, Resilience Amid Change: Our Engagement in North Africa', The Abraaj Group, 2014, https://s3-us-west-2.amazonaws.com/ungc-production/attachments/76641/original/North_Africa_Private_Sector_Impact_Report.pdf?1398166488.

7   Abraaj annual report, 2015.

8   'Fostering Development Through Private Equity', IFC, May 2016, https://www.ifc.org/wps/wcm/connect/news_ext_content/ifc_external_corporate_site/news+and+events/news/fostering+development+through+private+equity.

9   *The Abraaj Group 2018*, p. 14.

10  Private information.

11  Private information.

12  See The Giving Pledge website: https://givingpledge.org/.

13  'Pledge Signatories', Pledger List – The Giving Pledge, https://www.givingpledge.org/PledgerList.aspx.

14  Private information.

15  Greg Roumeliotis, Simon Meads, 'Apax Partners senior dealmaker exits as losses loom', Reuters, 27 September 2012, https://www.reuters.com/article/apax-mann-idUKL5E8KRCBZ20120927.

16  Mihajlo B. Jakovljevic and Olivera Milovanovic, 'Growing burden of non-communicable diseases in the emerging health markets: the case of BRICS', Frontiers in Public Health, 23 April 2015, https://www.frontiersin.org/articles/10.3389/fpubh.2015.00065/full.

17  The UN's SDG 3 is as follows: 'Ensure healthy lives and promote well-being for all at all ages.' See: https://sdgs.un.org/goals/goal3.

18  Toby Mitchenall, 'Abraaj nears $1 billion target for healthcare fund', Infrastructure Investor, 8 November 2016, https://www.infrastructureinvestor.com/abraaj-nears-1bn-target-for-healthcare-fund/.

19  Dennis Price, 'What we know about Abraaj's $1 billion health fund – and the mystery of the firm's finances', Impact Alpha, 7 February 2018, https://impactalpha.com/what-we-know-about-abraajs-1-billion-health-fund-and-its-dispute-with-the-gates-foundation-and-17f1abb6c2a4/.

20  Ibid.

21  Much of the information about the general working of APEF VI, its stated purpose and the change it marked in the firm are taken from internal documents, for example, 'Abraaj Private Equity Fund VI', The Abraaj Group, which is a presentation given as part of materials to prospective investors during the fundraising process. There is also a pitch deck, 'Abraaj Long Form Deck' from April 2018 compiled for the attempted sale of the company during the crisis.

22  Toby Mitchenall, 'Emerging markets Africa: The Abraaj pitch', *Private Equity International*, 5 December 2017.

23  Ibid.

24  Private information.

26 'Promotion Carry Memo', The Abraaj Group, an internal document sent around the company by Arif Naqvi after the Dubai meeting and the new structure of the firm had been laid out.

27 Private information from multiple sources in Abraaj management.

28 See Toby Mitchenall, 'Emerging markets Africa: The Abraaj pitch', *Private Equity International*, 5 December 2017:

> For investors looking to commit to global emerging markets – and in volume – there are not many options for 'one-stop shopping'. Actis closed its last global private equity fund on $1.6 billion in 2012, currently the largest single pool of capital in the market, but the other mega-funds capturing emerging markets returns are region-specific.

29 Private information from multiple sources confirmed the figures with slight variations.

30 Simeon Kerr and Henry Sender, 'Private Equity: Inside the fall of Abraaj', *Financial Times*, 9 September 2018.

31 'After pride, the fall. Abraaj, a private-equity firm, files for provisional liquidation', *The Economist*, 23 June 2018.

32 Mark Kolakowski, 'The World's Top 10 Private Equity Firms', Investopedia, updated and revised from current figures, February 2021, 2021 https://www.investopedia.com/articles/markets/011116/worlds-top-10-private-equity-firms-apo-bx.asp.

## Chapter 7: A string of pearls
Sources available here: https://wp.me/Pd2ymq-R.

1 John Perkins, *The New Confessions of an Economic Hitman: How America Really Took Over the World* (London: Penguin, 2016), p. 236.

2 For an excellent analysis of the Chinese geopolitical and economic interface see The China Project podcast, https://chinaafricaproject.com/podcasts/, and the Panda Claw, Dragon Claw blog, https://pandapawdragonclaw.blog/.

3 David Murphy, 'One Belt One Road: International Development Finance with Chinese Characteristics', in Gloria Davies, Jeremy Goldkorn, Luigi Tomba (eds), *Pollution* (Canberra: ANU Press, 2019), pp. 245–252.

4 There is much debate on whether China will actually take control of the ports in Kenya and Sri Lanka with some reports arguing that Chinese banks allow terms to be restructured and questioning the existence of the debt-trap paradigm. In both cases Chinese banks have controlled interests derived from debt collateral, but the issue is whether this constitutes sovereign control by one state of another state's port. See for example Deborah Brautigam and Meg Rithmirehttp, 'The Chinese "Debt Trap" Is

a Myth', The Atlantic, 6 February 2021, https://www.theatlantic.com/international/archive/2021/02/china-debt-trap-diplomacy/617953/. The alternative argument is put by Aditi Taswala, 'Peeking Behind China's "Debt Trap Diplomacy" in Kenya and Sri Lanka', The China Guys, 24 September 2020, https://thechinaguys.com/peeking-behind-chinas-debt-trap-diplomacy-in-kenya-and-sri-lanka/. To an extent both arguments are true depending on the time frame you apply. China's strategic patience means that, in my view, the debt trap is not a short-term intervention but will always come second to economic interests, but, in the long-term, control will become ownership because of the needs of the Chinese Navy.

5 For a full exploration of the strategic implications of this see: David Brewster, *Strategic Asia 2019: China's Expanding Strategic Ambitions* (The National Bureau of Asian Research, 2019). For a shorter analysis accessible see: Oliver Miles, 'The flag follows trade', *London Review of Books*, 16 December 2011, https://www.lrb.co.uk/blog/2011/december/the-flag-follows-trade.

6 Gurpreet S. Khurana, 'China's "String of Pearls" in the Indian Ocean and Its Security Implications', *Strategic Analysis*, Vol. 23, No. 1, 27 February 2008, pp. 1–39.

7 Azizullah Sharif, 'Karachi population to hit 27.5 million in 2020', *Dawn*, 10 July 2007, https://www.dawn.com/news/255587/karachi-karachi-population-to-hit-275-million-in-2020

8 'Global City GDP Rankings', *PricewaterhouseCoopers*, 2008–2025 the figures used come from Maria Saifuddin Effendi, 'Karachi: The backbone of Pakistan', *The Nation*, 1 September 2020.

9 Josh Lerner, Asim Ijaz Khwaja and Ann Leamon, 'Abraaj Capital and the Karachi Electric Supply Company', 6 March 2012. Harvard Business School Strategy Unit Case No. 812-019, Available here: https://ssrn.com/abstract=2034956.

10 'The China–Pakistan Economic Corridor', United States Institute of Peace, 25 October 2017, https://www.usip.org/publications/2017/10/china-pakistan-economic-corridor, p. 19.

11 'Karachi Ongoing Power Outages Leads to Cause for Nationalization', 2009, and 'New CEO And Changes In KESC Leadership And Future Of Karachi's Power System', 2009, both from Wikileaks.

12 Figures as quoted in Josh Lerner, Asim Ijaz Khwaja and Ann Leamon, 'Abraaj Capital and the Karachi Electric Supply Company – Case Solution', *Harvard Business Review*, 9 February 2012.

13 Ibid.

14 All quotes from the Harvard study are from Josh Lerner, Asim Ijaz Khwaja and Ann Leamon, 'Abraaj Capital and the Karachi Electric Supply Company – Case Solution'.

15 Laurent Gayer, 'Political Turmoil in Karachi: Production and Reproduction of Ordered Disorder', *Economic and Political Weekly*, Vol. 47, No. 31, 4 August 2012.

16 'KARACHI: KESC to launch "name and shame" drive against power thieves', *Dawn*, 30 August 2009, https://www.dawn.com/news/975415/karachi-kesc-to-launch-name-and-shame-drive-against-power-thieves.

17  Irfan Aligi, 'Cutting costs: KESC workers bite the hand that gave the golden handshake', *Express Tribune*, 21 January 2011.
18  'KESC Annual Report', 2013, https://www.ke.com.pk/download/financial-data/Annual-Report-2012-2013.pdf, p. 84.
19  There are a number of videos of members of the team making this kind of point still online on the Abraaj YouTube channel, also see Tom Speechley, 'Responsible investing: In growth markets, it's common sense', Pensions & Investments, 21 July 2015, https://www.pionline.com/article/20150721/ONLINE/150719916/responsible-investing-in-growth-markets-it-s-common-sense.
20  'KESC Annual Report', 2013, p. 101.
21  Salman Siddiqui, 'The Abraaj Group considering divesting stake in K-Electric', *Express Tribune*, 29 August 2016.
22  Mustafa Yağci, 'Rethinking Soft Power in Light of China's Belt and Road Initiative', *Uluslararası İlişkiler*, Vol. 15, No. 57, 2018, pp. 67–78.
23  'Abraaj sells K-Electric shares to Shanghai Electric worth $1.77 billion', ARYNews, 30 October 2016, https://arynews.tv/en/abraaj-sells-k-electric-shares-to-shanghai-electric-worth-1-77-bn/.

## Chapter 8: The geopolitics of selling Karachi Electric

Sources available here: https://wp.me/Pd2ymq-U.

1  Muhammad Munir, 'Pakistan–China Strategic Interdependence: Post-9/11 Imperatives', *Strategic Studies*, Vol. 38, No. 2, 2018, pp. 21–42.
2  'Timeline: History of US–Pakistan relations', *Dawn*, 4 July 2012.
3  This sense of closeness, occasionally veering into the saccharine, is by no means a thing of the past. When visiting in 2015, President Xi Jinping declared that 'I feel as if I am going to visit the home of my own brother'. Ankit Panda, 'Xi Jinping on Pakistan: 'I Feel As If I Am Going to Visit the Home of My Own Brother', *The Diplomat*, 20 April 2015, https://thediplomat.com/2015/04/xi-jinping-on-pakistan-i-feel-as-if-i-am-going-to-visit-the-home-of-my-own-brother/
4  Imran Ali Kundi, 'Pakistan's trade deficit with China shrinks by $3.2 billion', *The Nation*, 16 August 2019.
5  'S. 1707 (111th): Enhanced Partnership with Pakistan Act of 2009', United States Senate, 24 September 2009, https://www.govtrack.us/congress/bills/111/s1707.
6  Muhammad Akbar Notezai, 'What Happened to the China–Pakistan Economic Corridor?' *The Diplomat*, 16 February 2021.
7  'Sixty years of US aid to Pakistan: Get the data', *The Guardian*, 11 July 2011.
8  Naga Malleswara Rao, 'China's "New Maritime Silk Route", What it is for Asian Neighbors?', Chennai Centre for China Studies, 30 May 2015, https://www.c3sindia.org/archives/chinas-new-maritime-silk-route-what-it-is-for-asian-neighbors-by-naga-malleswara-rao/.

9   'The Strait of Hormuz is the world's most important oil transit chokepoint', US Energy Information Administration, 20 June 2019, https://www.eia.gov/todayinenergy/detail.php?id=39932.

10  Gurpreet Singh Khurana, 'China's Yuan-Class Submarine Visits Karachi: An Assessment', *Center for International Maritime Security*, 28 July 2015, https://cimsec.org/chinas-yuan-class-submarine-visits-karachi-assessment/17627.

11  Ibid.

12  Shuaihua Wallace Cheng, 'China's New Silk Road: Implications for the US', Yale University: YaleGlobal Online, 28 May 2015, https://yaleglobal.yale.edu/content/chinas-new-silk-road-implications-us.

13  Yen Nee Lee, 'Biden's team talks tough on China as early signs show policies won't differ sharply from Trump's', CNBC, Thursday 21 January 2021, https://www.cnbc.com/2021/01/22/us-china-relations-bidens-team-talks-tough-on-china-.html.

14  Private information.

15  'Encouraging Gulf Investment in Karachi's Power System', WikiLeaks, 25 August 2009, https://wikileaks.org/plusd/cables/09ISLAMABAD2022_a.html.

16  'United States and Pakistan Energy Cooperation Strategy: Priorities Through 2020 For The US-Pakistan Clean Energy Partnership', US Department of State, 24 May 2016, https://2009-2017.state.gov/p/sca/rls/press/2016/257718.htm.

17  Private information.

18  'The President's Speech in Cairo: A New Beginning', The White House, 4 June 2009, https://obamawhitehouse.archives.gov/issues/foreign-policy/presidents-speech-cairo-a-new-beginning.

19  Thomas Lynch, 'Imagining Pakistan in 2020', EastWest, 29 February 2012, https://www.eastwest.ngo/idea/imagining-pakistan-2020.

20  'USAID launched Pakistan private investment initiative to mobilize at $150 million in private equity investment', press release, USAID, 25 June 2013, https://2012-2017.usaid.gov/news-information/press-releases/usaid-partners-abraaj-and-jspe-150-million-private-equity-pakistan.

21  See his LinkedIn profile: https://www.linkedin.com/in/pramamurthy1/.

22  Alan Jones and Mary Fanning 'What could possible go wrong?', An Occasional Paper of the Center for Security Policy, 23 December 2016, https://archive.org/stream/20161223PortCanaveralOccasionalPaper122316/20161223_Port_Canaveral_Occasional_Paper_122316_djvu.txt.

23  'Vinay Chawla', World Economic Forum, https://www.weforum.org/people/vinay-chawla.

24  Private information.

25  Private information.

26  'The Kerry Peace Plan?' Middle East Policy Council, https://mepc.org/commentary/kerry-peace-plan

27  As an aside, I have seen the documents that Naqvi and de Boer developed and it

is ironic that Trump continued with a similar approach to Obama in relation to the Palestinian peace process in that economic peace and collaboration needed to be pursued first in order to build the trust that would be needed for a political solution to eventually be reached and a significant part of the thinking can be seen in the Kushner Plan that was unveiled in 2020.

28   Private information.
29   Private information.
30   Asian Infrastructure Investment Bank, https://www.aiib.org/en/index.html.
31   'Xinhua Power Co Ltd – Company Profile and News', Bloomberg News, https://www.bloomberg.com/profile/company/1278830D:CH.

## Chapter 9: More than meets the eye
Sources available here: https://wp.me/Pd2ymq-X.

1   Atika Rehman, 'Footprints: Arif Naqvi – the man who flew too close to the sun', *Dawn*, 1 February 2021.
2   Alan Jones and Mary Fanning, 'WikiLeaks Email Ties Apparent Clinton Pay-To-Play to Port Canaveral Deal with Family of Saddam Hussein's Nuclear Mastermind', Breitbart News, 7 November 2016, https://www.breitbart.com/national-security/2016/11/07/wikileaks-email-ties-apparent-clinton-pay-play-port-canaveral-deal-family-saddam-husseins-nuclear-mastermind/. This then spread around the American right-wing news ecosystem, see by the same authors, 'Jafars' Abraaj Group paid Clinton Foundation; Jafars rewarded with Port Canaveral Gulftainer deal', 1776 Channel, 5 October 2016, https://1776channel.com/2016/10/05/national-security/jafars-abraaj-group-paid-clinton-foundation-jafars-rewarded-port-canaveral-gulftainer-deal/, and Roger Aronoff, 'Gulftainer Scandal Connects Obama, The Clintons And The Media', GOPUSA, 6 January 2017, https://www.gopusa.com/gulftainer-scandal-connects-obama-the-clintons-and-the-media/.
3   Haroon Janjua, '"Nothing but lies and deceit": Trump launches Twitter attack on Pakistan', *The Guardian*, 1 January 2018.
4   'OPIC to finance up to $250 million in support of K-Electric', The Exporting Source, 21 October 2015, https://www.exportprac.com/sites/exportingsource.com/ht/display/ArticleDetails/i/59150.
5   Muhammed Rizwan Dalia to Naveed A. Sethi, 'Minutes of 109th Annual General Meeting (AGM) of K-Electric Limited (KE)', 3 June 2020, https://www.ke.com.pk/assets/uploads/2020/06/AGM-109-minutes.pdf.
6   Littlefield was the tenth president and CEO of OPIC and openly saw OPIC's primary goal 'to support US businesses investing in emerging markets', Rahim Kanani, 'Elizabeth Littlefield of the Overseas Private Investment Corporation: An In-depth Interview', *Forbes*, 12 October 2011.

7   'Trump attacks Pakistan "deceit" in first tweet of the year', BBC News, 1 January 2018, https://www.bbc.co.uk/news/world-us-canada-42536209.

8   Mercy A. Kuo, 'The Power of Ports: China's Maritime March', *The Diplomat*, 8 March 2017.

9   'US–China trade war and its implications on CPEC', *Pakistan Observer*, 14 April 2018.

10  Andrew Small, 'Returning to the Shadows: China, Pakistan, and the Fate of CPEC', The German Marshall Fund of the United States, 23 September 2020, https://www.gmfus.org/publications/returning-shadows-china-pakistan-and-fate-cpec.

11  'No need to convince anyone on CPEC: Planning Minister Asad Umar', CPECInfo, 19 December 2019, http://www.cpecinfo.com/archive/news/no-need-to-convince-anyone-on-cpec-planning-minister-asad-umar/ODQ5OA==.

12  Mian Abrar, 'China, Pakistan to adopt zero tolerance policy against corruption in CPEC', *Pakistan Today*, 25 November 2015.

13  Faseeh Mangi, 'Belt and Road Re-Emerges in Pakistan With Flurry of China Deals', Bloomberg News, 15 July 2020, https://www.bloomberg.com/news/articles/2020-07-15/belt-and-road-re-emerges-in-pakistan-with-flurry-of-china-deals.

14  Muhammad Akbar Notezai, 'CPEC 2.0: Full Speed Ahead', *The Diplomat*, 10 September 2020.

15  Private information.

16  'Continuous Excellence is Key to Growth and Sustainability: Annual Report 2017', Karachi Electric, August 2017, https://www.ke.com.pk/download/financial-data/Annual-Report-2017.pdf.

17  The official programme includes up to 10,000 places, see https://www.hec.gov.pk/english/scholarshipsgrants/US-Pakcorridor/Pages/default.aspx. There have been repeated questions asked about the fairness of the distribution of these scholarships by the Higher Education Commission of Pakistan.

18  See Veena Kukreja, *Contemporary Pakistan: Political Processes, Conflicts and Crises* (London: Sage Publications, 2003), p. 73 and *Military Intervention in Politics* (New Delhi: NBO Publishers, 1985).

19  Hasan-Askari Rizvi, *Military, State and Society in Pakistan* (New York: Palgrave MacMillan, 2000), pp. 236–7.

20  Ayesha Siddiqa, *Military Inc.: Inside Pakistan's Military Economy* (Oxford: Oxford University Press, 2007), p. 1.

21  Shahbaz Rana, 'K-Electric stake sale: Abraaj Group to get only half of receipts', *The Express Tribune*, 27 April 2017.

22  NEPRA has the authority to 'specify procedures and standards for investment programmes by generation companies and persons licensed or registered under this Act, settle disputes between licensees in accordance with the specified procedure, submit reports to the Federal Government in respect of activities of

generation companies and persons licensed or registered under this Act, review organizational affairs of generation companies and persons licensed or registered under this Act to avoid any adverse effect on the operation of electric power services and for continuous and efficient supply of such services'. All are legal powers which could be easily abused with ulterior motives. From 'About Us', National Electric Power Regulatory Authority, https://nepra.org.pk/.

23 See N. B. Shahab, 'Government interference in power sector regulation: a case of Pakistan', *Pakistan Administrative Review*, Vol. 3, No. 1, 2019, pp. 51–60.

24 Shahbaz Rana, 'K-Electric's fate lands in PM's Office', *The Express Tribune*, 27 March 2018, and Imran Ali Kundi, 'Cabinet to decide about KE-SEPL deal', *The Nation*, 31 March 2018.

25 For a general discussion of the power of the military from which this judgement is made, see S. Inderjit, 'The Pendulum of Leadership Change and Challenges of Civil Democracy and Military Rule in Pakistan', *International Journal of Education and Research*, Vol. 1, No. 12, December 2013.

26 Dipanjan Roy Chaudhury, 'Pakistan slows down CPEC to keep US happy', *The Economic Times*, 8 October 2019.

27 'Today Privatization Commission Stops The Sale Of Karachi Electric Shares', *Profit Pakistan Today*, April 2017.

28 Javed Mirza, 'Shanghai Electric withdraws offer to buy K-Electric stake', *The News International*, 14 June 2017.

29 Private information.

30 'Top Pakistani politicians found linked with Abraaj founder Arif Naqvi billion dollars fraud in US', *Times of Islamabad*, 10 July 2019.

31 Syed Muhammed Ali (ed.), 'Pakistan: Mapping the Policy Agenda: 2018–2023', Islamabad Policy Institute, August 2018, https://www.slideshare.net/ipipk/pakistan-mapping-the-policy-agenda-20182023.

32 Ibid.

33 Mian Abar, 'PM Khan to take final decision on IMF bailout', *Pakistan Today*, 18 November 2018.

34 'US' Pompeo warns against IMF bailout for Pakistan that aids China', Reuters, 30 July 2018, https://www.reuters.com/article/us-imf-pakistan-idUSKBN1 KK2G5.

35 'PM Imran Khan may decide against going to IMF', *Times of Islamabad*, 19 November 2018.

36 'Pakistan to get $3 billion loan from UAE, eyes deferred oil payments', Reuters, 21 December 2018, https://www.reuters.com/article/emirates-pakistan-economy-cenbank/pakistan-to-get-3-billion-loan-from-uae-eyes-deferred-oil-payments-idINKCN1OK0NS?edition-redirect=in.

37 'Dr Abdul Hafeez Sheikh appointed Finance advisor to PM Imran', Dunya News, 18 April 2019, https://dunyanews.tv/en/Pakistan/487662-Dr-Abdul-Hafeez-Sheikh-appointed-Finance-advisor-to-PM-Imran.

## Chapter 10: Strangled by a string of pearls
Sources available here: https://wp.me/Pd2ymq-10.

1   Shahbaz Rana, 'Defence ministry clears sale of K-Electric to Chinese firm', *The Express Tribune*, 29 September 2017.

2   Massoud A Derhally, 'Abraaj whistleblower emails warned investors ahead of scandal and collapse of firm', National News Business, 5 May 2019, https://www.thenationalnews.com/business/abraaj-whistleblower-emails-warned-investors-ahead-of-scandal-and-collapse-of-firm-1.857332.

3   Private information.

4   Massoud A Derhally, 'Abraaj whistleblower emails warned investors ahead of scandal and collapse of firm'.

5   See 'DECISION NOTICE: Abraaj Investment Management Limited (in Provisional Liquidation)', 29 July 2019, https://365343652932-web-server-storage.s3.eu-West-2.amazonaws.com/files/6416/0551/0509/Decision_Notice_AIML_final.pdf, paragraphs 207 to 215.

6   'Behind the Spectacular Demise of Private Equity Firm Abraaj', *Arabian Business News*, 30 July 2018.

7   Adam Le, 'Secondaries firms shun Abraaj stake sales', Secondaries Investor, 12 June 2018, https://www.secondariesinvestor.com/secondaries-firms-shun-abraaj-stake-sales/.

8   William Louch and Simon Clark, 'Abraaj Investors Hire Auditor to Trace Money', *Wall Street Journal*, 3 February 2018 and Landon Thomas Jr, 'Leading Private Equity Firm Accused of Misusing Funds', *New York Times*, 2 February 2018.

9   Landon Thomas Jr, 'Leading Private Equity Firm Accused of Misusing Funds'.

10  Ankura, https://ankura.com/.

11  Ankura chairman, Philip Daddona, is financial adviser to the SEC and the DoJ and the head of innovation is Vincent Stewart, former deputy US Cyber Command and director of the Defense Intelligence Agency, see: https://ankura.com/people/. The pattern continues lower down: 'Former FBI Special Agent and Branch Chief of Cyber-Integrity, Ted Theisen, Returns to Ankura's Cyber Practice as a Senior Managing Director', press release, CISION PR Newswire, 2 February 2021, https://www.prnewswire.com/news-releases/former-fbi-special-agent-and-branch-chief-of-cyber-integrity-ted-theisen-returns-to-ankuras-cyber-practice-as-a-senior-managing-director-301219549.html. On MDC ownership see: https://www.mdcp.com/portfolio/ankura.

12  Muhammad Aurangzeb, 'JPMorgan downgrades Hamilton Lane over Abraaj insolvency', S&P Global, 1 November 2018, https://www.spglobal.com/market-intelligence/en/news-insights/trending/vcewbuhkxuj1s0ypfilj9q2.

13  'Embattled Abraaj frees private equity investors from capital commitments', *Reuters Business News*, 2018, https://www.reuters.com/article/instant-article/idUSKCN1GJ0C0.

14  AppliedCG, 'Abraaj: one man, one vision, two faces...', Applied Corporate Governance, 15 June 2020, https://www.applied-corporate-governance.com/case-study/abraaj-one-man-one-vision-two-faces/.
15  'Abraaj to shed 15 percent jobs globally', *Pakistan Today Profit*, 30 March 2018.
16  William Louch and Nicolas Parasie, 'Development-Finance Groups Widen Inquiry Into Abraaj Funds', *Wall Street Journal*, 29 March 2018.
17  Private information from multiple sources.
18  'Introduction: President's Intelligence Advisory Board and Intelligence Oversight Board', https://obamawhitehouse.archives.gov/administration/eop/piab.
19  Daniel Lippman, 'Trump cuts off one of his closest friends', Politico, 19 August 2018, https://www.politico.com/story/2019/08/19/donald-trump-cuts-off-tom-barrack-1467191.
20  Dinesh Nair, Matthew Martin, Kiel Porter and Archana Narayanan, 'Abraaj to Consider Sale of Stake in Fund Unit to Raise Cash', Bloomberg News, 26 March 2018, https://www.bloomberg.com/news/articles/2018-03-26/abraaj-is-said-to-consider-sale-of-fund-unit-stake-to-raise-cash.
21  'Dana Gas appoints advisers for $700 million sukuk restructuring', Reuters, 4 June 2017, https://www.reuters.com/article/dana-gas-restructuring-idUSL8N1J10HC.
22  'UAE's Dana Gas raises loan, avoids another restructuring', Reuters, 15 October 2020, https://www.reuters.com/article/dana-gas-loan-sukuk-idUSL8N2H61H4.
23  Stephen Witt, 'Stephen Feinberg, the Private Military Contractor Who Has Trump's Ear', *The New Yorker*, 13 July 2017.
24  Private information.
25  See for example, 'Failing to Honour Bounced Cheques in Loans and Other Trans-actions', Legal Advice Middle East, 15 January 2020, https://legaladviceme.com/legal-blog/166/uae-failing-to-honour-bounced-cheques-in-loans-other-transactions.
26  Simeon Kerr and Henry Sender, 'Private Equity: Inside the fall of the Abraaj Group', *Financial Times*, 9 September 2018.
27  See the filing announcement here: http://enterprise.press/wp-content/uploads/2018/06/ABRAAJ-SUBMITS-APPLICATION-FOR-COURT-SUPERVISED-RESTRUCTURING-TO-FACILITATE-ACQUISITION-PROCESS-AND-PROTECT-INTERESTS-OF-ALL-CREDITORS.pdf.
28  Simeon Kerr and Henry Sender, 'Private Equity: Inside the fall of the Abraaj Group'.
29  Private information.
30  Private information.
31  Matthew Martin, Dinesh Nair, Stephen Morris, and Archana Narayanan, 'Abraaj's Alleged Misuse of Money Said to Go Beyond Health Fund', Bloomberg News, 20 May 2018, https://www.bloomberg.com/news/articles/2018-05-19/abraaj-s-alleged-misuse-of-money-said-to-go-beyond-health-fund.
32  Simeon Kerr, 'TPG in talks to take over Abraaj's healthcare fund', *Financial Times*, 24 September 2018.

33  Tom Arnold, Saeed Azhar, Davide Barbuscia, 'Exclusive: Abraaj founder Naqvi pitches last-ditch rescue bid to investors', Reuters, 28 November 2018, https://www.reuters.com/article/us-abraaj-founder-restructuring-exclusiv-idUSKCN1NX23S.

34  Kenneth Rapoza, 'Dubai Emerging Market Maverick Abraaj Gets A Lifeline', *Forbes*, 26 November 2018.

35  Private information.

36  Nicolas Parasie, 'Kuwait Pension Fund Tries to Force Abraaj Into Bankruptcy', *Wall Street Journal*, 30 May 2018.

37  Davide Barbuscia, Tom Arnold, Saeed Azhar, 'Abraaj expects deal on secured debt, Kuwaiti creditor holds out', Reuters, 4 June 2018, https://www.reuters.com/article/us-arbaaj-debt-idINKCN1J02J5?edition-redirect=in.

38  Ibid., and Kenneth Rapoza, 'Dubai Emerging Market Maverick Abraaj Gets A Lifeline', *Forbes*, 26 November 2018.

39  Simeon Kerr, 'Abraaj launches restructuring plan as court appoints liquidators', *Financial Times*, 19 June 2018.

40  Adam Le, 'Cerberus return with knockdown bid for Abraaj', *Private Equity International*, 10 July 2019. This was reported as a $20 million offer, but sources close to the transaction say it was $5 million.

41  Private information.

42  Private information.

43  'World Business Quick Take', *Taipei Times*, 12 June 2018.

44  Stefania Bianchi and Arif Sharif, 'Colony Capital Agrees to Buy Some of Abraaj's Key Funds', Bloomberg News, 21 June 2018, https://www.bloomberg.com/news/articles/2018-06-21/colony-capital-agrees-to-manage-several-of-abraaj-s-key-funds.

45  'Abraaj Holdings – In Provisional Liquidation (the Company)', PwC: Cayman Islands, 2018, https://www.pwc.com/ky/en/services/abraaj-holdings.html.

46  'ABRAAJ Investment Management Limited – In Provisional Liquidation (AIML)', Deloitte, 18 June 2018, https://www2.deloitte.com/ky/en/pages/about-deloitte/solutions/aiml-liquidation.html.

## Chapter 11: Liquidations and betrayals

Sources available here: https://wp.me/Pd2ymq-13.

1  Nicolas Parasie, 'Abraaj Gets Closer to Selling Off Some of Its Funds', Bloomberg News, 3 July 2019, https://www.bloomberg.com/news/articles/2019-07-03/actis-said-to-get-investor-approval-to-take-over-2-abraaj-funds.

2  'TPG Closes Transaction to Take Over the Abraaj Group's Growth Markets Health Fund', press release, TPG, 20 June 2019, https://tpggloballlc.gcs-web.com/news-releases/news-release-details/tpg-closes-transaction-take-over-abraaj-groups-growth-markets.

3  'Colony Capital Completes Acquisition of Abraaj Group's Private Equity Platform

in Latin America', businesswire, 18 April 2019, https://www.businesswire.com/news/home/20190418005133/en/Colony-Capital-Completes-Acquisition-of-Abraaj-Group%E2 per cent80 per cent99s%E2%80%99s-Private-Equity-Platform-in-Latin-America.

4   Will Louch, 'Franklin Templeton in Talks to Buy Abraaj's Turkey Business', *Wall Street Journal*, 9 May 2016.

5   'Actis assumes management rights on Abraaj Private Equity Fund IV and Abraaj Africa Fund III', press release, Actis, 15 July 2019, https://www.act.is/media-centre/press-releases/actis-assumes-management-rights-on-abraaj-private-equity-fund-iv-and-abraaj-africa-fund-iii/.

6   Melissa Gronlund, 'Fire sale of Abraaj art at auction: Million dollar work on the block starting at $66,000', National News Business, 9 October 2018, https://www.thenationalnews.com/arts-culture/art/fire-sale-of-abraaj-art-at-auction-million-dollar-work-on-the-block-starting-at-66-000-1.778917.

7   See my human rights brief on the extradition aspects of Naqvi's case at: https://charlwood-review.com/2021/03/02/the-case-of-arif-naqvi-and-uk-us-extradition-treaty/.

8   'Hedge Fund Founder, CEO, And CIO Anilesh Ahuja And Former Trader Jeremy Shor Convicted Of Securities Fraud Related Offenses In Manhattan Federal Court', press release, Department of Justice, US Attorney's Office, Southern District of New York, 11 July 2019, https://www.justice.gov/usao-sdny/pr/hedge-fund-founder-ceo-and-cio-anilesh-ahuja-and-former-trader-jeremy-shor-convicted and Alicia McElhaney, 'Convicted Hedge Fund Exec Alleges Federal Prosecutor "Suppressed Evidence"', *Institutional Investor*, 8 July 2020, https://www.institutionalinvestor.com/article/b1mdvscgrq8frs/Convicted-Hedge-Fund-Exec-Alleges-Federal-Prosecutor-Suppressed-Evidence.

9   'District Court urges the DoJ to investigate misconduct by SDNY prosecutors', Federal Defenders of New York Blog, Friday 19 February 2021, https://blog.federaldefendersny.org/district-court-urges-the-doj-to-investigate-misconduct-by-sdny-prosecutors/ and 'Botched Iran case adds to woes of SDNY, office upended by Barr', KYC360, 15 July 2020, https://www.riskscreen.com/kyc360/news/botched-iran-case-adds-to-woes-of-sdny-office-upended-by-barr/.

10   Lauren Briggerman, Aiysha Hussain and Katherine Pappas, 'SDNY Grapples with Judicial Rebukes', Bloomberg Law, 10 November 2020, https://news.bloomberglaw.com/us-law-week/sdny-grapples-with-judicial-rebukes.

## Chapter 12: The *Wall Street Journal* and the death of Abraaj
Sources available here: https://wp.me/Pd2ymq-16.

1   'Abraaj's millions went to Arif Naqvi's own account: US paper', *The News International*, 18 October 2018.

2    Ben Protess and Michael Corkery, 'Just how much do the top private equity earners make?' *New York Times*, 10 December 2016.
3    Fahim Badal, 'Private Equity Buys Out 2020 Election', Take On Wall Street, 3 December 2019, https://takeonwallst.com/2019/12/private-equity-2020-election/.
4    'Abraaj founder offered businessman $20 million to buy influence with Sharifs: WSJ', *The Express Tribune*, 18 October 2018.
5    This was widely reported in the media and in the memoirs of Imran Khan's former wife Reham Khan, 'Top Pakistani politicians found linked with Abraaj founder Arif Naqvi billion dollars fraud in US' *Time of Islamabad*, 10 July 2019.
6    Naqvi further denied this in a public statement to the media, see 'Abraaj founder Arif Naqvi slams WSJ report, denies corruption claims', *Arabian Business*, 17 October 2018.
7    'Corruption Perceptions Index, 2016', Transparency International, https://www.transparency.org/en/cpi/2016/index/nzl.

## Chapter 13: Legacy
Sources available here: https://wp.me/Pd2ymq-19.

1    APEF VI pitchbook, The Abraaj Group, p. 9.
2    'Introduction to The Abraaj Group: Memorandum', The Abraaj Group, p. 10.
3    The Abraaj Group 2018, p. 33.
4    Ibid., p. 34.
5    'Introduction to The Abraaj Group: Memorandum', The Abraaj Group, p. 10.
6    The Abraaj Group 2018, p. 49.
7    Ibid., p. 81.
8    Ibid., p. 78.
9    Ibid., p. 95.
10   Ibid., p. 10.
11   All on 'One Firm' from 'Introduction to The Abraaj Group: Memorandum', May 2017.
12   The Abraaj Group 2018, p. 6.
13   APEF VI pitchbook, p. 3.
14   'Track Record', The Abraaj Group, slide 6.
15   'Seeing like a citizen: the experience of mind changing projects', https://charlwood-review.com/2021/02/24/seeing-like-a-state/.

## Chapter 14: Reckoning
Sources available here: https://wp.me/Pd2ymq-1c.

1    *United States of America v Arif Naqvi, Waqar Siddique, Rafique Lakhani, Mustafa*

*Abdel-Wadood, Ashish Dave and Sivendran Vettivetpillai: Affidavit in support of request for the extradition of Arif Naqvi and Sivendran Vettivetpillai.*

2 Alex Ward, 'The battle over Trump's huge UAE arms deal, explained', Vox, 1 December 2020, https://www.vox.com/2020/12/1/21755390/trump-uae-f35-israel-weapons-sale.

3 Desmond Butler and Tom Lobianco, 'Emails reveal secret lobbying effort to alter US policy in Middle East', *Chicago Tribune*, 22 May 2018.

4 Ibid.

5 Ludovic Phalippou, 'Modifying The Carried Interest to Do What It Is Said to Do', 12 February 2019, available at Social Science Research Network: https://dx.doi.org/10.2139/ssrn.3333053.

6 The WhatsApp messages appear on pp. 34–5 of the DoJ indictment; see Chapter 14, note 1.

7 Michael McDaniel, Cupola's inhouse counsel, quoted in Josh Lerner, 'Cupola and the Inchcape Transaction', Harvard Business School, Case Study, 812-045.

## Postscript: Abraaj and private equity; private equity and Abraaj
Sources available here: https://wp.me/Pd2ymq-1f.

1 This term has been given academic credibility largely through the work of Professor Josh Lerner at Harvard through a string of publications. See his Harvard profile: https://www.hbs.edu/faculty/Pages/profile.aspx?facId=9961/.

2 'Our History', CDC: Investment Works, https://www.cdcgroup.com/en/about/our-history/.

3 All these sectors and their interactions are laid out in Abraaj materials, for example, its 2017 introductory memorandum for prospective investors: 'Introduction to The Abraaj Group: Memorandum', May 2017, The Abraaj Group.

4 The importance of this is highlighted in Darek Klonowski (ed.), 'Emerging Market Private Equity, Its Recent Growth and Differences with Private Equity in Developed Markets', in *Private Equity in Emerging Markets: The New Frontiers of International Finance* (New York: Palgrave Macmillan, 2012).

5 Anh Khoi Pham, 'The Dynamics of Returns and Volatility in the Emerging and Developed Asian Reit Markets', *Journal of Real Estate Literature*, Vol. 20, No. 1, 2012, pp. 79–96.

6 'Sectors and Approach to Value Creation', The Abraaj Group, September 2017.

7 Kim Kelly, 'This Is a Horror Story: How Private Equity Vampires Are Killing Everything', *The Nation*, 5 November 2019.

8 David Scott and Michael Kupfer, 'General Partnership vs Limited Partnership', Harvard Business School Blog, 7 December 2020, https://www.delawareinc.com/blog/general-partnership-vs-limited-partnership/.

9 By using balance sheet capital, creating this 'excess inventory' had a two-fold

purpose. As well as ensuring that reputational damage in failure to make up the fund target was avoided, it essentially stocked up capital liquidity for later in the progress of the fund, which could then be made up with later investment enticed by success. Much like the commingling of funds, it worked as long as the firm did not overreach itself and bite off more than it could chew in the amount of capital it used to make up shortfalls.

10   Dinesh Nair, Loni Prinsloo and Nicholas Parasie, 'Emerging Markets Pioneer Actis Rethinks Private Equity Model', Bloomberg, 2 October 2020, https://www. bloomberg.com/news/articles/2020-10-02/an-emerging-markets-champion-shifts-focus-in-sign-of-times.

11   Rajibul Hasan, 'Private Equity Investment Practices: A Comprehensive Study', *The Journal of Private Equity*, Vol. 18, No. 1, Winter 2014, pp. 73–101.

12   'Limited Partnership agreement', British Private Equity & Venture Capital Association, October 2002, https://www.bvca.co.uk/Policy/Tax-Legal-and-Regulatory/ Industry-guidance-standardised-documents/Other/Limited-Partner-agreement.

13   Josh Lerner et al., 'Majority and Minority Ownership in Global Growth Markets', The Abraaj Group, February 2014.

14   'Carried interest: Taking your slice of the pie', Private Funds CFO, 29 November 2019, https://www.privatefundscfo.com/carried-interest-taking-your-slice-of-the-pie/.

15   'Growing Businesses in Growing Markets', The Abraaj Group, May 2017.

16   This was told to me by almost every former Abraaj employee that I talked with.

17   Acquisition valuation is often, but not always, determined as a multiple of the cash earnings of the target company, which could, hypothetically, be a multiple of eight times EBITDA (the valuation multiple), which implies that the EBITDA is $12.5 million.

18   'Special Purpose Vehicle (SPV)', Corporate Finance Institute, https://corporate-financeinstitute.com/resources/knowledge/strategy/special-purpose-vehicle-spv//.

# Index